SCHOPENHAUER'S PHILOSOPHY OF RELIGION

STUDIES IN PHILOSOPHICAL THEOLOGY
43

Philosophical theology is the study of philosophical problems which arise in reflection upon religion, religious beliefs and theological doctrines.

SCHOPENHAUER'S PHILOSOPHY OF RELIGION

THE DEATH OF GOD AND
THE ORIENTAL RENAISSANCE

by

CHRISTOPHER RYAN

PEETERS
LEUVEN – PARIS – WALPOLE, MA
2010

A CIP record for this book is available from the Library of Congress.

© 2010 – Peeters, Bondgenotenlaan 153, 3000 Leuven, Belgium.

ISBN 978-90-429-2215-0
D/2010/0602/38

CONTENTS

ACKNOWLEDGEMENTS

The spirit of many is present in this work, but unfortunately I can acknowledge the contribution of only a select few.

Of intellectual influences I have benefited greatly from the criticism, advice and support of Professor George Pattison. George has the distinction of not merely awakening my interest in Nietzsche, but of complicating this by directing my attention to Schopenhauer a few years later. George has exerted a strong intellectual influence on me, and his share in this work is therefore very great. I hope he welcomes its publication and takes due pride in the part he played in its realisation.

Thanks are also due to Christopher Janaway and Douglas Hedley. I have learnt much about Schopenhauer from Professor Janaway's publications, and am also grateful for the consistent support he has extended to me. As for Dr. Hedley, my gratitude to him is very great. My understanding of the wider currents of nineteenth-century philosophy of religion has been profoundly deepened by our intellectual exchanges, and he has also been a tremendous source of support, guidance and advice. His efforts and encouragement have been particularly invaluable in the production of this book.

Many friends have entered into and departed from the horizon of my experience since I first began to entertain the reflections resulting in this book, all of whom have played their own unique part in its production. Many have offered kind words of encouragement as well as enduring with equanimity my occasional descents from yogic contemplation to Dionysian excess. James Alexander has been a consistent source of friendship, encouragement, criticism, irritation and provocation, and even, on occasion, a source of material support during my more impecunious periods. I can honestly say that without his disinterested and generous friendship, this work would never have been completed. Sincere thanks are due to Matthew Neale for his heroic efforts in reading and commenting on the final manuscript at short notice, for the interest he has taken in my research, and for his consistently insightful remarks and suggestions. I would also like to acknowledge the help, support, friendship and contribution of James Blackstone, Jonathan Mair, Aitoru Terenguto, Pilar Ortega Miguel and Simon Susen, as well as my sisters, Rosemarie, Elizabeth and Margaret and my niece Eleanor Jennings.

Finally, however, this book is dedicated to Mary Ryan, who unfortunately did not live long enough to witness its publication. Although I fear that she would have frowned at its main theme and several of its arguments, I know that she would have nevertheless celebrated its very existence.

KEY TO TEXTUAL CITATIONS FROM WORKS BY SCHOPENHAUER

FR1 *On the Fourfold Root of the Principle of Sufficient Reason, 1ˢᵗ edition, 1813.*

FR *On the Fourfold Root of the Principle of Sufficient Reason, 2ⁿᵈ edition, 1847.*

WWRI *The World as Will and Representation Vol.1.*

WWRII *The World as Will and Representation Vol. 2.*

WN *On the Will in Nature.*

BM *On the Basis of Morality.*

FW *Prize Essay on the Freedom of the Will.*

PPI *Parerga and Paralipomena Vol. 1*

PPII *Parerga and Paralipomena Vol. 2.*

MRI *Manuscript Remains Vol. 1.*

MRII *Manuscript Remains Vol. 2.*

MRIII *Manuscript Remains Vol. 3.*

MRIV *Manuscript Remains Vol. 4.*

MRAR *Manuscript Remains from vols. 1-9 of Asiatick Researches.*

PVI *Philosophische Vorlesungen Vol. 1.*

HNV *Handschriftliche Nachlass Vol. 5.*

GB *Gesammelte Briefe.*

PRESENTATION OF THE TEXT

Quotations from works not originally in English, including those by Schopenhauer, are from English translations cited in the Bibliography, unless otherwise indicated. For the sake of simplicity, key terms from the Indian religious traditions, Hinduism and Buddhism, are in all cases rendered in Sanskrit rather than Pali, unless otherwise stated. I have also taken the liberty of standardising Sanskrit concepts and the titles of Sanskrit works that appear in quotes from Schopenhauer and other writers.

INTRODUCTION

I. The Death of God and the Oriental Renaissance

As the title of this book announces, it is a study of Arthur Schopenhauer's philosophy of religion. It opens out onto this aspect of his thought by way of investigating his relation to the classical religions of India, Hinduism and Buddhism (or, as he called them, "Brahmanism and Buddhism"). Schopenhauer's relation to and presentation of these religions has elicited a substantial amount of secondary analysis, criticism and debate since his works first began to attract attention in the second half of the nineteenth century.[1] The greater proportion of the literature on this topic has adopted the speculative perspective of cross-cultural comparative philosophy or religion, with the purpose of either confirming or denying Schopenhauer's insistence that the doctrines and practices of the Indian religions are in fundamental agreement with his own philosophical system. This study eschews the method of speculative comparison and develops, instead, a contextual account of Schopenhauer's presentation of Hinduism and Buddhism, with the aim of exhibiting its continuity with other areas of his thought — such as his theory of metaphysical need, epistemology, metaphysics and ethics — and, in particular, his analysis of the nature and destiny of historical Christianity. By placing the main features of Schopenhauer's interpretation of Hinduism and Buddhism within the wider framework of his philosophy and his diagnosis of the religious and cultural situation of his time, this book sets out to illustrate the logic of his philosophical appraisal of Indian thought and to elucidate the motives that prompted his turn to this ancient religious tradition.

This contextual approach to Schopenhauer's interpretation of Hinduism and Buddhism reveals that his philosophy of religion was dialectical and comprised of two main phases or moments, one negative and one positive. The negative phase consists of Schopenhauer's repudiation of

---

[1] A — by no means comprehensive — bibliography of works dealing with various aspects of Schopenhauer's relation to the religions of India would include those by Mainländer (1876); Deussen (1894); Hecker (1897); Mockrauer (1928); Merkel (1948); von Glasenapp (1960); Conze (1963); Dauer (1969); Ñāṇajīvako (1970); Dumoulin (1981); Sedlar (1982); Gestering (1986); Halbfass (1988); Nicholls (1999); Meyer (1994); Hacker (1995); Scholz (1996); Kiowsky (1996); Pol-Droit (2003); App (1998b), (2003), (2006); Berger (2004a), (2007); Atzert (2007); Meisig (2007); Raj Singh (2007).

the prevailing system of metaphysics in Europe — that of Judaeo-Christian monotheism — to refer to which I have used Nietzsche's phrase 'the death of God' in the subtitle of this study. My appropriation of this phrase is likely to appear controversial to some, eccentric to others and overly literal to the remainder, since Nietzsche's pregnant formulation proclaims not merely the demise of the God of Christianity, but of all 'true world' theories that relegate change to the level of appearance — irrespective of whether they locate truth in the supersensory realm, such as the Platonic Good, or in some sort of immanent principle, such as the Hegelian *Geist* or the scientific lodestone of 'immutable truth'. Nietzsche regarded such theories as lower-order or attenuated versions of theism, or, in his poetic phrase, the 'shadows' of God,[2] since they are similarly the means by which human thought and language have domesticated the cosmos. He considered the appearance and proliferation of various 'shadows' of the divine in the nineteenth century as a rebuttal to the vaunted self-image of the age as an era of clear-eyed, scientific enquiry. Their tendency to warrant the selfless and ascetic values previously justified by the will of God testifies to the human psyche's need for and predisposition to believe in fixed truths and ideals after millennia of training, but they therefore stand as barriers to the development of new principles of evaluation based on a non-deified view of nature.[3]

And Nietzsche consistently remarked on the extent to which the shadow of the old God obscured even Schopenhauer's atheistic philosophy. On the one hand Schopenhauer was "the *first* admitted and inexorable atheist among us Germans", someone for whom the "ungodliness of existence was…something given, palpable, indisputable", while on the other Schopenhauer remained in thrall to "precisely those Christian-ascetic moral perspectives in which one had *renounced faith* along with the faith in God."[4] Nietzsche's characterisation is undoubtedly correct, for Schopenhauer did combine atheism with commitment to the pessimistic and world-denying features of Christian morality. His enthusiasm for the religious traditions of India stemmed from his conviction that they were repositories of religious stories and allegories capable of sustaining and recommending the spiritual and ethical values of Christianity after its metaphysics had been exposed as false and without foundation. It

---

[2] Nietzsche (1974) §108 (references to the works of Nietzsche are to section and aphorism rather than page number).
[3] Ibid. §109.
[4] Ibid. §357.

might therefore be acknowledged that, in Nietzsche's sense, the old God still haunted Schopenhauer's godless philosophy.

Why, therefore, if I recognise that Schopenhauer's opposition to and critique of the doctrines of monotheism is not equal to the radical connotations of Nietzsche's 'death of God', do I insist on using the phrase?

My reasons for doing so are not simple, but consist of a number of considerations. In broad terms, while acknowledging the contrasts between Schopenhauer and Nietzsche, my aim is to emphasise the *continuities* between them also, as these are too frequently overlooked in the secondary literature.[5] My study of the context or *sitz im leben* in which Schopenhauer formulated his philosophy of religion locates it firmly within the German tradition of *Kulturkritik*, a tradition in which Nietzsche has rightly been accorded a central position, while Schopenhauer's contribution has been overlooked.[6] The many polemical asides and meta-commentaries surrounding and accompanying Schopenhauer's more philosophical statements amply demonstrate that, like his more famous disciple, he too was concerned with the stability, health and unity of European culture. At an early stage in his intellectual development, Schopenhauer arrived at the conviction that the idea of God was no longer capable of grounding ideals or providing a fixed point of orientation for human life. This motivated his attempt to establish and recommend alternative conceptions, for the purpose of forestalling the advent of the "uncanniest of all guests",[7] nihilism — which for Schopenhauer wore the guise of metaphysical and moral materialism. The discontinuity between the *Kulturkritik* of Schopenhauer and that of Nietzsche consists

[5] For example, Walter Kaufmann set out to sever the umbilical cord connecting Nietzsche to Schopenhauer by arguing that Nietzsche's will-to-power was based "on empirical data and not on any dialectical ratiocination about Schopenhauer's metaphysics, as is so often supposed erroneously" (Kaufmann (1974) p. 207) and that "Nietzsche's position is best elucidated by comparing it, not with Schopenhauer's, as has generally been done, but with Hegel's" (Ibid. p. 236). But if this were so, it seems that it was inadvisable for Nietzsche to have chosen a phrase that so clearly invites comparison with Schopenhauer's characterisation of the inner being of nature as "will-to-life". Kaufmann and other Nietzsche enthusiasts too frequently take Nietzsche's attempts to disown his Schopenhauerian legacy at face value. Commentators who start out from Schopenhauer and only subsequently draw Nietzsche into their scholarly net are usually exceptions to this tendency, such as Christopher Janaway (1998), (2007) and Julian Young (1992), (2006).

[6] Georg Simmel's pioneering study of 1907, *Schopenhauer und Nietzsche*, is one of the few to place Schopenhauer's cultural criticism alongside Nietzsche's.

[7] The phrase is, once more, from Nietzsche (1968) §1, and I use it to emphasise the formal continuity between his concern for the integrity and health of European culture in the modern period and Schopenhauer's.

mainly of their contrary conceptions of the relation between Christian belief and Christian values. Whereas Schopenhauer regarded the latter as historical instantiations of immemorial or 'true' value, capable of philosophical justification in the absence of God, Nietzsche viewed them as local or historical errors, and as the symptoms of modern decadence and contemporary nihilism. More importantly, Nietzsche arrived at this position as a result of reading Schopenhauer's works.

This latter observation brings me to the core of my rationale for applying Nietzsche's formulation to Schopenhauer's assault on monotheism. This is because it was precisely Nietzsche's encounter with Schopenhauer's defence of Christian values in a godless and meaningless world that led him to regard European morality as a problem, and to set out to expose and eradicate the remaining shadows of God as the necessary prelude to his revaluation of values. When the 21 year-old Nietzsche came across Schopenhauer's *The World as Will and Representation* in a Leipzig bookshop, what he discovered therein was the image of a cosmos conditioned by a blind and insatiable inner principle named after the individual human will. Once magnified to the proportions of the universe (and presented powerfully in Schopenhauer's masterful prose), the characteristics of this inner reality assume horrific and demonic aspects, as a consequence of which value — political, aesthetic, moral and religious — is purchased at the cost of 'that which is'. The final consummation of all effort to suppress the essence of the self and world and instantiate value in the phenomenon is a mystical state beyond subject and object, and therefore beyond language and thought. Schopenhauer used negations to refer to it, such as the "relative nothingness" that "hovers behind all virtue and holiness" (WWRI p. 411). Nietzsche was an immediate but short-lived convert: having initially hailed Schopenhauer as his "educator" he soon repudiated the anti-naturalism of the latter and began to style Schopenhauer as his "antipode".

But apart from acting as a counterpoint in opposition to which Nietzsche could fix the central tasks of his philosophical project, Schopenhauer's philosophy was also, and paradoxically, a source for many of the presuppositions of Nietzsche's attack on Christian and Schopenhauerian values. Virtually every commentator has remarked on the putative contradiction between Schopenhauer's metaphysics of the will and ethics of its denial,[8] and it might be said that Nietzsche has the priority in this

---

[8] To quote just one, Luis Navia, "[t]he *Widerspruch* of [Schopenhauer's] metaphysics is the inevitable fruit of the opposition of his determinism and his ethical aspirations.' — Navia (1980) p. 180.

regard. His philosophy ends up rejecting Schopenhauerian morality as a consequence of assimilating a psychological version of Schopenhauer's metaphysics. For both thinkers egoism is the primary motive. Whereas, however, Schopenhauer maintained that acts of compassion and asceticism were mysterious and ultimately incomprehensible instances of the will's self-suppression and ultimate denial, Nietzsche's psychology of the will-to-power exposed them as subtle and subterranean self-affirmations, subterfuges by which a degenerating but still fundamentally egoistic form of life preserves itself.[9] By formulating explanations of morality and ethics that presuppose rather than displace the will, Nietzsche trumped his "educator" and "antipode" and revealed himself to be the more comprehensive and consistent volitionist of the two.[10] Since, therefore, Nietzsche's notion of the "death of God" was not merely a reaction to but also a development from Schopenhauer's atheism and metaphysics of will, I have retroactively applied the phrase to the negative moment of Schopenhauer's philosophy of religion.

As for the positive moment of Schopenhauer's philosophy of religion, this consists of his claim that the doctrines and practices of the classical Indian religions are both historical antecedents to and religio-allegorical counterparts of his own philosophical insights, and is indicated by the phrase the 'oriental renaissance' in the subtitle of this study. I have borrowed this from the title of Raymond Schwab's book surveying the nineteenth-century reception of Indian literature among linguists, artists, writers, philosophers, historians and other theorists. Schwab explains his use of the term as referring to

> the revival of an atmosphere in the nineteenth century brought about by the arrival of Sanskrit texts in Europe, which produced an effect equal to that produced in the fifteenth century by the arrival of Greek manuscripts and Byzantine commentators after the fall of Constantinople.[11]

However, since this book narrows the range of Schwab's study by exclusively focusing on *Schopenhauer's* conception of an oriental renaissance through Sanskrit literature, it is necessary to emphasise a crucial differ-

---

[9] Nietzsche (1989) III.13.

[10] This argument is not intended to discount the distinction between Schopenhauer's monist metaphysics of the will and Nietzsche's plurality of drives characterised as will-to-power. It merely emphasises that Nietzsche's psychological egoism was taken over from Schopenhauer's metaphysics, and that whereas Nietzsche remained faithful to this theory, Schopenhauer was obliged to limit the will in order to allow for morality and salvation.

[11] Schwab (1984) p. 11.

ence between the renaissance of the fifteenth and that of the nineteenth century not mentioned by Schwab. Whereas the reintroduction of Greek learning in the fifteenth century was, as Schwab comments, stimulated by the arrival of both manuscripts *and* commentators skilled in their exegesis, the nineteenth-century encounter with Indian literature was limited to the manuscripts alone, and only a small number at that. As a result, the burden of explanation and commentary fell upon a select circle of European philologists. They performed the difficult tasks of translating Sanskrit terms and conceptions into alien categories and schemas, making informed guesses about the historical provenance of Indian texts, movements and ideas, and constructing conjectures about the meaning and significance of central doctrines and practices. These speculative difficulties were further hampered by the fact that many of these early philologists were unsympathetic to the system of ideas contained in the great works of Sanskrit religious literature, especially the Buddhologists.[12] In the absence of Indian commentators able to explain the relation between the developed traditions of Hinduism and Buddhism and foundational texts such as the *Upaniṣads* and the *Dhammapada*, conjecture and supposition held the field. It was as if the Bible had been introduced into India without missionaries to explain and justify the connection between its narratives and teachings and the systematic and creedal statements of Christianity.[13] When, therefore, the creative thinkers of Europe encountered Sanskrit literature in translation, they naturally imposed their own meanings on the available texts, approaching them as repositories of primordial wisdom, capable of addressing the concerns and resolving the problems of their own time and context. In Schopenhauer's case, Europe's encounter with oriental wisdom provided an opportunity for resolving the crisis in faith and morals that had been brewing since at least the seventeenth century. He viewed the Indian religions as having anticipated some of his own philosophical positions — idealism, atheism, pessimism and asceticism — and hoped they might fill the religious and spiritual vacuum opened up by the decline of Church Christianity. Moreover, Schopenhauer did not regard the possibility of an oriental renaissance

---

[12] Friedrich Schlegel maintained that Buddhists stand to Christians as apes stand to man (Schlegel (1849) p. 517), while the works of the French Buddhologist Barthélemy Saint-Hilaire are littered with disdainful references to the "strange and deplorable doctrines" of his area of research expertise — see Welbon (1968) p. 69.

[13] And even with the presence of missionaries, Indian intellectuals from Rammohan Roy up to Gandhi persistently interpreted the maxims and narratives of the Bible and the figure of Jesus in accordance with Hindu categories — see Thomas (1969).

through Sanskrit literature as a betrayal of European culture in favour of an alien form of wisdom, but as the revival of the "old, true, profound, and original" religio-metaphysical *Weltanschauung* of the forefathers of modern Europe (FR p. 146).

II. Schopenhauer's Philosophy of Religion

Schopenhauer was born in Danzig (now Polish Gdansk) in 1788 and died in Frankfurt-am-Main seventy-two years later in 1860. His father Heinrich Floris Schopenhauer was a successful merchant and patrician, and his mother Johanna Schopenhauer (née Trosiener) — a vivacious woman twenty years younger than her husband — had also grown up amidst bourgeois comforts earned through commerce. Schopenhauer is therefore an exception to Nietzsche's otherwise accurate observation that the "Protestant pastor is the grandfather of German philosophy",[14] for his family home and schooling were almost totally lacking in the atmosphere of church and piety that formed the early experiences of the majority of modern German philosophers — including Kant, Fichte, Schelling, Hegel, Nietzsche himself, and into the twentieth century Heidegger: and, unlike the aforementioned philosophers, Schopenhauer also never studied theology. Arthur's father Heinrich Floris was a true representative of the cosmopolitan and mercantile spirit of Danzig, one of the foremost cities of the Hanseatic trading league. A republican opponent of Prussian absolutism and admirer of the French and British Enlightenment, Heinrich (like his son after him) read the London *Times* daily and named his first child Arthur because it was transferable from German to English and French without modification. Heinrich calculated that this would facilitate his son's future prospects in making and sustaining a network of foreign trading contacts; for Heinrich had decreed that the future philosopher would eventually assume control of the family business and live out the life of an affluent burgher. Arthur contemplated his destiny with some trepidation and when, at the age of 16, he was apprenticed to work with one of his father's business associates, he fulfilled his duties with great difficulty and self-sacrifice. After Heinrich's early death (and suspected suicide), Arthur shook off his paternal destiny and in 1807 went to the University of Göttingen to study medicine. Once there he came under the influence of the Professor of Philosophy, Gottlob Ernst Schulze,

---

[14] Nietzsche (1976b) §10.

author of the most acute of the early criticisms of the Kantian philosophy.[15] Under Schulze's guidance Schopenhauer transferred to the full-time study of philosophy, reading Kant and Plato alongside their contemporary incarnations Fichte and Schelling. In 1810 Schopenhauer went to the newly-established University of Berlin in order to study under Fichte, where he also attended Schleiermacher's lectures on the history of philosophy. His lecture notes from the period chart his growing disillusionment and exasperation with the philosophical assumptions and outlooks of both thinkers (MRII pp. 16-233, pp. 240-6).

In autumn 1813 Schopenhauer submitted his doctoral dissertation, *On the Fourfold Root of the Principle of Sufficient Reason*, to the Faculty of Philosophy at the University of Jena. The work was a Kantian-inspired work on epistemology that examined the various powers of the subject of knowledge, their correlative objects and the different forms of the principle of sufficient reason as it governs connections between objects of the same class. Having completed his doctorate, Schopenhauer moved to Weimar where his mother had settled after Heinrich's death, and where she had formed an acquaintance with no less a cultural luminary than Goethe. She had also established herself as a popular travel-writer and romantic novelist, which was later to stimulate great envy in her philosopher son, whose works failed to attract attention until late in his life. In Weimar Schopenhauer was initially overlooked by Goethe, but after briefly perusing a copy of Schopenhauer's dissertation, Goethe recruited him as a co-worker in the promotion of his anti-Newtonian colour theory. Schopenhauer's supreme self-confidence is demonstrated by the fact that, even as a young man, he remained unbowed by the reputation of such an Olympian figure, and in his relations with Goethe Schopenhauer displayed little of the tongue-tied hero-worship that was to characterise Nietzsche's association with Wagner. Schopenhauer eventually alienated Goethe by treating the great man's observations on the phenomenon of colour as so much raw data supporting a theoretical scheme of his own devising, which Schopenhauer published in 1816 in his second work *On Vision and Colours*.

By this time Schopenhauer had left Weimar and settled in Dresden, where he was working on the system eventually published in late 1818 as *The World as Will and Representation*, when he was 30. He remained faithful to the broad outlines of this system for the remainder of his life, his subsequent works modifying only some of the finer detail and

---

[15] Published anonymously in 1792 as *Aenesidemus*.

occasionally varying some of the original expression. The 1818 edition of Schopenhauer's chief work contains no systematic statement of his philosophy of religion, but a brief perusal of the original reveals he had already developed the habit of drawing explicit parallels between his own philosophical positions and the beliefs and practices of the world's religions.[16] Unfortunately, its reception among the philosophical fraternity and the reading public in general did not live up to Schopenhauer's expectations. The fate of Schopenhauer's work parallels Hume's description of the immediate career of his *A Treatise of Human Nature* published in 1739; they both fell "*dead-born from the press*; without reaching such distinction, as even to excite a murmur among the zealots."[17]

To cope with this disappointment, Schopenhauer began to develop the conviction (and, one might say, the face-saving hypothesis) that his philosophy failed to attract acclaim or provoke opposition not because of its flaws, but because of its virtues. He began to regard his philosophy as the supplement to and even completion of Kant's negative assault on the prevailing metaphysics of monotheism, insofar as it had not merely confirmed and expanded on Kant's exposure of the transcendental illusions of natural theology, but had defended a contrary, immanent metaphysic incompatible with belief in God and the soul. Schopenhauer claimed that the 'zealots', and the university 'professors' of philosophy who served them, were therefore forced to resort to the only means in their power of combating his influence — to suppress his philosophy by ignoring it. In the 1820s Schopenhauer set out to challenge this tacit conspiracy against his system with a number of failed attempts to publicise its main claims, including the foolhardy decision to lecture at the University of Berlin at the same time as its greatest philosophical luminary and the vessel of the *Zeitgeist*, Georg Wilhelm Freidrich Hegel. When a cholera epidemic swept through Berlin in 1831 (and, in one of the world-spirit's more inscrutable ruses, took Hegel with it) Schopenhauer fled the city to take up residence in Frankfurt-am-Main, where he remained until his death in 1860. From hereafter, Schopenhauer's life and daily routine were as solitary and ordered as that of his philosophical mentor Kant.

The lack of interest generated by his philosophy, combined with his flight from Berlin, might have heralded the close of Schopenhauer's career as a philosopher and his retreat into private individuality. However,

---

[16] For a copy of the German text of the first edition of *Die Welt als Wille und Vorstellung* see Malter (1987).
[17] Hume (1993c) p. 4.

his ongoing interest in the latest findings of various intellectual disciplines cemented his conviction that his metaphysics of the will and ethics of its denial was no fable forwarded by a solitary crank. On the contrary, recent scientific theories of a single natural force animating the operations of matter, in tandem with the latest scholarly researches on the world's religions, led him to believe that his philosophy had solved the riddle of existence and discovered the metaphysical truth underpinning all honest theoretical endeavours. In 1835, after a seventeen-year silence on philosophical issues, Schopenhauer published the short treatise *On the Will in Nature*, in order to draw attention to the "corroborations" his metaphysics of the will had obtained from "unprejudiced empiricists who are not familiar with it", and to demonstrate how his "metaphysics and the sciences meet of their own accord and without collusion at the same point." (WN p. 19) In one chapter of the treatise — entitled 'Sinology' — Schopenhauer developed various points of comparison between his non-theistic metaphysics and the religions of China and in the following chapter claimed that Buddhism, the *Upaniṣads* and "old and genuine Christianity" confirm the orthodoxy of his ethics of the denial of the will (WN p. 143).

In 1844, on the publication of a second edition of *The World as Will and Representation* accompanied by a collection of supplementary essays larger than the original volume, Schopenhauer outlined a theoretical framework for his formerly piecemeal assertions of parallels between his philosophy and specific religious doctrines and practices. In one of the chapters in the supplementary volume — 'On Man's Need for Metaphysics' — he located the origin of religion and philosophy in the human need for a metaphysical interpretation of life, while also differentiating between religious and philosophical metaphysics with respect to variations in medium of communication, form, intellectual scaffolding and function. This theory became the kernel of Schopenhauer's explicit philosophy of religion, and from 1844 onwards it provided the central presuppositions of his statements on the topic. It pervades the essays and aphorisms of his last work *Parerga and Paralipomena*, published in 1851, as well as the revisions he made of his earlier works — the second, 1847 edition of his doctoral dissertation, *On the Fourfold Root of the Principle of Sufficient Reason*; the third, 1859 edition of his "chief work", *The World as Will and Representation*; and the second, 1860 edition of his essay *On the Basis of Morality* (first published in 1841 under the title *The Two Fundamental Problems of Ethics*, along with his prize-winning essay of 1839, *On the Freedom of the Will*).

Schopenhauer naturally offered his philosophy of religion as a detached and timeless reflection on the nature of religion in relation to its wiser brother philosophy, and although it can be read as a purely conceptual exercise of great insight and explanatory power, it also lends itself to an historical interpretation. Schopenhauer's philosophy of religion was, in part, a reflection of his personal apprehensions regarding the reception and destiny of his philosophical system, but on a broader level it mirrors his understanding and diagnosis of the changing situation and concerns of his time — its cultural mood, intellectual climate, social upheavals and religious crises. Schopenhauer formulated the negative moment of his philosophy of religion in a period of intellectual ferment, in response to new forms of knowledge and the rise of a critical attitude in many respects hostile to traditional Christianity. The well-founded theories and critical methods of the natural sciences were making their authority on matters of truth seem unassailable. While some nineteenth-century Churchmen aimed to avert a confrontation between science and theology by formulating highly speculative theories that presented the conclusions of natural science as so many additional confirmations of Christian doctrine, in other circles it was gradually dawning that the conclusions of science were undermining the antique cosmology and anthropology that Christianity had inherited from the ancient world and authenticated with the stamp of orthodoxy. In addition to this, scientific method was discrediting the modes of reasoning and argumentative procedures by which Christian theology had originally been established, and on the basis of which it had traditionally defended itself against opponents. In the wake of the indisputable successes obtained through the application of natural scientific method, the new faith of metaphysical and moral materialism (a 'scientistic' rather than 'scientific' world-view) was threatening to supplant traditional forms of belief and practice in Europe.

The cultural supremacy of Christian doctrine and practice had lately come under attack from another direction, from sceptical and anti-clerical currents stemming from the Enlightenment. The eighteenth-century French *philosophes* had been notoriously hostile to God and the Church, but Hume's carefully reasoned assault on Christian doctrine and morals exerted a greater influence on Schopenhauer's philosophy of religion. Hume's critique was two-pronged, aimed first at undermining the demonstrative ambitions of natural theology and the miraculous props of revealed religion, then at the "whole train of monkish virtues" justified by these — "[c]elibacy, fasting, penance, mortification, self-denial, humility, silence, solitude".[18] Although Schopenhauer learnt and borrowed a great deal from Hume's critique of natural and revealed theology, he considered Hume's catalogue of "monkish virtues" independent of Christian doctrine and capable of justification without it.

In addition to challenges from the external disciplines of science and philosophy, the integrity of Christian doctrine was suffering erosion at source and *from within*, through philological studies of the Bible. Originally refined for research into Graeco-Roman literature, methods of historical and text critical analysis had led biblical theologians, such as Johann Semler,[19] to develop theoretical reconstructions of the collection of the biblical canon that tended to puncture its traditional, iconic status as the sole, unique and authoritative revelation of God's saving word to humankind. The historical reliability of the Old Testament narratives and the world-historical significance they attributed to events in ancient Israel were exposed as tendentious. Viewed within the wider context of the civilisations and societies of the ancient Middle East, the Old Testament and the religion of Israel began to look parochial, no longer a suitable basis for the values of a cosmopolitan, universal culture. In 1835 David Friedrich Strauss made the radical and sacrilegious step of applying the methods of philology and the assumptions of Hegelian philosophy to the New Testament, and in the process developed the thesis that the narratives of the Gospel and their various portraits of Jesus were products of a religious rather than historical mode of understanding. Strauss thereby stimulated a flood of activity aimed at unearthing the Jesus of history from the layers of myth putatively attending his representation in the Bible.

Many of the categories, contrasts and claims found in Schopenhauer's mature philosophy of religion were previously rehearsed in works of biblical criticism such as Strauss' *Life of Jesus* — including the allegorical approach to understanding religious doctrines as a *via media* between rationalism and supernaturalism, and the related theory that Jesus' disciples obscured his historical figure and ethical significance by clothing his person in supernatural and mythical attributes drawn from the religious milieu of the Old Testament.[20] The influence of biblical

---

[18] Hume (1966) p. 108.

[19] Professor of Theology at Halle and author of the four-volume *Abhandlung von freier Untersuchung des Kanons* (1771-75).

[20] Strauss (1906) pp. 83-6. Schopenhauer read Strauss' work, and commended its mythical approach to the New Testament narratives (PPI p. 269; PPII p. 385).

philology on the death of God is often underestimated, but a case might be made for arguing that more nineteenth-century thinkers lost their faith as a result of the paradigm shift in attitude towards the Bible inaugurated by the conjectures of Form, Tradition and Higher criticism, than as a result of the argumentative assaults on Christian doctrine formulated by natural scientists and philosophers.[21] It is, furthermore, telling that the most militant currents in twentieth-century theology have been biblicist, sustaining their positions and composing multi-volume dogmatic works while blithely overlooking or denying the relevance of biblical criticism to the practice of theology.[22]

The negative phase of Schopenhauer's philosophy of religion was also influenced by his allegiance to the critical philosophy of "the great Kant", the "all-pulveriser" who had undermined the realist assumptions of the traditional proofs of the existence of God and exposed the theoretical weaknesses of natural theology.[23] But Schopenhauer considered Kant's "greatest merit" — the distinction between phenomenon and thing-in-itself — to have deprived not merely natural theology but also its principal opponent, materialism, of its central assumptions. Schopenhauer regarded theism and materialism as companions in error rather than opponents, insofar as both are species of realism that deny the mutual dependence of subject and object established by idealism and attempt to derive the existence of one from the other. Hence, theism aims to resolve everything on a hyper-subject represented as spiritual substantiality, while materialism raises the alleged atomic substrate of objects to the level of the thing-in-itself and explains the subject as a modification thereof (WWRII p. 16). Since, in Schopenhauer's view, Kant's transcendental idealism can be condensed into the complementary formulas "no object without subject" and "no subject without object", its thesis of the ideality of the forms and laws of the phenom-

---

[21] George Eliot's commitment to evangelical Christianity was famously crushed as a result of translating Strauss' *Leben Jesu* and Feuerbach's *Das Wesen des Christentums* into English. And although Nietzsche was to vilify Strauss' later works as embodiments of cultured-philistinism, as a theology student in 1865 he warned his friend Paul Deussen of the atheistic implications of Strauss' New Testament scholarship, remarking that it has "a serious consequence — if you give up Christ, you will have to give up God too." — quoted from Hayman (1995) p. 63.

[22] I am thinking primarily of Karl Barth and his followers.

[23] The eighteenth-century Jewish philosopher, Moses Mendelssohn, had originally coined the term "all-pulveriser" to describe Kant's effect on the metaphysical tradition to which Mendelssohn himself belonged.

enon had undermined the very sense of the presuppositions of eighteenth-century disputes between theism and naturalism, teleology and chance, spirit and matter, and God and immorality (WWRI p. 513; PPII p. 105; BM p. 45). However, in Schopenhauer's estimation the significance of Kant's distinction between phenomenon and thing-in-itself was not merely critical or negative but also creative. In addition to destabilising the realist assumptions of theological and materialist metaphysics, it also supplied the occasion, and to an extent the premises, for taking the age-old metaphysical task of solving the riddle of existence in a new direction (BM p. 209).

The positive phase of Schopenhauer's philosophy of religion had another source in the late eighteenth-century reaction to Kant and the *Aufklärung* represented by Johann Georg Hamann, Friedrich Heinrich Jacobi and Johann Gottfried Herder. In various ways these thinkers disputed the Enlightenment's rational anthropology and confidence in the impartiality, universality and objectivity of reasoned enquiry with the counter-claim that reason always operates within the limits of concrete interests and needs, and ought therefore to recognise its subordination to and inability to criticise tradition. Their anti-Enlightenment subordination of reason to deeper instincts operating in the human breast bears comparison with Schopenhauer's theory of human nature as the objectification of blind, non-rational will. The early nineteenth-century Romantic heirs of Hamann, Jacobi and Herder — Friedrich Wilhelm Joseph von Schelling, Friedrich Daniel Ernst Schleiermacher, the brothers Friedrich and August Wilhelm von Schlegel, Johann Ludwig Tieck and Friedrich von Hardenberg (a.k.a. Novalis) — turned to religion, art and poetry as containers of the untrammelled operations of immediate inspiration and volitional faith, undisturbed by the sophistications of reason, including their manifestation in the literary sources of ancient and exotic folk cultures. They thereby made the German cultural scene receptive to a development which was to be one of the most crucial factors in determining the positive content of Schopenhauer's philosophy of religion, as well as his understanding of a possible solution to the religious and moral crisis of his time — the translation and systematic study of classical Indian texts. In the next chapter I will survey the rise and growth of the academic discipline of Indology from the late eighteenth century onwards, as well as the reception of its labours by important German thinkers previous to and contemporary with Schopenhauer, in particular Herder, Friedrich Schlegel and Hegel.

III. Hermeneutics vs. Comparison

This book is therefore a study of the interpretative, philosophical and historical issues relevant to Schopenhauer's philosophy of religion in its two moments, the death of God and the oriental renaissance. Its primary task is to reconstruct Schopenhauer's philosophy of religion and only secondarily to assess its adequacy, so that I will not be outlining my own understanding of Christianity, Hinduism or Buddhism in order to oppose this to Schopenhauer's representation, and will for the most part put the question of his interpretative fidelity to the 'objective' essence of these religions to one side. This is because from a non-sectarian perspective, Christianity, Hinduism and Buddhism are simply too large, multi-faceted and variegated for a thinker with a specific agenda such as Schopenhauer to have represented them exactly in every instance, so that for every general description he offers of their 'true spirit' or 'inner meaning', a contrary example is easily found. However, the reverse is equally true, since the multi-faceted and variegated nature of these religions entails that it is possible to find examples that match and confirm his presentation. For example, Schopenhauer argued that Hinduism and Buddhism teach the ideality of the many and the reality of the one (PPII p. 378; WWRII p. 463), and on this basis claimed them as religious counterparts of his philosophical idealism and metaphysical monism. If we test the validity of this claim in relation to Pali Canon Buddhism only, its falsity is easily demonstrated. As Peter Abelson points out, the ontology of the Pali Canon, and of the Abhidharma philosophers who systematised its teachings, was realist and pluralist rather than idealist and monist.[24] According to them, mental and physical life is a temporary assemblage of ultimate, extra-mental elements called *dharmas*. Even *nirvāṇa* is classified as a *dharma* by these schools, and subsumed under the sub-category of undefiled and unconditioned *dharmas* in contrast to the defiled and conditioned *dharmas* that make up *saṃsāra*. On the basis of this summary of Abhidharma, the immediate conclusion follows that Schopenhauer's characterisation of Buddhism as a religious instance of idealism and metaphysical monism is simply and unequivocally false.

However, Schopenhauer knew very little about Pali Canon Buddhism. Most of the earliest European sources on the religion came from the Mahāyāna tradition, and Schopenhauer himself seems to have been generally unaware of the division between Pali and Sanskrit or Southern and

---

[24] Abelson (1993) p. 258.

Northern Buddhism. Two Mahāyāna schools, Mādhyamika and Yogācāra (also known as Vijñānavāda), are generally recognised as idealist and monist in some sense, but whether they are idealist and monist in exactly Schopenhauer's sense is another question. When Nāgārjuna, the founder of Mādhyamika, states that where "the sphere of thought has ceased, that which is to be designated also has ceased",[25] there are very strong parallels with Schopenhauer's summary of his subject-object correlativism as "it is all one whether we say 'sensibility and understanding are no more,' or 'the world is at an end'" (FR p. 210). However, Nāgārjuna roundly rejected any metaphysical interpretation of the objects of experience by arguing that their appearance is the result of mutual conditioning, so that they lack, or are 'empty' (śūnya) of inherent existence or the property of self-subsistence (svabhāva). It might, therefore, be inferred that Nāgārjuna would have objected to Schopenhauer's metaphysics on account of its erroneous attribution of aseity to the will, which, for Nāgārjuna, cannot be separated from its causes and conditions (i.e., its motives).[26]

However, if Schopenhauer and Mādhyamika ultimately diverge, then the parallels between Schopenhauer and Yogācāra or Vijñānavāda seem to be much closer. In common with Schopenhauer, Vijñānavāda relegates the world of ordinary experience to the level of appearance, and although the language and terms of its metaphysics — such as its central concept, the ālaya-vijñāna (usually translated as 'storehouse consciousness') — suggest that it is a form of absolute idealism or consciousness-monism, T.R.V. Murti's summary of its position establishes surprising parallels with Schopenhauer's metaphysics. Murti says that when the Vijñānavādin

> uses the terms jñāna, vijñāna, vijñapti, citta, svasamvedana, etc. he is really meaning by these terms the creative act, Will. His Vijñāna is really Pure Act; pure as it is not conditioned by anything outside it with regard to its existence and function; it is act, as it is not a static passive Being like the Vedāntic Brahman, but an incessantly self-active creative entity...the Vijñānavāda is the only genuinely idealistic school in India. Vijñāna is Cosmic, Impersonal Will, realising itself through the projection and retraction of the object.[27]

Murti's gloss of the metaphysics of Vijñānavāda seems to be an unequivocal confirmation of Schopenhauer's claim that Buddhism is in

---

[25] Nāgārjuna (1991) 18.7 (references to Nāgārjuna's Mūlamadhyamakakārikā are to chapter and aphorism rather than page number).
[26] "An agent proceeds depending upon action and action proceeds depending upon the agent. We do not perceive any other way of establishing them." (Nāgārjuna (1991) 8.12)
[27] Murti (1974) p. 316.

fundamental agreement with his own philosophy. However, caution ought to be taken when we reflect that Murti's study stands firmly within what Gadamer would have called the 'history of effect' (*Wirkungsgeschichte*), or ongoing tradition of Schopenhauer's interpretative project of establishing parallels between Indian thought and German Idealism. Moreover, several of Murti's glosses seem to serve the cultural agenda of demonstrating that Indian philosophy is either equal or superior to European, and his characterisation of the *ālaya-vijñāna* as *"creative act, Will"* seems to be, in part, a riposte to the claims of nineteenth-century Europeans such as Hegel that Indian metaphysics supports an ethics of stupor and passivity.[28] However, even if we grant objective validity to Murti's presentation, what consequence would this have for Schopenhauer's claim that Buddhism "is strictly idealistic" (FR p. 184) and in fundamental agreement with at least the monist aspect of his metaphysics of will? Does it mean he was right, or are the contrary examples of Abhidharma and Mādhyamika sufficient to show he was wrong? Or is it more exactly the case that Schopenhauer was simply cavalier in presenting one of the many options and tendencies offered by the history of Buddhism as its essential teaching? The same is true for his claim that Hinduism is not strictly a theistic religion, or that Christianity, Hinduism and Buddhism are 'in essence' pessimistic and ascetic. In every case such generalisations are as easily confirmed with particular examples as falsified. In the absence of any foundational or presupposed norm that might settle what Christianity, Hinduism or Buddhism 'really' are or ought to be, the comparative or anti-comparative approach to Schopenhauer's relation to Indian thought is not merely fraught with hermeneutical difficulties, but also, perhaps, of uncertain merit.

For these and other reasons, the substance of this book is concerned with the coherence of Schopenhauer's presentation of these religions rather than its correspondence, offering a contextual account that illustrates its inner consistency and continuity with his wider philosophical project and aims. However, in the course of indicating from where and how some of Schopenhauer's understandings of particular religious doctrines arose, the implication occasionally arises that they serve interests of his own and are, therefore, non-veridical and unsupported by his sources. On a few occasions, when the point in question merits it, I will signify how Schopenhauer's presuppositions and aims have distorted his overall view and presentation of certain key doctrines. However, my

---

[28] Hegel (1956) p. 169.

main purpose in doing so is to elucidate the hermeneutical logic of his interpretation of Indian thought, rather than to demonstrate its erroneousness.

In seeking to understand the various forces at play in Schopenhauer's philosophy of religion, and his treatment of Christianity, Hinduism and Buddhism in particular, I have found Gadamer's philosophical hermeneutics useful for conceptualising the limitations of historical understanding within and across intellectual traditions. Gadamer recommends we relinquish the idea stemming from the Enlightenment that we can jump outside our own historicity, slough off the particular prejudices we have received from our tradition, and enjoy an unmediated understanding of the material or textual artefacts of another culture. Gadamer actually defends the necessity of prejudices or "fore-understandings" (*Vorverständnisse*) as the conditions of the possibility of knowledge.[29] He construes attempts at understanding as a kind of dialogue between three parties — text, tradition and interpreter — involving a constant and circular exchange and reappraisal of meaning on the part of the hermeneutical subject.[30] This has been especially helpful in thinking about the various issues relevant to Schopenhauer's presentation of Hinduism and Buddhism, for the evidence suggests that his encounter with them was dialectical, and a possible source of certain shifts, re-articulations and revisions in the statement of his philosophy that appeared after the mid-1830s.

With the exception of Chapter 1, the content of which is largely historical and contextual, each chapter of this book examines an aspect of Schopenhauer's thought relevant to his philosophy of religion. Unfortunately, and on account of considerations of space, this work contains no self-contained exposition or critical analysis of Schopenhauer's transcendental idealism, metaphysics of will, morality of compassion or 'higher' ethics of asceticism. Instead, doctrines belonging to these areas of Schopenhauer's philosophy are introduced when the occasion requires. Although this procedure is partly a response to certain constraints, it also supports one of the main theses of this study, which is that Schopenhauer's presentation of Christianity, Hinduism and Buddhism is intimately related to his philosophical project, and is distorted and easily presented as either false or foolish when assessed independently of this context. Explicit illustration of how Schopenhauer's writings on religion

---

[29] Gadamer (1989) pp. 277f.
[30] Ibid. p. 293.

reflect his philosophical doctrines will, I hope, facilitate understanding
of the reasons and motivations that governed his rejection of dogmatic
theism and concurrent appropriation of the religious systems of Hinduism
and Buddhism, and therefore provide a framework for assessment of his
contribution to the philosophy of religion.

Chapter 1 begins with an historical overview of the growth of European Indology from the late eighteenth century onwards, including its
reception by prominent thinkers in Germany prior to and contemporary
with Schopenhauer, especially Herder, Friedrich Schlegel and Hegel.
This exposition provides the groundwork for examining how Schopenhauer's specific philosophical outlook led to the development of a unique
diagnosis and understanding of the intellectual, cultural and religious
upheavals of early nineteenth-century Europe, which in turn shaped the
very different expectations he brought to and distinct questions he asked
of the available literature on India. This chapter closes with a brief survey
of the effects of Schopenhauer's Indian interpretation and a discussion of
some of the scholarly literature on the topic, with the aim of demarcating
their methodological assumptions from those of this study.

Chapter 2 is an examination of Schopenhauer's theory of metaphysical
need, which he identifies as the causal origin of religion and philosophy,
the two species of metaphysics found in all civilised nations. Schopenhauer's discovery of a common ground for religion and philosophy in
human nature enabled him to argue that they are essentially identical, that
they serve the same function and ought, ideally, to communicate the same
content. However, he also argued that religion was the intellectual junior
of the two, since it satisfies the metaphysical needs of the many by presenting the demonstrative and conceptual knowledge of philosophy on
the basis of authority and in the medium of mythical and allegorical
imagery. However, contrary to his normative account of their relation,
Schopenhauer observed that political and cultural circumstances prevailing in Europe after Augustine, or more exactly after the fall of the Roman
Empire, had facilitated a situation in which the proper relation between
religion and philosophy had been reversed, with the latter subordinated
to the popular religion and obliged to work in its interests. The advent of
modernity had upset this relation, for its cultural and intellectual advance-
ments had challenged the dogmatic claims of the prevailing religion,
permitting philosophy to extricate itself from its former servitude and
promulgate doctrines of its own, without regard for their agreement with
the orthodoxies of popular religion. Although Schopenhauer welcomed
philosophy's new-found liberation, he also regretted the concomitant

intellectual marginalisation of the popular religion, for this had rendered it incapable of performing its traditional function of satisfying the metaphysical needs of the many by threatening to bring about its complete decline. In Schopenhauer's rather conservative outlook, the least desirable outcome of this development was the secularisation of European culture and the triumph of materialism. However, his theory of metaphysical need maintains that the instinct for religion goes deeper than social or historical conditioning, so that the death of one religion is likely to be succeeded by the introduction of a new form, one that is more compatible with the intellectual and cultural outlook of the age. And Schopenhauer thought that a suitable replacement for Judaeo-Christianity was currently and fortuitously being introduced into Europe through the academic study of Sanskrit texts.

Chapter 3 is an extended analysis of Schopenhauer's critique of the transcendent part of the prevailing religion of Europe — Judaeo-Christianity. In his view, the combined effect of the natural sciences, the philosophy of Kant, the rise of historical awareness and the general critical spirit of the age had, by the early nineteenth century, rendered belief in the transcendent doctrines of Christianity — God, the creation of the world, the soul and its freedom and immortality — untenable.

And in Chapter 4 we see Schopenhauer intensifying his critique of transcendent monotheism by setting the immanent doctrines of Christianity against it, doctrines such as the Christian teachings of the ubiquity of suffering and evil, the Fall, original sin, and the need for salvation from the human condition through selflessness and ultimate denial. He regarded these latter doctrines as allegorical illustrations of important truths, accounting for Christianity's ability to displace Greco-Roman paganism and cater to the spiritual and metaphysical needs of Europeans for almost eighteen centuries. In the interests of preserving the insights conveyed by these doctrines and the moods and values they inculcate, Schopenhauer thought it necessary to separate them from the system of theism currently in decline and append them to a more adequate metaphysics, such as the popular religious cosmology of the Indian religions, "Brahmanism and Buddhism". And, in his view, this was no arbitrary or *ad hoc* manoeuvre, but the correction of an historical error, insofar as research into the Indian faiths was not merely revealing their fundamental agreement with the ethical outlook of Christianity, but was also indicating that they were among the historical sources of Jesus' ethical religion.

In Chapter 5 we review the type and variety of Indological sources available to Schopenhauer, and recount the stages in his intellectual development at which he encountered them. This is partly for the purpose of establishing a foundation for subsequent exposition and analysis of his presentation of their content, but also to assess the claim proposed by some scholars that Schopenhauer's philosophy was influenced by Indian thought. This chapter also considers Schopenhauer's account of the historical standing of Indian thought in relation to European, and reconstructs his theory of its sources, nature and methods.

Chapter 6 is an exposition of the theoretical basis of Schopenhauer's expectation of an oriental renaissance in detail, and is in the main a reconstruction and contextual analysis of his interpretation of the key doctrines of the Indian religions. Since Schopenhauer thought that the Indian religions represented the best of Christianity in its purest and original form, and expressed the hope that, with the decline of theism, Europeans might embrace Hinduism and Buddhism as the sacred vessels for the indestructible ethics and true view of life that had hitherto been sustained by Christian doctrine, the structure of this chapter parallels the exposition of Schopenhauer's treatment of Judaeo-Christianity in Chapters 3 and 4.

The Conclusion summarises the main themes arising from the study of Schopenhauer's repudiation of theism and concomitant endorsement of the religions of India, and examines Schopenhauer's religious and philosophical legacy in relation to the themes of the death of God and the oriental renaissance.

CHAPTER 1

EUROPE AND INDIA

I. The Scholars

Schopenhauer attributed the critical or negative side of his philosophy of religion to three recent developments in the intellectual history of Europe: the rise of the natural sciences, Kant's critique of the realist presuppositions of natural theology, and the expansion of historical and cultural knowledge generally, but especially "acquaintance with Sanskrit literature, Brahmanism, and Buddhism" (BM p. 44). The positive moment of his philosophy of religion makes use of two of the aforementioned sources: the philosophy of Kant — this time its distinction between phenomenon and thing-in-itself — and the religious doctrines and ethical outlook of Hinduism and Buddhism. On account of limitations of space, this study presupposes Kant's arguments for transcendental idealism and its distinction between appearance and thing-in-itself, as well as Kant's exposure of the transcendental illusions of dogmatic metaphysics.[1] In this chapter, however, we begin with an account of the rise of academic Indology in Europe, since this had a very great effect on the form and content of the positive moment of Schopenhauer's philosophy of religion.

In 1784 a group of British employees of the East India Company in Calcutta founded the Asiatic Society of Bengal, "for the Purpose of enquiring into the History, Civil and Natural, the Antiquities, Arts, Sciences, and Literature of *Asia*".[2] Since the time of Alexander the Great's Indian Campaign of 327-325 B.C.E., the wisdom of India and the practices and attainments of its Holy Men — the "gymnosophists", "Brachmanes" and "Sarmanes" of myth and historical legend — had waxed and waned in the imagination of Europe,[3] but a radical change

---

[1] However, I shall, as the occasion requires, discuss specific points of Schopenhauer's understanding and estimation of Kant's contribution to philosophy and the philosophy of religion.

[2] Quoted from a letter by the Society requesting the patronage of Sir Warren Hastings, governor-general of British India, reprinted in *Asiatick Researches vol.I*, p. v.

[3] In the late fourth century B.C.E. the Greek historian Megasthenes coined the terms "gymnosophists", "Brachmanes" and "Sarmanes" to refer, respectively, to the naked renunciates of India, Hindu Brahmins and Buddhist monks (*śramaṇas*). These terms were

occurred with the foundation of the Asiatic Society. Its members viewed the artefacts of Indian civilisation as a scholarly research project and their studies as a contribution to knowledge, rather than as the scholarly arm of missionary strategy, which had been the primary motive for Jesuit studies of the religions of China and India from the sixteenth century onwards.

This is not to state that the members of the Asiatic Society were initially or always pure, disinterested enquirers. Sir William Jones, the Society's founder and president and editor of its journal *Asiatick Researches*, arrived in India to take up the post of judge at the Supreme Court in Calcutta. Already a scholar of Persian literature, Jones initially studied Sanskrit so that the British judiciary might have direct access to the law-codes of the Hindus. Prior to this, executors of British rule had been dependent upon the exegetical expertise and trustworthiness of local paṇḍits for interpreting and applying the maxims of Sanskrit legal texts to specific cases, in accordance with British colonial policy that indigenous subjects be held accountable before their own laws. Jones' major translation from a Sanskrit manuscript was of the *Mānavadharmaśāstra* (*The Laws of Manu*), which appeared in 1794, under the very classical and Justinian title *Institutes of Indian Law*.

However, prior to 1794 Jones had undertaken translations of texts with a less obvious political application. In 1789 he translated Kālidāsa's classical drama *Śakuntalā*, which was received with great enthusiasm by Herder and Goethe, and in 1792 an English version of the *Gītāgovinda*, whose allegorical depiction of the soul's union with the Godhead resonated with the sentiments of many Romantics. Prior to this, in 1785, Charles Wilkins had earned the distinction of being the first member of the Society to translate a work direct from a Sanskrit manuscript with the appearance of his English *Bhagavad-Gītā*, which he followed in 1787 with a translation of the collection of animal fables known as the *Hitopadeśa*. In 1802 Wilkins' *Bhagavad-Gītā* and Jones' *Gītāgovinda* were translated from English into German by a student of Herder, the orientalist Friedrich Majer, lecturer at Jena and advocate of Indian literature to the poets and thinkers of the Weimar circle. In addition to translating primary sources, the Society's members published articles on an array of topics in its journal *Asiatick Researches*, from ancient Indian astronomy and mathematics, through India's flora and fauna, up to the classical

---

later adopted and made canonical by Arrian, Strabo and Clement of Alexandria — see Batchelor (1994) p. 7.

languages of Indian literature and the doctrines and practices of its religions. Henry Thomas Colebrooke, the third most prominent member of the Society and the most productive in the field of Indian religion and philosophy, published essays on the *Vedas* and on the religious ceremonies of Hinduism which contained long translations of hymns and passages from the *Vedas* and the *Upaniṣads*. His articles on the doctrines and practices of the six orthodox schools of Hinduism and the so-called "heterodox" systems of Buddhism and Jainism were published in London from 1827 onwards in the *Transactions of the Royal Asiatic Society*, and received as authoritative and approved sources by both Schopenhauer and Hegel, among others.

The most important hypothesis arising from the scholarly researches of the Asiatic Society was Jones' theory of India's formative relationship to European civilisation. His 1784 address to the Society, 'On the Gods of Greece, Italy, and India', posited a common origin for the pantheon of all three ancient systems of mythology, including the "Gothick system" as a fourth. Two years later, on the occasion of his Third Anniversary Address to the Society, Jones followed up his mythological speculations with his justly famous hypothesis regarding the common origin of Sanskrit and the central languages of European civilisation:

> The SANSCRIT language, whatever be its antiquity, is of a wonderful structure; more perfect than the GREEK; more copious than the LATIN, and more exquisitely refined than either, yet bearing to both of them a stronger affinity, both in the roots of verbs and in the grammar, than could possibly have been produced by accident; so strong indeed, that no philologer could examine them all three, without believing them to have sprung from some common source, which, perhaps, no longer exists; there is a similar reason, though not quite so forcible, for supposing that both the GOTHICK and the CELTIC, though blended with a very different idiom, had the same origin with the SANSCRIT, and the old PERSIAN might be added to the same family.[4]

In addition to its scholarly importance, Jones' hypothesis had a very strong impact on the imagination of Europe, for it suggested that further research into the ancient civilisation of India would simultaneously uncover the roots of European culture. It thereby acted as a great stimulus to the growth and popularity of comparative studies of language, myth and religion as the routes to European self-knowledge.

Independent of Jones and his colleagues, Abraham Hyacinthe Anquetil-Duperron, a French Persianist, had been pursuing solitary researches on

---

[4] Jones (1789c) pp. 422-3.

the ancient scriptures of India. In 1761, after a seven year stay in the sub-continent, Duperron returned to his homeland with a manuscript containing a Persian translation of the fifty most important *Upaniṣads*. This collection had originally been translated from Sanskrit in 1656 by a group of Brahmins commissioned by Dara Shikoh, Crown Prince of Delhi, son of the Moghul Emperor Shah-Jahan, great-grandson of Emperor Akbar, and unfortunate elder brother of Emperor Aurangzeb who, on his ascendancy to the throne, had Dara Shikoh executed for apostasy from Islam. Shikoh had commissioned the translation in the hope of discovering parallels between the scriptures of Hinduism and the *Qur'an*, thereby confirming the dictum of his great-grandfather Emperor Akbar that the different religions agree in spirit. Anquetil translated the entire fifty into Latin and published them in 1801-02 under the title *Oupnek'hat* (a corruption of the original '*Upaniṣad*'). The text has attained a degree of notoriety — not least because it remained the most comprehensive collection of Indian scriptures in a western language until 1897, when Schopenhauer's disciple Paul Deussen translated sixty *Upaniṣads* direct from Sanskrit into German[5] — but mainly on account of the palpable eccentricities of Duperron's approach. He chose to translate only the words into Latin while retaining the Persian grammar and syntax of the original manuscript. However, irrespective of its shortcomings, the *Oupnek'hat* provided an entire generation of European thinkers with their first substantial contact with the religious and philosophical ideas of ancient India. Anquetil's inclusion of scholarly appendices, in which he instituted the coming philosophical debate between east and west by pointing out comparisons between the doctrines of India and the ideas of Kant, Plato, Plotinus and the Gnostics, further facilitated the *Oupnek'hat's* reception among European philosophers. Anquetil's comparisons clearly had an effect on Schopenhauer, for in the 1818 Preface to his chief work he maintained that a preliminary reading of the works of Kant, Plato and the *Upaniṣads* constituted the best preparation for comprehension of his own system (WWRI p. xv).

Schopenhauer was introduced to Anquetil's *Oupnek'hat* in the winter of 1813-14 when, having submitted his doctoral dissertation to the University of Jena, he met Herder's disciple, Friedrich Majer, at his mother's home in Weimar. Majer recommended the *Oupnek'hat* to the young philosopher, and thereby initiated Schopenhauer's enduring love-affair with Anquetil's *Oupnek'hat* and his first substantial and mature

---

[5] See Deussen (1897).

contact with Indian thought.[6] Apart from August Wilhelm Schlegel's 1823 Latin translation of the *Bhagavad-Gītā* and Colebrooke's rather brief translations of some passages and hymns from the original *Vedas* and the *Upaniṣads*, Anquetil's *Oupnek'hat* was to remain Schopenhauer's chief and favourite sourcebook on Hinduism until his death in 1860. Other, incomplete translations from the *Upaniṣads* that appeared in European languages during his lifetime — by Rammohan Roy, Röer, Pooley, as well as Colebrooke — he considered inferior, occidental, and blighted by theism (PPII p. 397; BM p. 207n.8). Every time Schopenhauer refers his readers to the "*Upaniṣads* of the *Vedas*", he means the *Oupnek'hat*: every Upaniṣadic quote that appears in his works either translates or reproduces Anquetil's Latin. As an old man, Schopenhauer's evening routine was to play the flute and then spend a few hours pious reading of the *Oupnek'hat* before going to sleep.[7] In 1851, thirty-eight years after his meeting with Majer, Schopenhauer still had only rapturous praise for Anquetil's translation:

---

[6] Urs App has recently complicated the traditional story that Schopenhauer's first contact with India came through Majer's recommendation of the *Oupnek'hat*. In an impressive piece of scholarly detective work, App has published Schopenhauer's lecture notes from a course he attended on eastern ethnography given by Professor Heeren at Göttingen in the summer of 1811 (App (2003), (2006a)), as well as the 1813-14 records from the Weimar public library which show that Schopenhauer borrowed *Das Asiatisches Magazin* (containing Majer's German translation of Wilkins' English *Bhagavad-Gītā*) in December 1813, four months before he borrowed Anquetil's *Oupnek'hat* (App (2006b) pp. 40-61). However, App's findings are hardly sufficient to overturn the prevailing view that Schopenhauer's encounter with the *Oupnek'hat* was *the* event that secured his life-long interest in Indian thought and culture. The lecture notes of 1811 are a mass of unsynthesised factual material — now relating that China is divided into fifteen provinces, that the Japanese practice monogamy, the Tibetans polyandry and that India has "four sacred books, the Vedams" — but do not indicate that Schopenhauer learnt anything substantial from Heeren about the eastern doctrines to which he later attached significance. And App's contention that, because Schopenhauer read Majer's translation of the *Bhagavad-Gītā* before Anquetil's *Oupnek'hat*, the former text was central to Schopenhauer's understanding of Indian thought, and even "crucially important for the genesis of Schopenhauer's metaphysics of will" (App (2006b) p. 76), relies solely on the fact of chronological priority. References to Majer's *Bhagavad-Gītā* are completely outweighed by those to the *Oupnek'hat* in Schopenhauer's early notes and publications, and after the appearance of August Wilhelm Schlegel's Latin translation of the *Gītā* in 1823, Schopenhauer never again cited Majer's 1802 edition. As for App's claim that Majer's *Bhagavad-Gītā* was an important influence on Schopenhauer's metaphysics, its sole basis is that Schopenhauer and the *Gītā* shared a common commitment to metaphysical monism. But the distinguishing feature of Schopenhauer's metaphysics is not simply that it is monist, but that its unitary principle is blind *will*, and this has no parallel at all in the *Gītā*, which makes it a highly unlikely source.

[7] Merkel (1948) p. 164.

how thoroughly redolent of the holy spirit of the *Vedas* is the *Oupnek'hat*! How deeply stirred is he who, by diligent and careful reading, is now conversant with the Persian-Latin rendering of this incomparable book! How imbued is every line with firm, definite, and harmonious significance! From every page we come across profound, original, and sublime thoughts, whilst a lofty and sacred earnestness pervades the whole. Here everything breathes the air of India and radiates an existence that is original and akin to nature. And oh, how the mind is here cleansed and purified of all Jewish superstition that was early implanted in it, and of all philosophy that slavishly serves this! With the exception of the original text, it is the most profitable and sublime reading that is possible in the world; it has been the consolation of my life and will be that of my death. (PPII p. 397)

Inspired by his encounter with the *Oupnek'hat*, Schopenhauer began to seek out further materials on ancient India, borrowing the first ten volumes of *Asiatick Researches* from the public library at Dresden between November 1815 and May 1816. In 1814 he had begun work on his system, published in late 1818 as the first edition of *The World as Will and Representation*. His notebooks from 1816 onwards illustrate the extent of his engagement with Indian sources during this period, employing Sanskrit terms such as *māyā* as shorthand references for his own developing doctrines (MRI p. 113, p. 130, p. 247, p. 332, p. 419, p. 444). Commentators who argue that Schopenhauer's philosophy was indebted to the doctrines of classical Indian religion (or, at least, to his understanding of them) usually identify this period as the crucial period of influence. Schopenhauer himself remarked, in a manuscript note dating from 1816, "I confess that I do not believe my doctrine could have come before the *Upaniṣads*, Plato and Kant could cast their rays simultaneously into the mind of one man" (MRI p. 467), which might be taken as an admission of substantial dependence on themes and ideas he found in the *Oupnek'hat*. However, in an earlier note from 1813, pre-dating his meeting with Majer and exposure to the *Oupnek'hat*, Schopenhauer observed the formation in his mind of a system that is ethics and metaphysics in one (MRI p. 59), which has stimulated the counter-claim defended by Christopher Janaway that Schopenhauer's early encounter with Hindu sources only "contributed to the development of his philosophy, dovetailing with the rest of his thoughts towards the end of the process of completion."[8] The question whether or not Schopenhauer's system was, in origin, dependent upon Indian sources or not is a difficult one to resolve, since the data has been interpreted to support both the thesis of influence *and* the opposite. This is a question to which we will return later in Chapter 5.

---

[8] Janaway (1989) p. 29.

II. The Theorists

Schopenhauer's burgeoning interest in the literature on India had been pre-empted by a number of prominent figures in German cultural and intellectual life, for as Edward Said comments, there was a "virtual epidemic of Orientalia affecting every major poet, essayist, and philosopher of the period."[9] The scientific discipline of Indology may have been instituted by the British in Calcutta, but their countrymen back home were less supportive of their labours than the French or Germans. Britain did not establish a chair of Sanskrit until 1831. France established the first in Europe in 1814, with the Germans following in 1818 when August Wilhelm Schlegel was appointed Professor of Sanskrit at the University of Bonn. But although the French pre-empted the Germans at the scholarly and institutional level, German literary and cultural enthusiasm for the idea of ancient India surpassed anything comparable in France. From the outset many German thinkers possessed a strong sense of national and spiritual affinity with the ancient peoples of India. Academic Indology was disclosing a culture that pre-dated both Moses and the Greeks, yet which seemed not only to share the concerns of the present but to offer solutions to its problems. For the leading German thinkers at the turn of the nineteenth century Indology was more than a novel research discipline, a new area for European science to circumscribe and conquer, as it was for most of the French and had been for the British. It was, instead, the focus of hopes concerning the possibility of cultural regeneration, and a centre of opposition to the prosaic rationalism and pragmatism of the Enlightenment, which many Germans identified with the classicism of eighteenth-century France.

The intellectual underpinnings of these hopes — the hopes of Romanticism — had been laid at the end of the eighteenth century, during the height of the *Aufklärung*, by Johann Gottfried Herder. Herder turned from the ahistorical, transcendental perspective on the human subject favoured by his former teacher, Kant, to the study of the concrete life of particular historical cultures, in order to observe the various manifestations of his regulative idea of "humanity" — "distributed in a thousand forms, continually changing shape like an eternal Proteus throughout all continents and centuries."[10] In his main work, the *Ideas toward a*

---

[9] Said (1985) p. 50.
[10] Herder (1993) p. 44.

Philosophy of History of Mankind,[11] Herder opposed Kant's transcendental deduction of the categories with the immanent thesis that the faculties of understanding, reflection and thinking originate and take shape in specific cultural contexts, and find expression through the medium of language. In Herder's view language is more than merely a tool for outward expression of an inner, mental content. Instead, thinking is coeval with and dependent upon prior mastery of a specific language, for "not even the first, most elementary use of reason could take place without language."[12]

And Herder was sensitive to the extra-epistemological and cultural relevance of his theory of mind and language. He hoped it would stimulate investigation into the origins of culture and the roots of language, in order to correct what he saw as the one-sided intellectualism of the Enlightenment. In Herder's view language in its infancy had expressed the immediate impression of nature upon man and his awareness of the indwelling God, but the original, poetic vivacity of the human spirit expressed in words had since been lost. In the modern period language has become intellectualised, conventional, abstract, and no longer capable of expressing man's original sense of being-in-the-world and in relation to God.[13] Herder also encouraged the study of comparative mythology and religion, the results of which, he predicted, would be

> not only a history but also an applied critique of human reasoning about God, the world, creation, the order of things, destiny, purpose, and the historical changes and origin of everything that our eyes apprehend and our imagination dreams.[14]

He suggested that the most fruitful areas for research would be the mythologies and religions of "the pure, ancient, civilised nations", for these were symbolic vessels containing ancient man's original knowledge of God. Armed with Herder's theses that the study of language and ancient mythology was the route to uncovering founts of sensibility and knowledge since submerged in sophistication and complexity, his early nineteenth-century Romantic successors encouraged the development of comparative linguistics and mythology. Needless to say, the study of Sanskrit and ancient Indian mythology indubitably benefited from

---

[11] Published in four parts, 1784, 1785, 1787 and 1791 respectively. The later parts show evidence of the influence of the publications of the Asiatic Society on Herder's estimation of the historical significance of India and Asia.

[12] Herder (1993) p. 75.

[13] Ibid. pp. 161-2.

[14] Ibid. pp. 81-2.

Herder's theories, as the case of the Indologist and ancient mythologist, Friedrich Majer, Herder's former student and friend, illustrates.

However, Herder stimulated interest in the cultural artefacts of ancient India in a more direct manner, through his speculations on Asia's pivotal role in the development of European civilisation. He argued that humankind had originated somewhere in Asia, with the "most ancient kingdoms and states of the Earth" appearing on its foot-hills. He defended these suppositions on the basis of geographical and climatic assumptions, speculating that Asia in the most ancient times, as a mountainous plateau and "the mid-point of creation", was unlikely to have been covered in water like other parts of the earth, while its climate would have been sufficiently benign to support life and thereby facilitate the development of civilisation.[15] Herder traced the first alphabet and language and all the arts and sciences enjoyed by later civilisations to Asia, which had been brought to the west by the migrating inhabitants of the Asian fatherland, of whom Europeans are the descendants. And the flower of Asia for Herder was India. He speculated that Buddhism, or as he called it "the religion of Fo", was the original religion of all Asia, but that "the doctrine of the brahmins" was its most perfectly developed subspecies: "Of all the sects of Fo, which occupy the eastern world of Asia, this [Hinduism] is the flower: more learned, more humane, more useful, more noble, than all the bonzes, lamas, and talapoius." The Brahmin idea of God is "grand and beautiful", their morality "pure and sublime, and even their fables, when scanned by the eye of reason, are so refined and charming."[16] Herder's notion of India was highly lyrical and idealised: it was the cradle of the human race, and unlike Greece it had preserved its unspoilt and natural existence into the present. The Indian soul was mild, innocent and child-like, its morals the natural expression of a guileless constitution, far removed from the over-refined, concept-based morality of modern Europeans. Herder, like Schopenhauer after him, was severely critical of missionary activity in India. Although an ordained Christian minister, part of Herder's polemic against the universalism of the Enlightenment consisted of the claim that there is no over-arching route to happiness or holiness, since each culture posits its own notion of human perfection along with the means for its attainment. However, Herder was sufficiently Christian to express concern at the doctrine of trans-

---

[15] Herder (1800) p. 289.
[16] Ibid. p. 308.

migration and the caste system and the ways in which they challenged the unity of his regulative principle of humanity (*Humanität*). Transmigration's teaching that human souls have and will inhabit the bodies of plants and animals undermines the integrity of humanity by dispersing it throughout nature, while the caste system confirms this dispersion by projecting merely conventional and social divisions onto nature with its teaching of a hierarchy of human souls.[17]

Herder's theses on the authenticity and natural spontaneity of ancient language, myth and religion, combined with his theory that Europe's pristine and childhood state persisted undisturbed in India, were taken by many of the succeeding generation of German thinkers as pointing the way to the fulfilment of their ambition to bring about cultural renewal through revitalisation of the spiritual, moral and aesthetic standards of true religion. Hume and Kant had undermined the traditional arguments and assumptions of natural theology, while biblical criticism was doing the same for revealed. The Romantics thought that poetry and art had become mannered, and looked askance at the rise of science and technological industrialisation which, in their view, were threatening to make humans into machines. European culture seemed to have lost its harmonious centre and its instinct for religion. In 1802 Schelling maintained that the 'speculative' Idea of Christianity had been present in ancient India, prior to the appearance of the Old and New Testaments, and expressed the hope that knowledge of the Indian expression of the Idea might liberate Christian belief from its former dependence on revelation and empirical history.[18] In the same year Friedrich Schlegel went to Paris to learn Sanskrit, in the hope of encountering the origins of European language, literature and religion as they had immediately welled up from the natural soul of the Hindu. Schlegel had already assimilated the mythical image of India promulgated by Herder. For him it was a land of harmonious perfection, its culture enjoying an unbroken link with the ancient past, free of the dichotomies dividing that of modern European — reason and feeling, knowledge and religion, and philosophy and poetry. In 1800 Schlegel had already arrived at the conviction that "we must find the highest romanticism in the Orient."[19] In 1802 he set out to discover this pure romanticism for himself, and the fruit of his researches was the first work in the German language based on original study of

[17] Ibid. p. 309.
[18] Schelling (1966) pp. 94-7.
[19] Schlegel (1968) p. 320.

Sanskrit sources, *On the Language and Wisdom of the Indians*, published in 1808.[20]

Schlegel's dissertation testifies to the depths of his allegiance to Herder's theses on ancient language, mythology and religion, and to his expectation that the oldest available Indian sources contained Christianity in its unadulterated form. Jones' hypothesis and Herder's speculations encouraged the belief that an encounter with the thought-world and religion of ancient India was simultaneously an encounter with the root elements of European civilisation, but without the inauthentic and mannered sophistications they had assumed in the present. Schlegel was therefore the first of our thinkers to articulate explicitly the prediction from which this study takes the latter half of its subtitle — the prediction that Sanskrit sources would bring about an oriental renaissance, comparable to that witnessed earlier through the reintroduction of Greek learning:

> The study of Indian literature requires to be embraced by such students and patrons as in the fifteenth and sixteenth centuries kindled in Italy and Germany an ardent appreciation of the beauty of classical learning, and in so short a time invested it with such prevailing importance, that the form of all wisdom and science, and almost of the world itself, was changed and renovated by the influence of that re-awakened knowledge. I venture to predict that the Indian study, if embraced with equal energy, will prove no less grand and universal in its operation, and have no less influence on the sphere of European intelligence.[21]

The first book of Schlegel's treatise is devoted to exposition and analysis of the characteristics of Sanskrit and a comparison of these with analogous features of Greek, Latin, Persian and Gothic. Schlegel surpassed Jones' thesis that the Indo-European languages all derived from a common source since lost, by arguing that Sanskrit, though not the *Ur-Sprache* itself, is the source from which the others have descended, and is therefore the most ancient extant tongue.[22] He expressed great admiration for the structural perfection and internal consistency of Sanskrit, which he took as a counter-proof to naturalist and developmental theories regarding the near-animality of ancient man and his rudimentary capacity

---

[20] It is surprising that the Schlegels, Friedrich and August Wilhelm, were the only Germans to learn Sanskrit during this period. Friedrich Majer, who taught ancient Indian mythology at Jena, relied on the English translations of the Asiatic Society to mediate Indian literature to him, while Schopenhauer, who had a facility for languages and sufficient leisure to cultivate them, never attempted to learn Sanskrit.

[21] Schlegel (1849) p. 427.

[22] Ibid. p. 439.

for thought. Indeed, Schlegel seemed to have found the equivalent of Kant's *a priori* categories in the roots of Sanskrit:

> even in its simplest form it exemplifies the loftiest ideas of the pure world of thought, and displays the entire ground plan of the consciousness, not in figurative symbols, but in direct and immediate clearness and precision.[23]

Of all languages Sanskrit is the most spiritual and therefore the most suited to philosophy and religion. No other language, not even Greek, "is so philosophically clear and sharply defined."[24]

When, in the second book, Schlegel turned from the language of the Indians to their wisdom, his prior effusiveness is replaced by a cold, at times disapproving tone. He was clearly disappointed to find that the oldest Sanskrit sources available to him did not contain Christianity in its pristine form. However, rather than allow this discovery to cast doubt on his expectation that, originally, the ancient Indians knew God in the same way that Christians know him, Schlegel doubted the originality and purity of his sources, and his account of the history of Indian philosophy is a narrative of decline from an original knowledge which can, occasionally, be glimpsed in the oldest sources, but appears intermixed with all sorts of erroneous and superstitious notions. He identified as the oldest system of Indian wisdom that of "emanation combined with metempsychosis", as summarised in the opening chapter of Manu's law-book. It is, he tells us, a compound of "lofty wisdom" and "fearful and horrible superstition...profaning and polluting every thing it touched." This earliest of systems is "lofty" insofar as it contains a correct notion of God as "Eternal Spirit, the Supreme *One*, the Sovereign and Lord of Creation", and combines this with a "certain and decided" conviction of the soul's immortality,[25] but such truths are corrupted by an erroneously low estimation of creaturely existence, at odds with the Christian view of creation as God's gift to man:

> in that system [emanation] the condition of all created existences is rather counted unhappy, and the world itself ruined and guilty in its very essence; all is in a state of mournful degradation, sinking deeper and deeper into the abyss which divides it from the perfect bliss and purity of its divine Creator.[26]

Schlegel argued that such an amalgamation of divine truth and superstitious error is "totally inexplicable" if considered the offspring of idle

---

[23] Ibid. p. 454.
[24] Ibid. p. 457.
[25] Ibid. pp. 471-2.
[26] Ibid. p. 469.

reason or speculative fancy, but rendered intelligible if counted as the "perverted conception of revealed truth". Here we see the influence of Herder's thesis that the earliest myths, religions and systems of philosophy are vessels containing ancient man's original knowledge of God in symbolic form, but Schlegel's fidelity to Herder's principle of original purity left him with the difficulty of explaining how a patina of error and superstition had been superimposed upon truth in the earliest of religious sources. In the attempt, Schlegel affirmed his Herderian maxim that "the noble purity and simplicity" of the Indian idea of God proceeded from an original revelation, but argued that this was not a revelation in words "communicated by the immediate teaching of the Father, in symbolic and expressive language", but non-cognitive and consisting of a "glance into the mysterious depth" of God's being, conveyed through "an impulse" of ancient man's "inner feeling". According to Schlegel, therefore, the original revelation upon which Indian wisdom is based was not explicit and linguistic — as with the later revelation of Judaeo-Christianity — but implicit and mystical. And the intuitive medium of this revelation accounts for the palpable distortion of divine truth found in the earliest written sources of Indian religion, for these are merely human attempts to record and preserve the original revelation, but are not that revelation itself.

In combination with his theory accounting for the possibility of error in the scriptures of India, Schlegel developed an explanation accounting for its actual presence. He argued that when the ancient Indian attempted to fix his feeling of the immediacy of God's presence in symbolic or conceptual expression, he interposed his subjective awareness of the "unfathomable abyss" separating "the idea of infinite perfection in the creative essence and the visible imperfection of the world around".[27] The upshot was a metaphysical system combining a correct conception of God's sublime perfection and humanity's spiritual likeness to God, with a human all-too-human impression of anguish and sorrow concerning created existence, liberation from which is held up as the desired end of religion. To throw further light on this point, Schlegel called upon the Old Testament and Christian doctrine and maintained that the melancholy character of Indian thought was a symptom of the effect of the Fall and expulsion from Paradise on the psychology of ancient humans.[28] Contrary, therefore, to Schlegel's original expectation that research into Sanskrit sources would reveal divine truth in its pristine form, his exposition of

[27] Ibid. pp. 472-4.
[28] Ibid. pp. 515-6.

their contents suggests that he eventually came to see them as little more than illustrations of the appearance of error.

Schlegel evidently perceived no incongruity in using the scriptures and doctrines of Judaeo-Christianity as criteria for excavating the nuggets of divine truth from the superstitious veneer of Indian religion,[29] and his account of the later history of Indian wisdom is a narrative that reverses Hegel's dialectical ascent of spirit, a story charting the successive stages of descent into further error and the gradual degeneration and eventual eclipse of the divine idea given in original revelation. The system superseding emanation and metempsychosis is called by him "astrological superstition and fanatical materialism", in which the original nobility of the Indian conception of God is identified with ignoble and unworthy objects, such as the flora and fauna of the natural world. This system is in turn succeeded by dualism, which represents a reactive attempt to purify the idea of the divine by completely separating it from creation, which is supplanted in turn by its dialectical opposite pantheism, the nadir of Indian wisdom and the stage at which "the profound and vital idea originally entertained of the Eternal and his almighty power" was "greatly vitiated and enfeebled" through identification with "the nothingness of all matter". In Schlegel's view, pantheism's absorption of all finite existents "into an abstract and negative conception of the Eternal" refutes life and deprives human beings of moral discernment, imagination and the energy and curiosity to investigate nature.[30] The appearance of oriental pantheism, instanced in Vedānta and the teachings of "Fo, the Chinese philosopher" (i.e., the Buddha), marks the point when the ancient Indians finally abandoned revelation and religion, repudiated God and resolved instead to rely on their own resources. According to Schlegel pantheism is "the offspring of unassisted reason, and therefore marks the transition from the Oriental to the European philosophy. It is no less flattering to the self-conceit of man than to his indolence."[31]

Schlegel's conception of and assault on oriental pantheism owes far more to the *Pantheismusstreit*, or pantheism-controversy of the late eighteenth century, than to the content of his Sanskrit sources. This controversy

---

[29] Later we will see that Schopenhauer proposed the opposite course when he asserted a parallel between using Sanskrit to elucidate the structure and descent of Greek and Latin, and the doctrines of "Brahmanism and Buddhism" as standards for differentiating truth from falsehood in Church Christianity (PPII p. 381).

[30] Schlegel (1849) pp. 489-90.

[31] Ibid. p. 490.

had its origin in a dispute between Moses Mendelssohn and Friedrich Heinrich Jacobi over the alleged Spinozism of one of the central luminaries of the German Enlightenment and Mendelssohn's recently deceased friend, Gotthold Ephraim Lessing. Jacobi maintained that Lessing had privately confessed allegiance to Spinoza's pantheism to him, which Mendelssohn hotly disputed. However, the significance of the controversy was much broader than the question of the accuracy of Jacobi's revelation about Lessing, but reflected a cultural and intellectual debate regarding the nature and extent of reason and the limits of critical enquiry championed by the representatives of the *Aufklärung*, such as Mendelssohn and Lessing. In 1785 Jacobi published his exchange with Mendelssohn accompanied by an examination of Spinoza's philosophy, in which he paid tribute to the latter for having constructed the most consistent and rigorous system of speculative reason, but since, as Jacobi alleged, its practical consequences were scepticism, atheism, nihilism and fatalism, it also stood as a cautionary rebuke to those who rejected the need for faith and agitated for an untrammelled application of critical reason. Schlegel's reconstruction of the descent of ancient Indian intellectual history into oriental pantheism was simultaneously a polemic aimed at illustrating and confirming Jacobi's admonition against the follies of unfettered rationalism. The consequences were unfortunate, insofar as Schlegel thereby became the first prominent nineteenth-century thinker to establish an association between Indian thought and nihilism in the imagination of Europe.[32]

Schlegel may have ended his study as he started it, on a buoyant note, by predicting that a deeper study of oriental sources will "bring back a new idea of the Divinity" and reinvigorate Europe's intellect and soul by giving new impetus to "all art, science, and literature",[33] but his failure to discover a pristine form of divine revelation in Sanskrit sources seems to have left him disillusioned. In 1808, the same year in which *On the Language and Wisdom of the Indians* was published, Schlegel and his wife converted to Roman Catholicism, and his later works were more critical of Indian doctrines.[34] By the time Friedrich's brother, August Wilhelm, was appointed Professor of Sanskrit at Bonn in 1818, Romantic enthusiasm for India had passed over into methodical academic

---

[32] The works by Roger Pol-Droit (2003) and Guy Welbon (1968) are good accounts of the history of the association between Buddhism and nihilism in the nineteenth century.

[33] Schlegel (1849) p. 526.

[34] Schlegel (1846) pp. 155-161.

Indology. It was beginning to seem as if the oriental renaissance had exhausted itself at its inception.

But if Schlegel had simultaneously raised and crushed the possibility of an oriental renaissance in 1808, in the 1820s there arose a powerful force in the intellectual life of Europe which, by way of an *a priori* historicism, set out to consign the intricate detail of classical Indian thought to the dustbin of history: that force was Hegel.

Hegel agreed with Herder and Friedrich Schlegel on the issue of India's formative relation to European culture, and considered an understanding of its civilisation to be an important element in comprehending the conditions that had created the European present. As a result, his lectures on the various determinate shapes assumed by consciousness throughout history and on the cultural attainments of the human spirit included lengthy discussions of Indian thought, art and religion.[35] However, Hegel's appreciation of the immanent relations between thought and the wider — social, economic, political and cultural — conditions of its emergence led him to disparage the Romantic conviction that a revival of Indian wisdom might help to resolve the tensions of the present and institute a return to a mythical original wholeness.[36] For Hegel, intellectual culture is the reflective summary of an epoch, and has immediate value and meaning in relation to the context of its appearance.[37] For this reason, he was critical of the comparative project of tearing particular doctrines or ideas from the conditions of their becoming, since this makes what was once a system of living concepts into an empty shell or abstraction. Just as he argued that "there can be no Platonists, Aristotelians, Stoics, or Epicureans today",[38] so we can imagine him declaring that no

---

[35] Hegel only occasionally referred to Indian thought in the philosophical works he published during his lifetime. He discussed India's contribution to the doctrine of One-in-All in §573 of the third part of the 1830 edition of the *Encyclopaedia of the Philosophical Sciences*, and also composed a long article responding to Wilhelm von Humboldt's review of A.W. Schlegel's Latin translation of the *Bhagavad-Gītā*, which was published in the Hegelian journal *Jahrbücher für wissenschaftliche Kritik* in 1827. But the most substantial sources for Hegel's view of Indian culture are contained in the posthumously published collections of his lectures on the philosophy of religion, aesthetics, the philosophy of history and the history of philosophy.

[36] Hegel remarked that the worst kind of *a priori* history consisted of the "widely current fiction, that there was an original primeval people, taught immediately by God, endowed with perfect insight and wisdom" (Hegel (1956) p. 10), which seems to be a criticism of the Romantic view of India promulgated by Herder and Friedrich Schlegel.

[37] Hegel (1974) p. 53. However, this statement needs qualification, insofar as Hegel's teleological stance entails that the philosophies and religions of the past find their *ultimate* meaning and value in the extent to which they have contributed to present consciousness of the Idea.

[38] Ibid. p. 46.

contemporary western philosopher can respectfully and genuinely declare allegiance to Navya-Nyāya logic or Sāṃkhya philosophy of nature. Hegel's maxim that intellectual systems are best examined in relation to their context is now a generally undisputed axiom of historical method, but his evaluation of Indian thought and its role in history presupposed a metaphysics that is not merely questionable, but formulated to reassert the normativity and superiority of the culture of the European present in opposition to Schlegel's Romantic critique of the age.

Hegel's presentation of Indian thought and culture was informed by his integration of system and history, in accordance with which he treated temporal systems of thought as so many premises in the unfolding of a logical argument. Just as the meaning and value of a premise is determined by the contribution it makes to the *telos* or conclusion of an argument, so for Hegel a system of thought has value insofar as what is essential in it has been at once cancelled, preserved and taken up into (*aufgehoben*) succeeding systems that both supersede and fulfil it.[39] These processes of system and history are, in turn, aspects of the world-spirit's ascent to explicit knowledge of itself as reason and freedom. Hegel's developmental and totalising view of the history of thought was the basis for his opposition to and denigration of the Romantic glorification of origins, and led him to argue that the antiquity of classical Indian culture was not a mark of its greater authenticity and authority, but of its inferiority when inappropriately and anachronistically compared with the thought of a succeeding age. For Hegel, thought in its origin cannot be richer and more comprehensive than thought in the present, since present philosophy contains and comprehends what was essential in the thought of the past.[40]

In addition to its temporal direction, the odyssey of the world-spirit also moves with the sun, from east to west, so that India's relegation to the past is compounded by its geographical subordination to the civilisation of the west.[41] Eastern thought is therefore not only more adequately understood and represented in the works of western scholars, but its peoples are destined to be ruled by European powers such as Britain.[42] Compared with the richer and more developed civilisation of the west, the oriental world is static, having "remained stationary and fixed" from its inception.[43] Hegel thought that the study of Sanskrit sources was useful

[39] Ibid. p. 30.
[40] Ibid. p. 41.
[41] Hegel (1956) p. 103.
[42] Ibid. p. 142.
[43] Ibid. p. 139.

insofar as it acquaints us with the infancy of Europe and man's first rude attempts to liberate his thought from immersion in nature and ascend to the universal, but Romantic nostalgia for such a state of simplicity is mere flight "from the difficult...into mere sterility".[44]

Hegel traced the low level of Indian culture to its lack of a critical, historical tradition, which he regarded as the essential mark of a culture's awareness of the spirit's dialectical ascent to self-knowledge and freedom through mediation with finite individuality.[45] Cultural differences in social and political organisation in relation to individual freedom are therefore reflections of differentiated levels of historical awareness. The non-historical perspectives of China and India entail that Orientals assign freedom to one individual only (the despot); the emergence of an embryonic historical tradition among the ancient Greeks led them to bestow freedom on only a privileged few (the citizens); but the perfection of the historical sense in Europe at the dawn of modernity has issued in European (or Germanic) man's recognition that all men, or man as man, are free.[46] Hegel also characterised Christianity as the consummate religion, on the grounds that it not only includes what is essential in the religions of India, but surpasses them by truly representing the mediation between universal and individual, or infinite and finite, in the symbolic doctrine of the incarnation. Further to this, the speculative and historically informed philosophy of modern Europe comprehends the essential content of all religions, Christianity included, by having raised the implicit content of their images and pictures to the level of the concept (*Begriff*). As a result, Hegel disputed the existence of a tradition of free, philosophical reflection in India. He acknowledged that certain universal notions and a doctrine of One-in-All had been central features of ancient Indian thought, but judged them to have been too subordinate to practical — religious and soteriological — ends to constitute evidence of the existence of self-aware philosophical reflection. He argued that the speculative categories of the Indian religions demonstrate no more than that philosophy was potentially present in India, but explicit and actual philosophical awareness first appeared among the Greeks.[47]

We may ask what it was that Hegel considered defective about the speculations of classical Indian religion, since Hindu and Buddhist definitions of the concepts of *Brahman* and *nirvāṇa* seem *prima facie* equal

[44] Hegel (1974) p. 48.
[45] Hegel (1956) p. 163.
[46] Ibid. p. 18.
[47] Hegel (1974) p. 96.

to the sophisticated notions of Parmenides, Plato, Plotinus, Spinoza, and perhaps even those of Hegel himself. As just noted, Hegel acknowledged that the universal Idea to which all philosophical thought aspires was indeed known to ancient Indians, but, so he argued, not in its proper form. The ruling principle of the oriental world is substantiality or abstract unity, a unity that Indians experienced in absolute separation from finite particulars, as an alienating force standing over the existence of finites and refusing to incorporate their finitude into its own life. For Hegel, Hinduism is therefore the prototype of the "religion of substance": for this religious mode of understanding pure substance is indeterminate, abstract being-in-itself, lacking internal differentiations and external relations. More importantly, the Hindu Absolute is an impersonal, spiritless substance in-itself rather than a subjective for-itself. In other words, in its discovery of the One as substance, India had excluded the Many, depriving them of any mediation or reconciliation with their true essence. So, apart from being the religion of substance, the other side of Hinduism is that it is "the religion of phantasy", "the maddest of polytheisms" in which a riot of monstrous, contingent forms are idolatrously worshipped as divine.[48] This elevation of the abstract unity of substance to the highest, and its concomitant separation from finite life, has had an effect on the moral outlook of the Hindus. Their religious practices place no value on human life, but are predicated upon a negative death-wish manifested in customs such as suttee, mass self-immolation at the Juggernaut festival in Orissa, infanticide, and ultimately the asceticism of yoga, the aim of which is perfect union with substance through attainment of "the highest degree of abstraction — the perfect deadening of consciousness; a point from which the transition to physical death is no great step."[49] Hegel contrasted this with the relation between religion and morality in European Christianity, where the Highest is understood as personality and as the ground of human knowledge and volition.[50] Therefore, although Hegel took issue with Schlegel on the question of the possibility and desirability of an oriental renaissance, he converged with his view of oriental monism's practical nihilism and inability to support moral distinctions.

Hegel was far less conversant with Buddhist sources than he was with Hindu, since academic Buddhology had its most creative and productive

[48] Hegel (1985) pp. 307-8.
[49] Hegel (1956) p. 150.
[50] Ibid. pp. 157-8.

period after his death in 1831. As a result, his analysis of the historical transition from Hinduism to Buddhism in the last, 1831 organisation of his *Lectures on the Philosophy of Religion* pays little regard to the doctrinal differences or historical relations between the two religions, and owes more to the logical transition from being to nothingness in Hegel's *Logic* of 1830 (part one of the *Encyclopaedia of the Philosophical Sciences*). For Hegel Buddhism is that moment in the development of the Idea when the abstraction of pure Being — the substance of Hinduism — is experienced as absolute negativity, so that Buddhists cognise the infinite God through the most extreme of negative theologies, under the aspect of indeterminate nothingness.[51] The religious practices correlated with this mode of cognition seek absorption with ultimate nothingness by replicating it in life through "pure passivity", which is attained by observing the maxims "do nothing, wish nothing, desire nothing."[52] But irrespective of his convergence with Schlegel on the topic of oriental monism's theoretical vacuity and practical nihilism, Hegel's developmental perspective entails that neither Hinduism nor Buddhism is a fixed doctrine of nihilism. Each is a transient moment in the development of thought, whose rise and cultural dominance over the Orient was historically and logically necessary. But, for this very reason, the attempt to introduce Indian thought into Europe through an oriental renaissance is tantamount to reifying an ephemeral and — in comparison with that of the European present — inadequate mode of consciousness.

Ironically, Hegel's characterisation of classical Indian thought as abstract indeterminacy was to be turned against him by Schelling in the 1840s. We have seen how Schelling embraced Indian thought in the first decade of the nineteenth century, on account of the commonality of themes he presupposed it to share with his own philosophy of the time, such as pantheism.[53] In 1807 Hegel had honed his later objections to the abstract substantiality of Indian thought on Schelling's notion of the identity of all things in the Absolute, rhetorically referring to it as the night in which all cows are black, and as a reduction of cognition to vacuity.[54] In 1841, when Schelling had repudiated many of his former philosophical convictions and his expectation that Europe might learn from ancient

---

[51] Hegel (1975) p. 127; Hegel (1987) p. 568.

[52] Hegel (1956) p. 169.

[53] With barely veiled sarcasm Schelling hinted in his 1809 work that Schlegel's conception of pantheism in *On the Language and Wisdom of the Indians* was philosophically inadequate (Schelling (1936) p. 10n.1).

[54] Hegel (1977) p. 9.

Indian sources, he was summoned to Berlin and offered Hegel's old chair of philosophy, for the express purpose of eradicating the "dragon's seed of Hegelian pantheism" from German culture.[55] Schelling styled his position of the 1840s as "positive philosophy", a mode of thought that takes account of concrete existence and the facticity of monotheism and revelation. Just as Hegel recycled his early critique of Schelling's Absolute in his criticisms of Indian abstraction and substantiality, so the later Schelling's enumeration of the defects of classical Indian thought also drew upon his objections to the Hegelian philosophy. Schelling presented Hegel and the Indian religions as antitheses to his positive philosophy, as negative modes of understanding that leave factual life out of account by retreating into reflection and pure conceptuality.[56] In many respects Schelling's notion of positive philosophy simply appropriated Hegel's criteria of concretion and factuality in order to 'out-concretise' Hegel and turn the charge of vacuity against him. In doing so, he also adopted Hegel's habit of using an association with the putatively formal and abstract character of Indian categories as a species of philosophical refutation and a mark of conceptual inadequacy.

Schelling's 1841 assumption of Hegel's old chair in Berlin marked the decline of Hegelianism in German universities, but Hegel's evaluation of Indian thought and his historicist estimation of its contribution to culture and philosophy outlived the period of his philosophical supremacy. Influential historians of the later nineteenth century such as Windelband, Zeller and Überweg still adhered to Hegel's dictum that the Orient and India were merely preparatory in the development of thought, and were therefore rightly excluded from what Windelband referred to as the "self-consistent and self-contained course of European philosophy" that originated in Greece.[57] By the first part of the twentieth century, this historicist estimation of India's contribution to the history of thought had become a settled dogma. The phenomenologist Husserl claimed that Chinese and Indian thought were exclusively mythical and subordinated to religious practice, and contrasted this with the "wonder" (θαυμάζειν) of the Greeks, to which he traced the purely theoretical attitude of modern European science and philosophy.[58] This view was taken over and

---

[55] A phrase allegedly coined by the Prussian monarch Frederick William IV and quoted in the letter from the Ministry of Culture offering the Chair to Schelling, reprinted in Schelling (1977) pp. 408-9.

[56] Schelling (1857) p. 40, pp. 476-80.

[57] Windelband (1903) p. 22n.1.

[58] Husserl (1970) pp. 280ff.

repeated by Husserl's student Heidegger, for whom philosophy was also Greek in origin.[59] However, Heidegger was less affirmative of modernity's Greek inheritance than either Hegel or Husserl, claiming that the globalisation of quantifying and objectifying modes of thought had brought about the atomic age, the dominance of the technological perspective and the prevalence of modern nihilism. Heidegger's evaluation of modern culture has many affinities with Friedrich Schlegel's Romantic critique of the present. But although he occasionally sought rapprochement with oriental thought as a potential curative for the predicaments of modern Europe and a possible source for bringing thought in a new direction,[60] for Heidegger the best method of cleansing the nihilist perspectives of modern European civilisation was to reinvestigate its origins in Greek philosophy, rather than enter into dialogue with a separate tradition.

III. Schopenhauer and India

After Hegel and Schelling it seemed as if the Romantic hopes of an oriental renaissance through the study of Sanskrit sources had been brought to a close. Although academic Indology continued to be productive and gave birth to Buddhology in the late 1820s, in the universities it was largely a philological discipline confined to specialists, its researches having little impact on the creative and theoretical exertions of their professorial colleagues in departments of philosophy or theology. In the first half of the nineteenth century those who continued to view Indian thought as a serious corrective to western modes of apprehension were few in number. They were, moreover, generally solitary figures whose thought departed from the mainstream of contemporary philosophy in Europe, and who therefore lacked institutional positions or a public voice. Such a one was Karl Christian Friedrich Krause, who lamented the manner in which "the Indian science had...been given short shrift under the ignominious title of barbaric, i.e., non-Hellenic, philosophy."[61]

Krause was an enthusiastic reader of Anquetil's *Oupnek'hat* who had also taught himself Sanskrit and some Indian meditation techniques. Between 1815 and 1817 Krause resided in Dresden, and his neighbour

---

[59] Heidegger (1955) p. 33.
[60] Heidegger (1971).
[61] Quoted from Halbfass (1988) p. 145.

during this time was another solitary thinker newly-converted to the Indian cause — Arthur Schopenhauer. Rüdiger Safranski claims that Schopenhauer regularly consulted Krause on points of interpretation of Indian doctrines, and "also learned from him details of meditation techniques."[62] During this period Schopenhauer was working on the first statement of his philosophical system, published in late 1818 in *The World as Will and Representation*. In its Preface he expressed, a decade after Schlegel, the conviction that the nineteenth century would go down in history not as the age in which secularity and unbelief became the norm in Europe, nor exclusively as the age of the death of God and the revaluation of all values. Instead, he predicted that it would be the era of the oriental renaissance, since access to the *Vedas* and *Upaniṣads* was

> the greatest advantage which this still young century has to show over previous centuries, since I surmise that the influence of Sanskrit literature will penetrate no less deeply than did the revival of Greek literature in the fifteenth century; (WWRI p. xv)

But despite having this much in common with Friedrich Schlegel, Schopenhauer approached the Indian sources available to him with expectations and presuppositions markedly distinct from those of his predecessors and contemporaries. His conception of the broadness of the renaissance of European culture through oriental sources was far more limited than that of Schlegel and other Romantics, such as Tieck and Novalis. He never envisaged that the study of Sanskrit sources would have an effect on the canons of European art, poetry and literature, never attempted to learn Sanskrit, had no taste for India's plastic arts, and thought its poetry lost too much in translation. As a result, he recommended that translators from Sanskrit neglect Indian poetry in favour of its religious and metaphysical works, for whereas "there is now in Europe no lack of poetical works that directly appeal to us," there is "a very great dearth of correct metaphysical views" (PPII p. 395). And Schopenhauer did not turn to the ancient scriptures of India in the hope of uncovering an original revelation of God to primeval humanity, and was not disillusioned by the metaphysical and moral doctrines he found in texts such as Anquetil's *Oupnek'hat*. On the contrary, the Indian religions seemed to share fundamental themes with his godless philosophy, such as idealism, pessimism, a morality based on compassion and a higher ethics of ascetic denial. As a result, he did not champion the Indian religious traditions on account of their exotic 'otherness', but because they

---

[62] Safranski (1991) p. 202.

seemed to contain adequate metaphysical insights which had, in the east, served as the basis for popular religious traditions. For him, therefore, the introduction of Indian wisdom into Europe supplied the occasion for constructing a bridge leading back from philosophy to religion after Kant had deprived theism of the supports of dogmatic metaphysics.

Schopenhauer also invested little philosophical value in the antiquity of the Indian tradition. Faithful to Kant's doctrine of the ideality of time, he considered the external events of history as philosophically insignificant. History is neither decline from pristine origins and God's original revelation nor the world-spirit's ascent to knowledge of itself as reason and freedom. It is, instead, merely a kaleidoscope in which the same inner content — the blind metaphysical will — presents itself in various guises and different representational dress to the subject of knowledge (WWRII p. 444). Philosophical insight does not develop over time, but transcends the everyday procedure of relating effects to causes or actions to motives (of which science and history are the respective systematic elaborations). Instead, the material part of philosophy derives from intuitive apprehension of the universal in the particular (the Platonic Idea), while its formal part consists of the ability to raise the content of these intuitions to explicit reflection and deposit them in appropriate and communicable concepts. For Schopenhauer these capacities were eminently present in the artistic and philosophical genius, that freak of nature who is distinguished from the ordinary mass of people, including scholars, by a superabundance of intellect over will. Genius is therefore untimely, and subjectively independent of the external conditions of the age in which it appears. In opposition to Schlegel and Hegel therefore, Schopenhauer's conception of philosophy remained immune to the rise of historical studies and philosophies of history, and retained the more traditional view that philosophical genius is possible in all periods of history and in all geographical locations. As a result, Schopenhauer venerated neither origins nor the present, and approached his Indian sources as repositories of timeless metaphysical and moral insights realisable anywhere and in any age.

However, Schopenhauer did occasionally present the antiquity and originality of Indian culture as a characteristic favourable to its religions, which seems to contradict his ahistorical outlook and affiliate him to the Romantic veneration of origins. However, in the context of his thought such references are merely external considerations in support of the authenticity of the Indian religions, rather than intrinsic guarantees of their truth and value. He reiterated Herder's thesis that "Brahmanism and Buddhism" were the original religions of the human race and India the original homeland of European nations (WWRI p. 357). He claimed further that the "brown skin of the Hindu" was the natural colour of humanity, and that the forefathers of contemporary Europeans had lost their natural hue after migrating to northern lands, where, over the course of centuries, the harsh climate eventually turned their skin white (WWRII p. 547). However, these ancestors of Europe had not merely forfeited their original skin colour when they moved west, but also their original metaphysical world-view, and had accepted as substitutes less adequate modes of thought, such as the hyper-rationalism of Greek philosophy and the fictitious metaphysics of Jewish theism (WWRI pp. 47-8; PPII p. 226).

There is also a hint in Schopenhauer's works of a theory paralleling the Romantic postulation of an original revelation. He claimed that the "almost superhuman conceptions" recorded in the *Upaniṣads* had proceeded from an "immediate illumination" enjoyed by the ancient *ṛṣis* of India (WWRII p. 475). This illumination was made possible by the fact that the *ṛṣis* "stood considerably nearer to the beginning of the human race and to the original source of organic nature than do we", and therefore "possessed both greater energy of the intuitive faculty of knowledge, and a more genuine disposition of mind." (WWRII p. 162)

However, Schopenhauer's theory of the "immediate illumination" of the *ṛṣis* is — unlike that of Herder and Schlegel — non-theological, since for him the mental acuity of the *ṛṣis* stems from genius rather than illumination by God. Schopenhauer regarded the ahistorical, subjective condition distinguishing genius from other mortals — namely, "greater energy of the intuitive faculty" — to be possible in any age, and perceived evidence of its operation in the doctrines of thinkers from all times and circumstances, including Augustine, Scotus Erigena, Descartes, Spinoza, Berkeley, and pre-eminently Kant. However, in Schopenhauer's view, the difference between these more recent thinkers and the *ṛṣis* of old consists in the fact that the European thinkers lacked the external condition for an unfettered expression of genius — namely a "genuine disposition of mind". They had been indoctrinated from an early age to think and understand the world in accordance with a set of erroneous metaphysical pictures. When, therefore, they attempted to give thematic, reflective expression to their intuitive perceptions, the system of concepts they received with their early education led them to distort the true import of these experiences. Schopenhauer was far from agreeing with Gadamer that the prejudices and fore-understandings (*Vorverständnisse*) we receive from our culture are the conditions of the possibility of understanding.

He maintained that it is not false appearances that give rise to philosophical error, but *a priori* prejudices given through tradition (PPII
pp. 14-5). Therefore, according to his theory, the intuitive faculty of the
ṛṣis was more energetic and their disposition of mind more genuine
because, standing closer to the beginning of history, their thought was
unimpeded by the fetters and blinkers of false metaphysical pictures preserved through tradition and implanted in early education. Schopenhauer
may have stated that "wise men can live in any age", but he also thought
that "those of antiquity remain so for all the generations to come"
(WWRII p. 80). The natural genius of the *ṛṣis* was undisturbed by early
exposure to tradition and the social pressure to conform to its received
ideas: whereas Augustine, Scotus Erigena, Descartes, Spinoza, Berkeley
and Kant were obliged to reconcile their intuitions to a pre-existing tradition of metaphysical pictures and concepts, the *ṛṣis* had the luxury of
creating one.

Schopenhauer therefore approached Indian thought as a storehouse of
adequate metaphysical and ethical intuitions, and his oriental renaissance
was partly based on the expectation that Europe's encounter with ancient
Indian thought would support his own reappraisal of the content and
methods of European philosophy. What Eberhard Scheiffele says about
Nietzsche's appropriation of other cultural viewpoints is equally applicable to Schopenhauer's appropriation of Indian doctrines and perspectives: it was for the sake of "'*estranging' what is one's own by questioning it from behind, from the perspective of the foreign.*"[63] As Scheiffele
observes of Nietzsche's method, so Schopenhauer's interpretation of
Indian thought was not exclusively for the purpose of

> 'doing justice to' what is foreign than of seeing one's own *anew* from a
> different perspective, of questioning what is familiar so as to 'get behind'
> it and letting what is 'obvious' appear as something *strange*.[64]

From the novel perspective of Indian thought, what appeared strange to
Schopenhauer about the western tradition was its commitment to a metaphysical scheme not derived from reality, but from the ancient documents
of the Old Testament. This arbitrary scheme had endured and even
derived support from European philosophy's methodological commitment to an exaggerated form of abstraction and conceptualism. Hence
metaphysical theism posits an absolute distinction between the world and
its originating principle in the doctrine of *creatio ex nihilo*, and as a

---

[63] Scheiffele (1991) p. 32.
[64] Ibid. p. 33.

counterpart teaches ontological dualism, whereby the soul as transcendent hypostasis is set apart from and placed above nature. Theism also assumes the transcendental reality of the objects of perception and promulgates the "false" and "pernicious" doctrine of cosmological optimism. Schopenhauer considered all these elements of theism indefensible with reference to reality as encountered through perception, and even contradicted by it, but thought they had persisted for so long in the west because of the impotence of the philosophical tradition. European philosophers have obligingly demonstrated the existence of theism's main objects, God and the soul, using proofs that merely pile one abstraction upon another, and without enquiring after the intuitive or perceptual bases of the concepts they use. As a result, Schopenhauer viewed the predisposition towards insight and intuition encoded in the doctrines of India as a refreshing alternative to the material biblicism and formal rationalism of western metaphysics. His estimation of the merits of Indian thought in relation to European was therefore the reverse of Schelling and Hegel, insofar as he discovered a greater degree of concrete reality in the myths and allegories of India than in the second order abstractions of the greater portion of the European philosophical tradition.

However, in agreement with Hegel and Husserl, Schopenhauer did differentiate between philosophy as a theoretical discipline found only in Europe, and Hinduism and Buddhism as religions communicating the theoretical knowledge of philosophy in less adequate form, and for the attainment of practical (i.e., ethical and soteriological) ends. This is why he began his essay on the history of philosophy with neither *Vedas* nor *Upaniṣads* but with the pre-Socratics (PPI p. 32). Elsewhere he claimed that the "disconnected utterances" of the *Upaniṣads* find their systematic, scientific expression in his own work (WWRI pp. xv-xvi), and that his philosophy communicates in clear and distinct concepts the same content that Buddhism communicates to the mass of people under the veil of allegory (WWRII p. 169).

However, Schopenhauer's exclusion of the Indian religions from the history of philosophy has a different significance from that of Hegel and Husserl, and on account of his opposition to European hyper-conceptualism. As a result his criterion for demarcating western from eastern thought is closer to that of Schlegel and Heidegger. Schopenhauer invested greater epistemological value in the inarticulate and non-thematic knowledge (*Erkenntnis*) of intuitive perception (*Anschauung*), and characterised rational knowledge (*Wissen*) as merely an abstract *reflection* of this (WWRI p. 35). In agreement with Kant, Schopenhauer was critical of western philosophy's investment in pure reason (*Vernunft*), and lamented that

> [s]ince scholasticism, really in fact since Plato and Aristotle, philosophy has been for the most part a *continued misuse of universal concepts*, such as, for example, substance, ground, cause, the good, perfection, necessity, possibility, and very many others. (WWRII pp. 39-40)

He complained that the majority of philosophers had simply exploited the abstract nature and structural indeterminacy of concepts "for the purpose of metaphysical manoeuvring" (FR p. 226). Only since Locke have philosophers considered it necessary to enquire into the origin of concepts, and thus "back to what is *perceptive* and to *experience*" (WWRII p. 41). In opposition, therefore, to the rationalist model of philosophy as a "science *of* concepts", Schopenhauer proposed that it be understood as "a science *in* concepts, drawn from knowledge of perception, the only source of all evidence," the content of which is merely "set down and fixed in universal concepts" (WWRI p. 453). Philosophy has no special sources of knowledge and is subject to no revelations or intellectual intuitions from above, but merely brings to self-conscious awareness through concepts the content of perceptual experience of which everyone is pre-cognitively aware (WWRI p. 383). Although Hegel's conception of the task of philosophy was very similar, he differs from Schopenhauer by placing greater emphasis on the theoretical and practical benefits issuing from philosophy's conceptual explication of perceptual knowledge, heralding conceptual form as the medium through which knowledge attains greater validity, richness, and practical efficaciousness. Schopenhauer's view was the reverse, especially in the practical realm where, he argued that

> moral excellence stands higher than all theoretical wisdom; the latter is always only a patchwork which reaches the goal by the slow path of inferences and conclusions, whereas the former attains the goal all at once. (BM p. 210)

The sole benefit of transcribing material knowledge of perception into the formal and abstract knowledge of philosophical reflection is that it facilitates preservation, communication and demonstration to others. However, Schopenhauer also thought that this transcription necessarily involves a loss of richness and original vivacity, and tends to make knowledge more abstruse and nebulous. As a result, his demarcation of the philosophy of Europe from the religious traditions of India reflects less badly on the value of the latter than Hegel's similar demarcation, and is compatible with a higher estimation of the intuitive inner core he discovered within the allegorical casings of Indian doctrines.

Schopenhauer's philosophy first came to public and scholarly attention in 1853, when the *Westminster Review* published a survey of his system by John Oxenford. From this time until the early twentieth century Schopenhauer's name was, as Josiah Royce noted in 1892, "better known to most general readers, in our day, than is that of any other modern Continental metaphysician, except Kant."[65] Oxenford's article was the first to take the association that Schopenhauer had so assiduously cultivated between the Indian religions and his own philosophy at face value. He claimed that Schopenhauer was devoted to "the wisdom of the Oriental world",[66] and that his "religious faith wavers between Brahmanism and Buddhism".[67] Although Oxenford was generally sympathetic towards Schopenhauer, reserving special praise for the intelligibility of his style and his commitment to reasoning upon perceptual evidence, it was Schopenhauer's convergence with "the Indian Fakeer" that gave him the most difficulty, insofar as they seem to agree on hailing self-annihilation as "the greatest boon".[68] It is questionable whether this perception of a convergence between Schopenhauer and India did not turn out to be a burden to both in the long term.

On the one hand, with the rise to prominence of analytical philosophy in the Anglo-Saxon world, the association between Schopenhauer and Indian religion gave rise to the belief that his main doctrines lacked argumentative bases and were derived from exotic religious texts such as the *Upaniṣads*. Patrick Gardiner states that this led some to imagine that Schopenhauer's metaphysics

> sprang in the first instance from sources which have little or no relevance to the logical and epistemological problems that have typically occupied the attention of Western thinkers, and can in consequence be regarded as little more than a sort of exotic or freak growth in the evolution of European speculation, in essentials unrelated to issues that have constituted the central themes of Western philosophy.[69]

Such attitudes contributed to the erasure of Schopenhauer's philosophical pre-eminence in English speaking nations in the early twentieth century.

The reception of Indian thought by philosophers and theologians in the west was similarly hindered as a consequence of association with

---

[65] Royce (1892) p. 228.
[66] Oxenford (1853) p. 390.
[67] Ibid. p. 399.
[68] Ibid. p. 407.
[69] Gardiner (1963) p. 23.

Schopenhauer. While many enthusiastic and attentive readers of Schopenhauer were directed to the texts, doctrines and practices of classical India under his stimulus — including the Indologist Paul Deussen, the novelist Hermann Hesse and the psychologist Carl Gustav Jung — and irrespective of the fact that his interpretations of Indian doctrines appeared (often without acknowledgement) in the works of Neo-Vedāntins such as Vivekananda and Radhakrishnan, in some circles the popular image of Schopenhauer as cantankerous nihilist and pessimist reflected badly on Hinduism and Buddhism. Nietzsche maintained that Schopenhauer's popularity marked the advent of a Buddhist form of decadence in Europe, whereby "*a will to nothingness*, an aversion to life, a rebellion against the most fundamental presuppositions of life" is established as the highest ideal.[70] Related to this, Freud gave credence to the use of the phrase "*nirvāṇa* principle" as a reference to the pursuit of mental stasis, which he took as evidence for his postulation of a nihilistic death drive.[71]

Terms such as 'nihilist' and 'nihilism' are, of course, notoriously resistant to precise determination. They usually appear in a polemical context where they derive meaning from the unarticulated assumptions of the polemicist. Schopenhauer's argument that the suffering and evil of the world entail that its non-existence is preferable to its existence and that "it is something which at bottom ought not to be" (WWRII p. 576) does, indeed, come across as extremely nihilistic. However, the way in which he distinguishes his soteriology of the denial of the will from suicide indicates that he regarded mere self-annihilation as no solution to suffering and evil (WWRI p. 398).[72] How does this compare with the soteriological schemes of Hinduism, Buddhism and Christianity? It is true that none states explicitly that existence ought not to be, but insofar as they set out images of salvation they all implicitly claim that human nature *ought not to be as it is*. Their theories of salvation are therefore comparable with Schopenhauer's denial of the will, insofar as they presuppose change in the natural constitution of humanity, with Buddhism and Schopenhauer refusing to illustrate the soteriological state in anything other than negative terms. It is therefore sometimes easier for a

---

[70] Nietzsche (1989) III.28.

[71] Freud (1991) p. 261.

[72] However, Schopenhauer's soteriology is highly ambiguous, since his philosophical standpoint commits him to agnosticism concerning the nature of the will in its denial, as I discuss later. It may therefore be the case that he considered suicide "a quite futile and foolish act" precisely because "the thing-in-itself remains unaffected by it" (WWRI p. 399). This suggests that its futility consists in missing its annihilationist aim.

theologian attuned to the negative way to appreciate Schopenhauer's description of the saint in whom the will has turned and denied itself than a philosopher or historian. Don Cupitt summarises Schopenhauer's position in the following way:

> his religious outlook was ascetic, for he held that it is possible in oneself to turn the will back upon itself and extinguish it. One can thus enter into the impersonal bliss of *nirvāṇa*. But this final state of salvation is indescribable. From the point of view of the natural person who lives in the world, it cannot be distinguished from nothingness. Nevertheless, Schopenhauer did affirm this ineffable natural state, so that although he rejected God and was strongly naturalistic in his philosophy, he is still in an important sense a religious thinker.[73]

Of course to a contemporary secularist, and *a fortiori* to a dedicated Nietzschean, even Cupitt's explanation would be insufficient for acquitting Schopenhauer of the charge of nihilism if, at the highest level, the goal of renunciation can only be represented through a negation such as the denial of the will. But Nietzsche traversed so far in the opposite direction to Schopenhauer in his celebration of an untrammelled affirmation of the will, that he characterised even the moral instinct to act upon feelings of sympathy or pity as the first step on a path leading to nihilism.[74] And one of the central motivations behind Schopenhauer's commendation of the religions of India was to stave off the possibility of a secular culture in which all taste for religious, ethical and soteriological questions is lost, and in which people sink to "the absolutely physical viewpoint", seeking political or consumerist outlets for the satisfaction of metaphysical need, such as he saw occur in his own day among the "demoralised and corrupted" Socialists in England and the young Hegelians in Germany (WWRII p. 464).

Schopenhauer's portrayal of Hindu and Buddhist doctrine was highly unsystematic, so that representing his understanding presupposes a fair amount of hermeneutical reconstruction from the hints and piecemeal references littering his texts. The majority of his references to the Indian religions consist of simple assertions of their importance, profundity and nobility, with rarely any elucidation of what their importance, profundity and nobility consist in. At other times he briefly summarises their main ideas (or his understanding of their main ideas), while at others he directs interested readers to his favoured translations and secondary commentaries.

---

[73] Cupitt (1994) p. 75.
[74] Nietzsche (1989) III.14.

Most often we find Hindu or Buddhist themes and doctrines introduced in an incidental way in the midst of a philosophical argument, with the Indian reference acting as an independent confirmation of Schopenhauer's own position on the point in question, and a weighty ally against his opponents. Schopenhauer's philosophy attracted little attention for the greater part of his life, and he was highly sensitive to the fact that many of his positions departed radically from the European tradition and contradicted the outlook of his contemporaries, and might, therefore, appear as either foolish or repugnant. As a result, he availed himself of the independent testimony of the Indian religions to show that his theories were not the musings of an eccentric crank, but substantially identical with the oldest and — measured in terms of number of votives — largest religions in human history, addressing concerns and illustrating tendencies that are permanent features of the human condition as such. His tendency to seek independent confirmation of his views was not confined to Indian literature, but embraced the works of Plato, Plotinus, Augustine, Eckhart, Luther, Giordano Bruno, Spinoza, Berkeley and Kant, as well as quotations from Shakespeare and Goethe, the latest conclusions of empirical science and articles from the London *Times*. This may imply that Schopenhauer's use of and interest in Indian thought was opportunistic, and placed in the service of promoting his philosophy. But that he used the Indian religions to lend respectability to his own system is as unquestionable as his personal enthusiasm for them. He read almost everything published on the topic during his lifetime, and at his death in 1860 his personal library contained around two hundred works on oriental literature.[75]

Many of the scholarly commentaries on Schopenhauer's relation to the Indian religions have been content to analyse and confirm his assertion of an amazing confluence between the two, while others — predominantly the most recent — have sought to demonstrate the opposite. Many of the latter, anti-comparative works were written by scholars whose sympathies evidently lie with the religious traditions of India rather than with Schopenhauer, and whose tacit purpose is to exonerate Hinduism and Buddhism from all association with the atheist, cynic, pessimist, misanthropist, anti-Semite and misogynist of Frankfurt, by showing that his interpretation was simply 'wrong' or 'mistaken'. They have usually taken issue with Schopenhauer's method of isolating Hindu and Buddhist doctrines from their context, stripping them of their allegedly allegorical form, and then asserting that the bare remainder (or, in Schopenhauer's

---

[75] A comprehensive list is contained in HNV pp. 319-52.

idiom, the "kernel") essentially agrees with his own positions. For example, Joachim Gestering notes how Schopenhauer approached Hinduism and Buddhism "without any hermeneutic", and therefore looked upon the Indian tradition "as if it were some other European philosopher".[76] As a consequence of this lack of hermeneutical awareness, Gestering charges Schopenhauer with asserting uninformed parallels between aspects of his system and those of the Indian religions, specifically his claim that they shared the same conception of pessimism.[77] Gestering is correct to detect a divergence in the form and extent of Schopenhauerian and Indian pessimism, but his study oddly lacks hermeneutical awareness and appreciation of context by implying that it is a defect in a philosopher to have failed to anticipate a set of methodological principles that appeared one hundred years *after* he died.[78] However, we encounter a more unfortunate attitude of accusation and indignation in Roger Pol-Droit's claim that Schopenhauer not only completely misunderstood Buddhism,[79] but apparently also took

> malicious pleasure in seeing a convergence, even a similarity, between the teachings of Shakyamuni and his own…one could never overly emphasise the fact that this was a question of a belated — and in part even abusive — annexation.[80]

Schopenhauer's tone does frequently assume a mischievous air when he is extolling the greater merits of Indian doctrines over those of Judaeo-Christian monotheism, but Pol-Droit's attribution of malicious motives is clearly unwarranted. However, the latter's scornful presentation of the malice apparently motivating Schopenhauer's appropriation of Indian thought is completely put in the shade by Gerald Larson's casual assertion that the comparative approaches of Hegel and Schopenhauer to Indian thought are "hardly worth mentioning" and that the latter's "exuberant affirmation of matters non-European is clearly a case for the psychoanalyst."[81]

Schopenhauer's Indian interpretation has clearly stirred emotions in some quarters, and largely among those committed to the scholarly vogue for dialogue and dialectic promoted by Buber and Gadamer, compared with which Schopenhauer's interpretative stance appears arrogant and

---

[76] Gestering (1986) p. 59.
[77] Ibid. p. 262.
[78] Schopenhauer died in 1860: Gadamer's *Truth and Method* was published in 1960.
[79] Pol-Droit (2003) p. 93.
[80] Ibid. pp. 95-6.
[81] Larson (1988) pp. 7-8.

monological. His distinction between the explicit knowledge of philosophy and the implicit, intuitive knowledge of religion does tend to situate the classical Indian religions as junior partners in his encounter with them, with him assuming the role of a fully self-aware, neutral Cartesian subject, transcending the object of his scrutiny. In Gadamer's idiom, Schopenhauer's encounter with Hinduism and Buddhism might be characterised as less of a fusion of the horizons of east and west than an absorption of the former by the latter. But, however misguided or scandalous Schopenhauer's hermeneutical stance may seem to the heirs of Gadamer's ontological account of understanding, *ad hominem* and moralising attributions of sinister or unhealthy motives are neither insightful nor helpful, especially since the *what* or substance of Schopenhauer's Indian interpretation is still a matter of rumour and conjecture, and the *why* or motivations governing his interpretation have been largely overlooked. Schopenhauer was the first serious advocate of Indian thought to the west, and irrespective of the soundness of his guiding principles or the validity of his presentation, all westerners who attempt to comprehend the Indian traditions today stand within the "history of effect" (*Wirkungsgeschichte*) of his interpretation, and therefore owe him some recognition as a pioneer in this regard. Moreover, as previously noted in the Introduction, Schopenhauer's works provide evidence that his interpretation of Hinduism and Buddhism was dialectical and underwent modification as a result of his developing exposure to better sources, which undermines the view that he was impervious to their influence.

As a result, this study assumes that an epistemological and historical approach to understanding Schopenhauer's appropriation of Indian thought is preferable to the moral stance of recent works. This is because, when we take note of the interests and expectations that he brought to his Indian sources in conjunction with the prevailing hermeneutical models of his time, his choice of interpretative principles is completely justified. In agreement with his former teacher Schleiermacher, Schopenhauer's approach presupposes that the interpreter has the ability to awaken within himself the original intuitions inscribed within the concepts of textual sources, and to understand a text better than its original author, making connections and disclosing meanings of which the latter was unaware.[82] And although it might be conceded that Schopenhauer's representations of Hindu and Buddhist doctrines and practices are perhaps less accurate or objective than those of contemporary scholarship, the difference can

---

[82] Schleiermacher (1998) p. 266.

only be one of degree rather than kind. Andrew Tuck has shown how Indological studies from the nineteenth century onwards have interpreted Nāgārjuna's *Mūlamadhyamakakārikā* using the categories, concerns, objectives and schemas of the dominant philosophical fashion. Tuck narrates how Nāgārjuna has been successively represented as a nihilist by Eugène Burnouf and Louis de La Vallée Poussin, a transcendental idealist by Theodore Stcherbatsky and (as we saw previously) T.R.V. Murti, a Logical Positivist by Richard H. Robinson and a precursor of Wittgenstein's later philosophy by Chris Gudmunsen, Nathan Katz and Robert Thurman.[83] Tuck's study illustrates on a local level Gadamer's theory of the permanence of isogetical and unconscious presuppositions in our attempts to understand and explicate artefacts from cultures spatially and temporally removed from the here and now. And this insight equally applies to studies of texts from the same tradition, such as those of nineteenth-century German Idealism. It is, therefore, the assumption of this study that there is sufficient historical distance between Schopenhauer and the present to cease setting him up as the subject of philosophical hermeneutics in order to find him wanting. Instead we need to view Schopenhauer's interpretation of Hinduism and Buddhism as the object rather than subject of hermeneutical enquiry, as something that calls for understanding, and to explore the connections between his references to Indian doctrines and Christianity by placing them within the context of his wider philosophy and his diagnosis of the religious and philosophical situation of his time. In the words of Karl Popper, "[a] theory is comprehensible and reasonable only in its relation to a given *problem-situation*, and it can be rationally discussed only by discussing this relation."[84] Placing Schopenhauer's appropriation of Indian thought in the context of his understanding of the nineteenth-century crisis of religion throws more light on both the content of his interpretation as well as the motives governing it: this work is a contribution to this enquiry.

---

[83] Tuck (1990) Chapters 2-4.
[84] Popper (1968) p. 199.

CHAPTER 2

METAPHYSICAL NEED

I. Philosophy and Religion

According to Schopenhauer most people, most of the time, devote their attention to private interests and the objects serving these. Caught up in the struggle to secure survival, preservation, happiness and well-being, their intellect is locked *into* the pursuit of life and finds no time for reflection *on* it. Within the limitations of this pragmatic perspective they accept the world and their existence as matters of fact, and do not consider them questionable, problematic, or riddles. At some point, however, when the minimum necessary for existence has been secured, a person may raise his or her gaze, survey life and the world as a whole and enquire into their meaning, asking the questions 'why is there something rather than nothing?', and 'why does this something manifest itself under the conditions governing this, our world?' When a person truly attains this perspective, he or she is exposed to "wonder" (θαυμάζειν), the pathos that Plato and Aristotle identified as the genesis of philosophy (WWRI p. 32; WWRII p. 160).

But Schopenhauer's conception of wonder wears a gloomier cast than that of Plato or Aristotle. Denied the option of quenching wonder through contemplation of the Good or primary causes and principles of being *qua* being, Schopenhauer's philosophical investigator finds himself — in Heidegger's idiom — thrown into the world without special sources of knowledge, apart from the facts of inner and outer consciousness. Intensifying his scrutiny of phenomena, his wonder passes over into distress and dismay on the realisation that this world is ruled by the form of time, so that this being, this existence before which he experienced wonder, is forever passing over into nothingness. He notices that this ever-vanishing existence bears the characteristic of constant striving, that the striving is without end or aim, that it is accompanied by frustration and suffering, and that it finds its terminus in personal extinction rather than final satisfaction. He asks the further questions 'why do I suffer and why must I die?' With the arising of such awareness he finds himself in need of metaphysical consolation, of an interpretation of life that locates its significance beyond the boundaries of birth and death, and this "need for metaphysics" (*metaphysische Bedürfniß*) constitutes the human being as a "metaphysical animal" ("*animal metaphysicum*") (WWRII p. 160).

Schopenhauer's conception of the origin and status of metaphysics can be elucidated through comparison with similar lines of thought in two of his influential predecessors — Hume and Kant. In their view metaphysics was the argumentative and philosophical wing of Christian theology, its task that of demonstrating the existence and fixing the attributes of metaphysical objects such as God and the soul. Much of Hume's corpus can be read as an argumentative assault on the metaphysical project thus conceived, and he completes his assault with an unflattering account of the genesis of religious belief, tracing it to hope and fear regarding the unknown causes governing the fortune and destiny of individuals and society. The "ignorant multitude", says Hume, are incapable of conceiving of these unknown causes non-anthropomorphically, so that religion is a sort of primitive technology for attracting the favour of "invisible, intelligent power".[1] Although Hume was not as assured of reason's potential omnipotence as some of his contemporaries, his "wise man" who "proportions his belief to the evidence"[2] experiences no emotional shock on the discovery that the unknown causes are simply material particles operating with "regular and constant machinery".[3] Hume's philosopher remains contented with mitigated scepticism and the application of the experimental method, and observes without a sense of loss the exposure of the intellectual disreputability of Christianity and traditional metaphysics.

Whereas Hume traced the metaphysical instinct to the emotions of hope and fear, Kant discovered its origin in reason. According to Kant, reason's special task of synthesising representations leads up to the unconditioned ground of any given representation as its explanation, but this subjective necessity leads to illusion when the products of this process are mistaken for the real, objective principles of God, world and soul, the existence and nature of which metaphysical psychology, cosmology and theology set out to demonstrate and describe. In his first *Critique* Kant showed the impossibility of proving that these Ideas have real, transcendent referents, while in the second he put the Ideas to work as postulates of moral faith, belief in which arises from reason's practical need to bestow unity on our thought and action.[4] Kant acknowledged that

---

[1] Hume (1993b) p. 143.

[2] Hume (2000) p. 84.

[3] Hume (1993b) p. 141.

[4] Kant (1997) 5:142-5:143 (citations to Kant's works refer to the *Akademie* pagination).

popular religion originates in faculties other than reason, servile emotions analogous to Hume's superstitious hope and fear,[5] but he thought that the end of the eighteenth century — an age of enlightenment rather than an enlightened age — marked the cusp of humanity's extrication from childhood and tutelage, so that the religion of the future would replace belief in transcendent doctrines and ritual performance with theoretical agnosticism and moral practice in which duties are cognised *as if* divine commands.[6]

Kant's enlightened religious rationalism almost immediately came under fire from an opposite tendency, represented by Hamann, Jacobi and Herder. They developed a philosophical anthropology that resolved reason on feeling and located the intellect as a limited, even impotent epiphenomenon of the passions. Schopenhauer synthesised both views by, on the one hand, placing the intellect in the service of a vital and irrational element in human nature, while on the other rejecting the fideism of the Counter-Enlightenment and retaining the Humean and Kantian criterion that knowledge worthy of the name is attained only by way of reflection on sense-experience. But Schopenhauer's reversal of the will-intellect relation made him less confident of empirical or rational man's self-sufficiency.[7] For him humans are monstrously needy beings, prey to powers and forces more vital than reason. Metaphysical need is therefore ubiquitous, a "strong and ineradicable" instinct following "close on the physical." The history of civilisation testifies to its strength, for "all countries and ages" have had their creeds, philosophies, temples, churches, mosques and pagodas (WWRII p. 162). Schopenhauer's account of metaphysical need implies that whatever victories human ingenuity should wrest from nature, and irrespective of the improvements accruing from the application of critical reason to everyday affairs, the darker elements of life such as misery, suffering and death are constants, faced by the wise and the multitude alike with fear and trembling. The need for metaphysics cannot, therefore, be quietened by either scepticism or criticism, for it is "the knowledge of death, and therewith the consideration of the suffering and misery of life" that provides the strongest

---

[5] Kant (1960) 6:171-2.

[6] Ibid. 6:153.

[7] Hume may have concurred with Schopenhauer when he maintained that "reason is, and ought only to be the slave of the passions" (Hume (1978) p. 415), but his works are not haunted by the storm and stress of Schopenhauer's writings. Hume's philosopher is imperturbable in the face of his own mortality, as confirmed by Boswell's report of the philosopher's state of mind on his death-bed (Boswell (1992) p. 109).

impulse to seek metaphysical interpretations of existence, for their "strongest and essential point" are their various doctrines of a post-mortem existence. Schopenhauer maintained that theistic systems may seem to make the existence of the gods the main point and glory offered to these the main practice, but if it were possible either to show that immortality is independent of the gods or that the gods are an obstacle to immortality, "lively ardour for their gods would at once cool" (WWRII p. 161). The strength of metaphysical need and the consolation it seeks in the face of death entail that sceptical and materialist *Weltanschauungen* will never receive general approbation or prevail for long (WWRII p. 162).

For this reason, Schopenhauer observed with consternation the rise of materialism and the concomitant decline of religion and metaphysics in the nineteenth century. But whereas Nietzsche dismissed Schopenhauer's theory of metaphysical need as a hangover of Christian belief,[8] something that might persist for generations as the "shadows" of God before fading and giving way to new conceptions of existence, Schopenhauer's ahistorical view of human nature prompted him to regard the decline of one religion as the mere preliminary to the birth of a new form. As a result, he did not take the challenge of positivism and secularism seriously, or truly envisage the possibility of a civilisation that lacks an overarching communal religion and whose philosophical tradition spurns metaphysical enquiry. The spectacle of twentieth-century Anglo-American philosophers waging war against metaphysics and taking their bearings from physicalism, while those on the Continent confine philosophy to political and social questions and problems of textual interpretation, would have struck him as enigmatic and inexplicable. He assimilated the ancient religions of India to his own system in order to create a centre of opposition to positivism and materialism, and in order to fill the gap opened up by the decline of Christian institutions in the wake of the increasing awareness of the intellectual indefensibility of historical Christianity.

However, it is one thing to detect a metaphysical need in human nature, another to argue for its ineradicability, and yet another to suggest it can be satisfied cognitively. Schopenhauer defined metaphysics as

> all so-called knowledge that goes beyond the possibility of experience, and so beyond nature or the given phenomenal appearance of things, in order to give information about that by which, in some sense or other, this experience or nature is conditioned, or in popular language, about that which is hidden by nature, and renders nature possible. (WWRII p. 164)

---

[8] Nietzsche (1974) §151.

Pre-Kantian metaphysics had located the principle that conditions nature and renders it possible in a transcendent realm, reachable only by way of ratiocination on an alleged *a priori* content. In opposition to this, Schopenhauer redefined metaphysics as the "*science of experience in general*", a science with empirical sources whose aim is to comprehend the immanent essence of nature by connecting at the right point outer experience with inner "and making the latter the key to the former" (WWRII p. 181). In Schopenhauer's view, therefore, Kant's critical philosophy had not demonstrated the impossibility of all metaphysical enquiry, but had merely deprived "theism of its foundation" by undermining the realist presuppositions of the transcendent metaphysics allied to Christian theology. On the contrary, Schopenhauer thought that the most important feature of Kant's work — "*the distinction of the phenomenon from the thing-in-itself*" (WWRI p. 417) — had restored the issue of man's metaphysical need to the catalogue of live philosophical concerns, and thereby opened "the way to entirely different and deeper explanations of existence." (WWRI p. 513) Kant may have attempted to resurrect the old metaphysical picture in his moral theology, employing the practical postulates to sneak God in through the back door, as it were, but in the *Critique of Judgement* Kant referred to a "supersensible substrate (which underlies both nature and our ability to think), a substrate that is large beyond any standard of sense".[9] He also remarked that judgement

> finds itself referred to something that is both in the subject himself and outside him, something that is neither nature nor freedom and yet is linked with the basis of freedom, the supersensible, in which the theoretical and the practical power are in an unknown manner combined and joined into a unity.[10]

These quotations show the extent to which the later Kant had departed from traditional conceptions of metaphysics, since in the mainstream Christian tradition the supersensible, or God, had never been depicted as the immanent substrate of the self and world, but as their transcendent creator. The locus of human personality, the soul, had been morally and intellectually set apart from God by its finite creature-hood, and more so by its fallen nature. In the above passages, however, Kant places the human subject *within* the supersensible, and in the thought of his successors this encouraged the formulation of systems of metaphysical monism at odds with the predominant dualism of western metaphysics since the

---

[9] Kant (1987) 255.
[10] Ibid. 353.

scholastics. Fichte, Schelling and Hegel animated the substance-monism of Spinoza using themes from Kant's regulative philosophy, such as God, freedom and teleology, indicating that they took Kant's theoretical critique as relevant only to transcendent forms of metaphysics. Schopenhauer maintained that Kant had liberated metaphysics from the obligation to answer the transcendent questions of theology, such as by whom or why the world was made. Instead, post-Kantian metaphysics enquires into *what* the world is, and thereby gives content to the supersensible substrate or inner nature of the phenomenon. Metaphysics is therefore cosmology rather than theology, its method that of *immanent* interpretation rather than *transcendent* inference (WWRII p. 612). It is perhaps one of the greatest ironies of intellectual history that after Kant had shown that the human mind is incapable of cognising non-physical objects, his successors developed a host of exotic systems of metaphysics not seen in such variety and abundance since the ancient Greeks. For this short period in which post-Kantian philosophers developed strange and inspiring systems of metaphysics, before philosophy became ultra-sceptical, cynical, ironic and middle-aged, there is no better description than that used by Rüdiger Safranski in the subtitle of his biography on Schopenhauer: these were indeed "the wild years of philosophy", even perhaps its rebellious adolescence. Schopenhauer thought it especially fortuitous that Kant had done away with philosophy's obligation to systematise and justify Christian dogma at a time when scholars were publishing and expounding the contents of ancient Indian texts, for he read these as containing a religious metaphysic that similarly denies the ultimate reality of causal relations and the forms of the phenomenon.

II. Philosophy vs. Religion

But irrespective of his conviction of the strength and ineradicability of metaphysical need, Schopenhauer also thought that the intellect is not always equal to its demands. In origin the intellect is not an organ adapted for the reception or discovery of metaphysical knowledge, but a light for the will and its need to know the relations between representations, and their ultimate relation to the body as the will's visibility or objectification. As a result, the history of civilised nations shows the ubiquity of metaphysics as well as its division into two basic types. The first, esoteric and catering to an intellectual elite, is metaphysical philosophy proper; the other, exoteric and tailored to the needs of the majority, is the metaphysics of the people, commonly known as *religion* (WWRII p. 164).

Schopenhauer thought it imperative to separate philosophy and religion, and this conviction dates from his period as a student in Berlin. When Schleiermacher claimed in a lecture that "no one can be a philosopher without being religious", Schopenhauer wrote in the margin of his notes "[n]o one who is religious attains to philosophy; he does not need it. No one who really philosophises is religious; he walks without leading-strings, perilously but free." (MRII p. 243) Although Schopenhauer traced the two species of metaphysics to a common origin in human nature, and thought they responded to the same questions concerning the meaning of life and the necessity of suffering and death, he thought that the religions do not always give adequate metaphysical answers to these questions. For this reason, he inveighed against what he considered to be the tendency of his contemporaries in the universities to "weld philosophy and religion into one centaur which they call philosophy of religion [*Religionsphilosophie*]" (PPI p. 142), and against those who talk of a Christian philosophy, "which is much the same as if we were to speak of a Christian arithmetic" (PPI p. 143). He thought that the schoolmen in the Middle Ages had been justified insofar as they openly acknowledged that their philosophy was an *ancilla theologiae*, but in his view the university philosophers of the nineteenth-century were dishonest to claim intellectual independence while seeking to demonstrate, using slippery arguments cloaked in incomprehensible jargon, that the doctrines of the national religion are capable of rational defence (WN p. 16). They thereby betrayed philosophy's origin in wonder, reducing it to a trade *by* which they lived rather than an ideal to live *for* (FR p. 73). Schopenhauer thought that philosophy had been established on the right path when Descartes founded it on immediate self-consciousness, for this had led up to Kant's transcendental idealism (PPI p. 3). But a philosophy in the pay of the state and serving the interests of the national religion will necessarily profess the realism of the masses rather than the idealism of post-Kantian philosophy, and will thereby vitiate the great gains made in philosophy since it tendered its resignation as theology's handmaid. The purpose of university philosophy is to rationalise tradition rather than exercise genuine metaphysical thinking, since the state is unlikely to permit its hired philosophers to contradict from the lectern what its other employees, the priests, teach from the pulpit (PPI p. 139). For this reason, Schopenhauer argued that serious philosophy can only be pursued outside state institutions. The philosophical ideal for him was that of the economically self-sufficient gentleman amateur, characteristic of the ancients and the philosophers of the early modern period in Europe.

It is possible to adduce biographical and psychological causes for Schopenhauer's opposition to philosophy of religion, causes distinct from the reasons he assembles in justification of his view. Like Kant before him, Schopenhauer had no taste for religious ritual, and although responsive to nature, art and ethical phenomena, he betrayed no specifically religious yearnings. His upbringing and education left him without the sentimental attachment to Christianity found in contemporaries such as Fichte, Schelling, Schleiermacher and Hegel. Schopenhauer's early education was almost wholly secular,[11] and his initial course of study at the University of Göttingen was in medicine. As a result, Schopenhauer approached the religions from the standpoint of an external observer. A religious believer might consider his perspective overly intellectual, for he tended to look upon the religions as doctrinal systems and paid little attention to their communal rituals and institutions. However, while it is important to draw attention to Schopenhauer's biographical limitations and the manner in which they frame his perspective on religion, it is questionable to what extent they facilitate evaluation of his arguments: there is, moreover, always the danger that such explanations through causes may be used as a substitute for analysing the reasons he gives in defence of his position.

Current reflection on the methodological study of religion recognises three broad perspectives: religious theories of religion (occasionally confessional, but increasingly less so); naturalist or reductionist theories of religion; and a perspective that has been called methodological agnosticism.[12] Non-confessional practitioners of the first would include Rudolf Otto, Mircea Eliade and John Hick. Feuerbach, Freud and the majority of anthropologists after Durkheim can be identified as naturalists. McCutcheon identifies Ninian Smart as a methodological agnostic.[13] Schopenhauer's philosophy of religion fails to slip neatly into either of these categories. He was certainly not an agnostic in Smart's sense of limiting analysis of religion to phenomenological description, since he regarded the metaphysical questions to which the religions respond to be amenable to resolution through the methods of philosophy. Although there is a strong strain of metaphysical agnosticism in Schopenhauer's admission that we cannot say what becomes of the thing-in-itself after it

---

[11] The exception to this is the brief period he spent at a parson's school in Wimbledon, which left him with the conviction that Anglicanism was enforced by a politically influential clergy and practised in a spirit of hypocrisy (PPI pp. 15-6n.20).

[12] See McCutcheon (1999) pp. 1-8.

[13] Ibid. pp. 216-7.

has turned and denied itself (WWRII p. 612), this is not agnosticism about the soteriological schemes of religion, since he clearly thought that some (such as the Buddhist *nirvāṇa*) were preferable to others (such as reabsorption in *Brahman* or union with God — WWRII p. 608). Whether his perspective on religion can be categorised as a reductionist or a religious theory is more ambiguous. It is true that he traced religion to a cause in human nature — the need for a metaphysical interpretation of life — which, *prima facie*, suggests he is a causal reductionist or naturalist. However, Schopenhauer did not reduce religion to metaphysical need as its cause, since he looked upon some religious doctrines as practical vehicles of metaphysical truth, and therefore in harmony with the philosophical project of supporting metaphysical interpretations with reasons. By contrast, Freud regarded explanation in terms of wish-fulfilment as a sufficient causal reduction of religion and exposure of its beliefs as illusions.[14]

Consistent with his claim that religion and philosophy have a common origin, Schopenhauer's philosophy contains all the theoretical elements of a positive religion — a metaphysic, a theory of immortality, a doctrine of pure virtue and a soteriology. And although his epistemology was in many respects closer to that of Locke and Hume than it was to Kant's, Schopenhauer was neither an empiricist nor a positivist, and tended to expend equal portions of scorn on the naturalist ambition to replace metaphysics with a system of absolute physics as he did on Hegel and Hegelianism (WN p. 3, p. 13). The enthusiasm with which he embraced and championed the wisdom of the ancient religious traditions of the east shows that he was capable of appreciating determinate religious forms, but his conviction of the distinction in sources, methods and respective functions of philosophical and religious metaphysics made him alive to the need for a separation between them.

However, and irrespective of his censorship of *Religionsphilosophie*, Schopenhauer consistently philosophised *about* religion, and in many ways his objections to the discipline indicate a change in terminological meaning between his day and the present. What Schopenhauer understood by the term *Religionsphilosophie* was speculative theology, a confessional project that borrows the concepts, techniques and methods of argumentation formulated by philosophers in order to construct a theoretical prop for the doctrines of the established religion, presenting them as the conclusions of reason. Although many philosophers of religion still

---

[14] Freud (1985) p. 212.

adhere to this conception of the discipline, others regard it as a branch of philosophy that adopts a stance external to any particular religious tradition, and that employs philosophical methods to investigate the truth claims, meaning, and function of religious doctrines — a conception that harmonises with Schopenhauer's methodological approach. Schopenhauer's hostility to *Religionsphilosophie* also stemmed from his belief that, in the hands of the 'professors', it was insufficiently independent of state and religious authorities, and that its analysis of religious doctrines frequently spilled over into attempts at proof and demonstration. For this reason, and with vigour equal to a Tertullian or a Karl Barth, Schopenhauer maintained that Jerusalem should not consort with Athens. Religion is exposed to the "rifle-fire of scepticism, and the heavy artillery of the *Critique of Pure Reason*" when attempts are made to establish its doctrines on reasons (WWRII p. 168), while philosophy is brought into disrepute when its conclusions are determined by the doctrines of a particular tradition in advance (PPI p. 143).

It is clear, however, that Schopenhauer expected philosophy to profit most from his petition for a distinction between it and religion, and his statement that it would be mutually beneficial to both species of metaphysics if each remained "clearly separated" from the other, and confined "itself to its own province, in order there to develop fully its own nature" conceals imperialist philosophical ambitions (WWRII p. 168). His appeal for a strict demarcation was not simply an assertion of philosophy's freedom, but also the preliminary for philosophy's explanatory absorption of religion. In his view, religion has nothing to say about philosophy, its sources and methods limit it to a narrow sphere, whereas philosophy's status as universal knowledge gives it the right to lord it over religion, to submit its truth claims to verification, to compare doctrines belonging to different traditions, to explain the function of religion generally and to assess the adequacy of particular doctrines in relation to the demands of metaphysical need. Philosophy may even, on occasion, expose the inner, rational content of certain religious doctrines. It is not surprising to find Schopenhauer claiming that the results of philosophical reflection and religious belief often converge, since they have a common root in human nature, but he also thought it important to allow philosophy to develop without interference from religious authorities and dependence on religious sources. As such, although Schopenhauer was keen to press the analogy between the religious traditions of India and some of his own philosophical positions, he was simultaneously concerned to disavow the possibility that his thought had been influenced by his encounter with them.

However, Schopenhauer's proclamation of philosophy's freedom from religion extended no further than its right to *theorise* freely. In his view, philosophy's response to "wonder" (θαυμάζειν) takes the form of reflection rather than action, so that all philosophy, whether metaphysics, aesthetics or ethics,

> is always theoretical, since it is essential to it always to maintain a purely contemplative attitude, whatever be the immediate object of investigation; to enquire, not to prescribe. But to become practical, to guide conduct, to transform character, are old claims which with mature insight it ought finally to abandon. For here, where it is a question of the worth or worthlessness of existence, of salvation or damnation, not the dead concepts of philosophy decide the matter, but the innermost nature of man himself... (WWRI p. 271)

On this note he continues by stating that it is "as foolish to expect that our moral systems and ethics would create virtuous, noble, and holy men, as that our aesthetics would produce poets, painters and musicians." Given his exclusively theoretical conception of philosophy, the inference might be drawn that Schopenhauer never imagined it assuming the functions of the historical religions or otherwise making them redundant, since fulfilment of the practical obligations flowing from metaphysical need is essentially a religious task. The concepts of philosophy are incapable of transforming the inner character of the will, so religion uses abstract dogmas, myths and allegories to guide conduct from the outside (WWRI p. 368), setting up ideals of ethical worth and holiness as objects of aspiration to the many, and presenting images of salvation — such as that of the risen Saviour — as consolations for suffering and knowledge of the certainty of death (WWRI p. 329). Analysis, explanation and confirmation of the ethical and soteriological teachings of the world's religions may be a central part of philosophy's remit, but for illustration of its theories of virtue and holiness it turns not to intellectual history but to the mystics, saints, *sannyāsins* and holy-men of religion, such as St. Francis of Assisi or the Buddha (WWRI p. 384). Hence, although Schopenhauer thought that the cultural conditions of the nineteenth century had enabled philosophy to assert its freedom from and theoretical ascendancy over religion, he also thought that religion remained supreme in the sphere of practice.

Schopenhauer's demarcation between philosophy and religion as theoretical and practical metaphysics was paralleled by his estimation of the different methods they use in the fulfilment of their respective ends. As theoretical science, philosophy is a "doctrine of conviction", supporting its theories with proofs grounded in appropriate logical or perceptual bases. Philosophy can therefore give an account of itself. On the other hand, religion as practical technology is a "doctrine of faith", shoring up its creeds and dogmas by appealing to external factors, such as the authority of tradition, sacred texts and institutions (WWRII p. 165). In Schopenhauer's view the conditions that create the necessity for a twofold appearance of metaphysical truth are empirical, being "the great original difference in the powers of understanding [*Verstandeskräfte*]" between one person and another, as well as the varying levels of civilisation and intellectual attainment in different ages and nations (WWRII p. 164).

Schopenhauer's criterion for differentiating philosophy from religion has a number of points in common with Plato's and Aristotle's criterion for distinguishing dialectic from rhetoric. The truths of philosophy and dialectic are supported by arguments that issue in conviction, while religion for Schopenhauer and rhetoric for Plato and Aristotle aim to persuade others of the truth of certain opinions, their product being belief. The rationale for the division is the respective nature of the audience: philosophy addresses itself to trained minds moved by argument, while rhetoric and religion are aimed at "audiences of limited intellectual scope and limited capacity to follow an extended chain of reasoning."[15] For Schopenhauer, the proofs of philosophical metaphysics depart from material available to all — facts of inner and outer perception — while religion relies on feeling and respect for authority, so that its arguments appeal to the will rather than the intellect. Philosophy therefore "has its verification and credentials in itself," while the evidence for religious doctrines is external and grounded in revelation, which is in turn "authenticated by signs and miracles." (WWRII pp. 164-5)

Apart from differentiating philosophy and religion on the grounds of their respective sources, credentials and purposes, Schopenhauer detected a further criterion of distinction in the formal nature of their propositions. For him metaphysical philosophy has one obligation, "to be true *sensu stricto et proprio*" irrespective of whether its truths are pleasing, and it must present its truths in systematically arranged concepts, for it "appeals to thought and conviction." By contrast, religious doctrines need be no more than true "*sensu allegorico*", making use of mythic, parabolic and symbolic veils to impress metaphysical truth on the imagination of the masses. Schopenhauer thought that the religions naively announced the

---

[15] Aristotle (1991) 1357a (citations to Aristotle's works refer to the Bekker pagination).

allegorical nature of their doctrines by relying on mysteries, "found perhaps in every religion" (WWRII p. 166). However, Schopenhauer's conception of the various possibilities and uses of mysteries was rather more complex than he sometimes suggested. At one point he claimed that a mystery functions popularly as "an obviously absurd dogma which nevertheless conceals within itself a sublime truth" (PPII p. 334), which implies that mysteries are partially cognitive, being vehicles that communicate the transcendental truths of philosophical metaphysics in non-conceptual form. At another point he maintained that mysteries are "certain dogmas that cannot even be distinctly conceived, much less be literally true", which suggests the different view that mysteries have no cognitive content or function, but are useful for stimulating feelings of awe in the masses and thereby enforcing the point that metaphysics refers to an order of things wherein the laws of the phenomenon are annulled (WWRII p. 166).

However, Schopenhauer also gave his second definition of mysteries an esoteric interpretation, where they no longer function as substitutes for philosophical knowledge but as signs indicating the ineffable point beyond subject and object where all knowledge necessarily ends (WWRII p. 612). However, despite the suggestion that this esoteric use of mysteries surpasses the reach of philosophical enquiry, for Schopenhauer they are still nothing but signs useful for evoking emotions and attitudes, as opposed to conceptual units standing for possible perceptions. Mysteries and mystical paradoxes lack cognitive content and do not, therefore, convey knowledge, for they lack the determinacy and concretion of philosophical doctrines, and are, moreover, unsupported by proofs or arguments. Their sole ground is the authority of the mystic's private experience, which "is unable to convince." (WWRII p. 611) Since Schopenhauer traced the resort to mysteries to various types of limitations on knowledge, his theory is distinct from Rudolf Otto's thesis that the category of the *mysterium tremendum* — the "numinous basis and background to religion" — "can only be induced, incited, and aroused" by the non-rational medium of mysteries rather than adequately represented in concepts.[16] This is because Otto's theory assumes some sort of inchoate knowledge of the numinous basis of religion by presenting the resort to mysteries as necessitated by the inscrutability and immensity of the religious object, while Schopenhauer's interpretation has it that mysteries are either concessions to the non-philosophically minded or symbols indicating the margins of knowledge as such.

---

[16] Otto (1958) p. 60.

Since the allegorical propositions of religion are supported by authority, Schopenhauer maintained that it is not incumbent upon the guardians of religion to demonstrate their truth by other means. They need only ask for faith, which he defined as "a voluntary acceptance that such is the state of affairs." (WWRII p. 167) For those who have faith — who are content to satisfy their metaphysical need by maintaining belief in the doctrine and worshipping in accordance with the rites prescribed by the religion — eternal bliss is promised, which satisfies the most important criterion flowing from metaphysical need — the obligation to offer consolation for suffering and death. Schopenhauer also thought that religious or popular systems of metaphysics serve the purpose of raising a person's perspective from absorption in everyday physical needs and desires, thereby underscoring the moral significance of life and deposing the brutishness warranted by egoism and sanctified by metaphysical materialism. As a communal or national metaphysic, one of the main tasks of a religion is to recommend observation of public virtue. In this capacity, religious allegories take the place of abstract maxims of practical reason, providing external grounds for determination of the will by promising rewards and threatening punishments. Although Schopenhauer maintained that popular systems of religious morals could never be sources of genuine virtue, since they are powerless to bring about radical change in the nature of the egoist's will and must, instead, appeal to his sense of self-interest, he still thought they were useful adjuncts to social mores and state law. But from this perspective of social utility, Schopenhauer maintained that the specific content of religious allegories and their relation to truth and virtue is irrelevant. Insofar as they have the power to promote certain patterns of conduct and forbid others, they fulfil their purpose:

> there must be a public standard of right and virtue; and in fact this must at all times flutter high overhead. After all, it is immaterial what heraldic figures are put on it, if only it signifies what is meant. (PPII p. 331)[17]

Schopenhauer never explicitly outlined the epistemological presuppositions of his contrast between the allegories of religion and the concepts of philosophy, and a modern literary theorist might consider his employment of the term allegory somewhat indiscriminate. However, his contrast has a long pedigree in the philosophy of religion, and stems

---

[17] This view is similar to Richard Braithwaite's theory of religious propositions. Braithwaite maintained that Christian doctrines cannot be considered factual because they are not amenable to verification, but are rendered meaningful when taken as stories encouraging intentions to act in accordance with *agape* (see Braithwaite (1964) pp. 243-5).

from Philo of Alexandria's Platonic exegesis of the Hebrew Bible.[18] But although Schopenhauer never explained his conception of the difference between allegories and concepts, in the second edition of his doctoral dissertation he drew a distinction between concepts and "pictures of the imagination" (*Phantasiebilder*). Despite the fact that the latter denotes a broader category than that of allegory, his analysis can be applied to the problem under consideration. In the dissertation he states that "[a]ll thinking in the wider sense...requires either words [the sensuous correlates of concepts] or pictures of the imagination" (FR p. 153). Concepts and imaginative pictures are both, therefore, objects of self-conscious reflection, "representations of representations" or *reflections* of the individual objects of perception, the source and "real content of all our thinking" (WWRII p. 71). And if "thinking in the wider sense" combines picture and concept, then thinking "in the narrower sense" is pure cognition, when thought dispenses with all mental imagery and operates in the medium of concepts alone. Schopenhauer's nominalist view of concepts has it that they are formed by removing similar attributes (qualities and relations) from individual objects of perception and depositing them in a single item of thought (FR pp. 146-7). Therefore, in accordance with Schopenhauer's account, the concept 'red' is obtained by extracting this property from distinct objects of perception, such as a braeburn apple, a ripe tomato and the Chinese flag. Properties distinguishing these objects from one another (such as shape, size, texture, purpose, etc.) are dropped, while their common 'redness' is collected into one abstract unit (FR p. 151). Pictures of the imagination differ from concepts insofar as they are concrete, or "intuitive, complete, and thus individual" representations. They are therefore formally identical to the particulars known through perception (having shape, colour, texture, a specific size, etc.), but distinct from perceptual particulars insofar as they do not arise directly through an impression of sense, and do not, therefore, "belong to the complex of experience" (FR p. 152). Like scenes in a dream, imaginative pictures are flesh and blood images whose appearance in the mind has no direct causal relation to or dependence upon objective states of affairs.

---

[18] In his allegorical interpretation of the story of Cain and Abel, Philo defended a moral and spiritual contrast between love of self and love of God that is strongly paralleled by Schopenhauer's contrast between the moral significance of the symbols of Adam and Christ outlined below. For a discussion of Philo's allegorical method, see Armstrong (2007) pp. 49-53.

Although Schopenhauer argued that there is no necessity for imaginative pictures to accompany pure cognition or thinking "in the narrower sense", he acknowledged that they can and often do so, on which occasions they stand as symbols or representatives of concepts. However, when they do so the picture is never "adequate to the concept represented thereby, but is full of arbitrary determinations." (FR pp. 152-3) As an example Schopenhauer referred to the concept of 'dog', logical analysis of which may be accompanied by an imaginative picture of a dog of a certain size, colour, shape and breed. However, since this image is of a particular dog it does not fully represent the concept, since the latter is meant to stand for all dogs, irrespective of size, colour, shape and breed (FR p. 152).

Schopenhauer detected a similar asymmetry between the allegories of religion and the concepts of philosophy. Both species of metaphysics are required to represent the Platonic Ideas, the eternal forms and prototypes of the individuals of phenomena.[19] Philosophical genius communicates its vision of the Ideas through systems of concepts, while religious and artistic genius embodies them in imagery. However, since the narratives that religious genius uses for allegorical communication of the Ideas are usually and originally historical in nature, they are full of extrinsic and "arbitrary determinations." For example, Schopenhauer maintained that Christianity teaches

> the great truth of the affirmation and denial of the will-to-live in the garment of allegory by saying that, through the Fall of Adam, the curse had come upon all men, sin had come into the world, and guilt was inherited by all; but that through the sacrificial death of Jesus, on the other hand, all were purged of sin, the world was saved, guilt abolished, and justice appeased. (WWRII p. 628)

However, Christian theology has tended to present the historical portion of the allegory as its main part, teaching that Adam was an historical individual and the ancestor of the human race and Jesus the incarnation of the logos of God in first-century Palestine, so that the guilt of the former and the grace of the latter is transmitted through natural and divine causality respectively. Such over-emphasis on the realist or material part

---

[19] Schopenhauer's Platonic Ideas are not Platonic in the strict sense. They do not indicate abstract virtues such as the true, the good or the beautiful, all of which Schopenhauer considered to be ectypes rather than archetypes, nominal concepts created by the rational processes of division and collection (FR p. 169). Schopenhauer's Ideas are objects of perception rather than conception, and refer to the various grades of the will's objectification in nature — from original forces such as gravity and impenetrability, through animal and plant species, up to the character or will of individual human beings.

of the allegory has distorted Christianity by turning it into a propositional faith, in which salvation is promised to those who are able to maintain faith in specific historical claims and the theological conventions associated with these. In the process, the allegory's ability to express opposite determinations of the Idea or will of human beings has been obscured, vastly diminishing its capacity to guide conduct in accordance with the truths known to philosophy.[20] In opposition to this, Schopenhauer maintains that a religious interpretation of Adam and Jesus ought not to view them as "individuals according to the principle of sufficient reason" (WWRI p. 405), but as symbols or pure types according to which "every person is Adam as well as Jesus, according as he comprehends himself, and his will thereupon determines him." (WWRII p. 628)

III. A Post-Kantian Synthesis

However, Schopenhauer acknowledged that it was unlikely for a religion to confess openly to its allegorical nature. The guardians of religion are obliged to claim *sensu proprio* truth for their doctrines in order to retain the allegiance of the many, since it is this that guarantees their social influence and the politically underwritten monopoly of their species of metaphysical knowledge. Under this regime, Schopenhauer noted that philosophy is either tolerated "as a weed growing" by the side of religion, "an unauthorised worker...a horde of gypsies" (WWRII p. 186), or forcibly recruited to the service of religion and assigned the role of formulating proofs for its allegories. But, says Schopenhauer, a national religion need not concern itself with the separate existence of a doctrine of conviction, and needs no theoretical prop to authenticate its doctrines from within, having innumerable means for its promulgation:

> revelation, documents, miracles, prophecies, government protection, the highest dignity and eminence, as is due to truth, the consent and reverence of all, a thousand temples in which it is preached and practised, hosts of sworn priests...(WWRII p. 166)

---

[20] Schopenhauer's criticism of allegories in the plastic and pictorial arts has points in common with his analysis of religion allegories. Just as the latter tend to represent belief in the events of sacred history, rather than transformation of the will, as the condition of salvation, so allegorical art makes prior acquaintance with the arbitrary conventions connecting sign and signified, rather than aesthetic sensibility, the condition for appreciation of the art-work (WWRI pp. 238-9).

Schopenhauer is obviously indulging in irony here, but on a more serious note he observed that a national religion's most "invaluable prerogative" is its state guaranteed right to teach its dogmas to the young as *sensu proprio* truths, before judgement has matured. This prerogative ensures that religious doctrines receive more than mere outward consent, since the early impress of religious education inwardly determines the structure of the mind, and thereby retards its capacity to conceive of or even comprehend alternative metaphysical schemes. As a result, religious dogmas become fixed ideas, "a kind of second inborn intellect, like the twig on the grafted tree." (WWRII p. 165)

For this reason, Schopenhauer maintained that Kant was mistaken when he referred to the inconclusiveness of metaphysical disputes as evidence of the impossibility of establishing metaphysics as a science.[21] On the contrary, the lack of progress and permanent results in metaphysics is not the consequence of its obscurity or alleged impossibility, but of the political, cultural and educational privileges accorded to Christianity and its institutions. The state's political sponsorship of religious authorities has not merely enabled the latter to press philosophers into their service, but has also ensured that philosophers departing from the mainstream — such as Giordano Bruno, Spinoza, and Schopenhauer himself (WWRI p. 422n; WN p. 144) — have been deprived of a fair hearing and their systems rendered incomprehensible, since "nothing can so firmly oppose the comprehension of even the *problem* of metaphysics as a previous solution to it forced on the mind, and early implanted in it." (WWRII p. 186) A psychologist of religious belief such as Kierkegaard might defend the educational privileges of Christianity, arguing that people need to believe and cannot wait for metaphysicians to resolve their disputes,[22] but Schopenhauer held the traditional, Cartesian view that metaphysics is First Philosophy, and that its propositions

> affect the foundation of all our other knowledge and accordingly for this fix for all time the point of view. In the event of such statements themselves being false, the point of view is for ever distorted. Moreover, as their corollaries everywhere affect the whole system of our knowledge, this is then thoroughly falsified and adulterated by them. (PPII p. 329)

But if Schopenhauer thought that the guardians of Christianity have been either unable or unwilling to acknowledge the allegorical nature of their teachings and their explanatory dependence upon philosophy, he also

---

[21] Kant (1990) 255-6.
[22] Kierkegaard (1962) pp. 49-52.

thought that the growth in scientific knowledge from the seventeenth century onwards, combined with the recent revolution in philosophy instituted by Kant, had forced this recognition on them from the outside. These advances in intellectual culture had made the question of the integrity of the European metaphysical *Weltbild* an important issue, for if "it is the mind, if it is knowledge that makes man lord of the earth, then no errors are harmless, still less venerable and holy." (WWRI p. 36)

And Schopenhauer considered Christian doctrine to be full of harmful errors, irrespective of its antiquity and venerability. Christianity teaches that the world was created good for the benefit and happiness of humans, that nature and animals are *things*, or objects created for the satisfaction of the human will. It represents the originating principle as a transcendent and almighty personal creator, a fusion of thinking and willing, and the human as its analogue, a transcendent hypostasis or soul set apart from nature and operating in accordance with laws of its own making. As a result, Schopenhauer maintained that Kant could not have been in earnest when he attributed a regulative value to the transcendent doctrines of God, world and soul, as principles encouraging us to strive for the greatest unity and extension in our investigations of natural phenomena.[23] In Schopenhauer's view, an examination of the history of western thought shows that the intellectual dominance of these ideas has more frequently hindered than facilitated understanding (WWRI p. 514). The most promising minds of the Middle Ages and of the sixteenth and seventeenth centuries were "paralysed" by the "false fundamental notions" of metaphysical theism, so that "all insight into the true constitution and working of nature was, so to speak, boarded up for them." (PPII p. 329) For example, Descartes instituted the modern epoch in philosophy by repudiating the traditional authorities of Aristotle and the Bible and founding philosophy on the immediate witness of self-consciousness (PPI p. 3). When, however, Descartes discovered the proposition impervious to doubt — *cogito ergo sum* — he interpreted it as confirmation of the Christian myth he had learnt as a child, and divided human nature into a rational spiritual essence and a materially extended body. Similarly, argued Schopenhauer, Scotus Erigena's concrete perception of the world informed him that it was pervaded by evil and wickedness, but his fundamental intuition was contradicted by the theistic and purely conceptual dogma that almighty God created the world and judged it good (πάντα

---

[23] Kant (1998) A644/B672.

καλὰ λίαν[24]). To reconcile his intuition with his inherited conceptual scheme, Erigena made use of the theological equivalent of Ptolemaic epicycles, saving hypotheses that can be verbalised but not thought with any clarity, such as the non-being of evil and the freedom of the will (PPI p. 63). Even nineteenth-century physiologists, when they put aside "scalpel and scoop" and theorise about their subject, do so "with concepts they received when they were confirmed" (WWRII p. 199). Irrespective, therefore, of the greater achievements of the moderns in natural science and the mechanical and technical arts (PPII p. 405), Schopenhauer maintained that "the ancients are still our teachers in metaphysics." (WWRII p. 187)

And, in Schopenhauer's view, the politically enforced intellectual and pedagogical privileges of Europe's popular metaphysic had not merely hindered the progress of philosophy and understanding of the theoretical underpinnings of the *Naturwissenschaften,* but also limited cultivation of that breadth of understanding and sympathetic insight necessary for excellence in the *Geisteswissenschaften.* He cites as evidence an article on Chinese thought by the pioneering Sinologist Reverend Morrison, in which the author sets out to expose the falsehood of Chinese cosmology and ethics by pointing out its disagreement with Christian theism, and thereby "imagines that he has demonstrated the false nature of the alien creed." (PPII p. 330) And the failure to recognise that Christian truth is allegorical and pragmatic rather than conceptual and theoretical has not merely hindered appreciation of other religions, but understanding of the whole phenomenon of religion, including therefore Christianity. This has led to the aforementioned over-emphasis on belief to the detriment of practice, and to the scholarly tendency to classify religions in accordance with their transcendent dogmas, such as whether they are monotheist, pantheist or polytheist. But, Schopenhauer objects, this method presupposes the transcendent dogmas of Judaeo-Christianity as the norm, and thus the "positively scandalous" habit of presuming that religion and theism are synonymous, whereas "religion is related to theism as the genus to a single species." If we conduct an impartial survey of the world's religions, we will see that "only Judaism and theism are identical", but "all races who are not Jews, Christians, or Mohammedans are stigmatised by us with the common name of heathen." (FR p. 187) European scholars have thereby failed to appreciate the possible extent and diversity of

---

[24] The phrase used in the Septuagint, or Greek Old Testament, when God surveyed his creation and "saw that it was good" (Gen 1:31).

the religious forms capable of catering to metaphysical need, and in their eagerness to find variations on their own scheme fail to reflect on whether or not they "quite falsely" translate "the Brahma of the Hindus and the Tien of the Chinese" as God (WWRI p. 486).

In opposition to this method of defining and classifying religions in accordance with their supposedly foundational transcendent dogmas, Schopenhauer proposes that we take the "spirit and ethical tendency" as "the essentials of a religion, not the myths in which it clothes them." (WWRII p. 623) The negative presuppositions of this proposal are taken from Kant's exposure of the transcendental illusions of natural theology, and its positive part from Schopenhauer's metaphysics of will. In the *Critique of Pure Reason* Kant showed that transcendent or supernatural knowledge is beyond the powers of the subject, while Schopenhauer's metaphysics entails that most acts of knowledge proceed from the interests of the will rather than from the freely operating intellect. Religious dogmas cannot, therefore, be literal truths communicating information about the nature and actions of transcendent and divine beings, but are mythical encryptions of immanent truths, referring to feeling states and practical attitudes about the world and existence, for the purpose of inculcating moods and guiding conduct. In Kant's idiom, religious truth is regulative not constitutive. Or, in the words of the character of Demopheles in Schopenhauer's dialogue 'On Religion'

> [p]ossibly the metaphysical element in all religions is false, but in all the moral element is true. This can be surmised already from the fact that in the former they clash with one another, whereas in the latter they agree. (PPII pp. 340-1)

For Schopenhauer, therefore, religious dogmas are not to be taken as the theoretical justification of its practical or ethical part, but as mythical vehicles communicating the religion's basic evaluation of the world, life and the human condition, which constitutes the real, immanent or empirical ballast and warrant for its system of ethics. This becomes clear when we consider the foundational scriptures of the religions, which are simply ancient documents recording "the thoughts of sages" rather than revelations (PPII p. 361), for if a "being of a higher order" were to attempt to satisfy man's metaphysical need and communicate to him the solution to the riddle of existence, "we should be quite unable to understand any part of his disclosures." (WWRII p. 185) A revelation that purports to convey from whom and for what the world exists is not, therefore, to be taken at face value, but as an indirect articulation of the evaluatory spirit of the

religion to which it belongs, and a figurative justification of its ethics.[25]
The first chapters of Genesis ought not, therefore, to be read as the majority of theologians and Christians have read them, as a treatise on the
origin of the world and the nature of its originating principle, and thus
evidence for monotheism or creationism. Instead, its narrative of the
creation of the world by an almighty, personal being who judges it good
(πάντα καλὰ λίαν), indicates that Judaism is a religion with the characteristics of realism and optimism. By contrast, Schopenhauer argued that
the New Testament revelation is a gospel of pessimism, depicting a saviour who comes into the world to redeem us from its evil (WWRI p. 326).
These reflections encouraged Schopenhauer to propose a new typology
of religion, in which the criterion of distinction is their fundamental attitude towards life and the world, and hence whether they are optimistic
or pessimistic and

> present the existence of this world as justified by itself, and consequently
> praise and commend it, or consider it as something which can be conceived
> only as the consequence of our guilt, and thus really ought not to be, in that
> they recognise that pain and death cannot lie in the eternal, original, and
> immutable order of things, that which in every respect ought to be. (WWRII
> p. 170)

Presupposing this typology Schopenhauer detected an identity of inner
spirit between "true", "genuine" or "original" Christianity and the religious traditions of India, "Brahmanism and Buddhism".

Although he was not aware of it, Schopenhauer's non-supernatural and
pragmatic theory of the meaning of religious scriptures has much in common with that of Pūrva-Mīmāṃsā, one of the six orthodox schools of
classical Hinduism.[26] Theorists of this school maintained that religious

---

[25] Schopenhauer's post-Kantian theory of religious doctrine is very close to the anthro-
pological definition of religion of Clifford Geertz, as "a system of symbols which acts to
establish powerful, pervasive and long-lasting moods and motivations in men by formulating conceptions of a general order of existence and clothing these conceptions with such
an aura of factuality that the moods and motivations seem uniquely realistic." (Geertz
(2002) p. 63)

[26] Schopenhauer knew of Pūrva-Mīmāṃsā, or the prior school of Vedic exegesis, having read about it in Part III of Colebrooke's essay 'On the philosophy of the Hindus'.
However he rarely mentioned the school and never remarked on its distinction from the
later school of exegesis, Uttara-Mīmāṃsā or Vedānta. The Vedāntins emphasised the
Jñānamārga, or path of knowledge, and looked upon the *Upaniṣads* as a revealed source
of information concerning the nature and actions of supermundane beings, the discursive
propositions of which were confirmed in mystical experience. In opposition to this, the
exegetes of Pūrva-Mīmāṃsā emphasised the *Karmamārga*, or path of action, arguing that
Upaniṣadic descriptions of supermundane beings were simply myths prescribing and
encouraging performances of the sacrificial ritual (*yajña*).

texts — in their case Vedic — do not disclose knowledge of or describe divine beings and transcendent facts, but prescribe (ritual) action (*karman*).[27] Schopenhauer's theory of religious doctrines also bears comparison with that of recent anti-realists in the philosophy of religion. Braithwaite has already been mentioned, while D.Z. Phillips' theory or religious doctrines also has some points in common with that of Schopenhauer.[28] However, perhaps the greatest scope for comparison is with Don Cupitt's similarly Kantian-inspired opposition to supernatural forms of religion, and his recommendation that we cease taking doctrines as literal statements of fact, and interpret them instead as practical and spiritual guides.[29] Cupitt's description of his position as "Christian Buddhism" provides further grounds for comparison with Schopenhauer, for we will see later that Schopenhauer's philosophy of religion also attempts to assimilate Christianity to Buddhism.[30]

But, irrespective of his post-Kantian theory of religious doctrines, Schopenhauer thought that the social and political ambitions of the church, the needs of the state, and the psychology of religious belief had all hindered general recognition of the allegorical nature of religious truth, and was threatening to bring about a schism between the culture of Europe and its traditional religion. Modern scientific education produces students with critical and intellectual ability but no training in metaphysics apart from youthful indoctrination in the catechism: noticing the disharmony between science and the doctrines of Christianity, they "become scoffers of religion, and are soon turned into shallow and absurd materialists." (WN p. 4) Schopenhauer identified a twofold theological response to this situation, both of which he considered inadequate. On the one side are the supernaturalists, whose "orthodox Tartuffian hypocrisy" has led them to refuse any concession to the critical outlook and advanced culture of the age (WN p. 5), and to a reassertion of the literal truth of the fundamentals of the faith without deduction, or "with skin and hair as it were" (WWRII p. 167). The supernaturalists have, however, achieved little

[27] Lipner (1998) p. 39.

[28] See especially Phillips (1976) Chapter 11.

[29] Cupitt (1980) Chapters 2-3.

[30] In his subsequent works Cupitt tended to cite Nietzsche as an influence (Cupitt (1982) Chapter 3), irrespective of the fact that Nietzsche contemplated the approach of a European form of Buddhism with horror, as portending nihilism and the exhaustion of our culture (Nietzsche (1989) Preface, 5). Cupitt's non-supernatural Christianity is, however, Nietzschean insofar as it is affirmative rather than world-denying, and his 'expressivist' theory of religion might be considered a response to Nietzsche's lament that "[i]n religion the constraint is lacking to consider *ourselves* as value-positing" (Nietzsche (1968) §19).

more than to transform what was once a living faith into a programmatic banner for rhetorical polemics against the intellectual and ethical culture of the age. But Schopenhauer judged the modernising schemes of the rationalist enemies of supernaturalism to have fared no better. Rationalist attempts to regenerate Christianity have simply evacuated it of its sublime mysteries, offering instead a minimalist version of the faith centred on the putatively demonstrable doctrines of God and the soul. They have thereby reduced Christianity to "a shallow Pelagianism...an infamous optimism, absolutely foreign to Christianity proper." (WWRII p. 168) However, the opposition between supernaturalism and rationalism is the consequence of an erroneous assumption common to both parties — namely, the view that religious doctrines are, or ought to be, true *sensu proprio* rather than *sensu allegorico*. As a result of holding to this false assumption, together they have made Christianity into a cultural irrelevance, with one side marginalising it and the other surrendering its distinctive and salvific message.

Schopenhauer predicted that the temporary and initial effect of the decline of Christianity would be Europe's cultural abandonment to a "moral materialism...even more dangerous than the chemical one" (WN p. 5). However, as we have seen, he also thought that man's need for metaphysics is ineradicable and cannot be satisfied by positivism, utilitarianism or "washing-machine materialism".[31] For him, the rise of science and the growth of new forms of knowledge required not a restriction of philosophy's scope but an expansion and "a real progress", for

> this nineteenth century is a philosophical one; though by this we do not mean that it possesses philosophy or that philosophy prevails in it, but rather that it is ripe for philosophy and is therefore absolutely in need of it. This is a sign of a high degree of refinement, indeed a fixed point on the scale of the culture of the times. (WWRI p. 47)

This is so because true philosophy's

> lofty goal is the satisfaction of that noble need, called by me the *metaphysical*, which at all times among men makes itself deeply and ardently felt, but which asserts itself most strongly when, as at the present time, the prestige and authority of dogma have been ever more on the decline. (PPI p. 147)

After fifteen centuries of philosophy's subordination to a now discredited theological scheme, Schopenhauer thought that its first freely undertaken task should involve wholesale revision of the methods and content of

---

[31] A coinage taken from Sprigge (1991) p. 34.

metaphysical enquiry. However, he was doubtful whether the same could be done for Christianity and whether it might be restated in such a way that it could continue to inculcate moods and guide conduct, for, even as allegories, he regarded many Christian doctrines as distortions of rather than representatives of truth. But, in opposition to the deists and natural theologians of the eighteenth century, it was precisely the transcendent doctrines of God, creation and the soul that Schopenhauer regarded as no longer tenable beliefs, whereas the sublime mysteries of Christianity — original sin, predestination and the need for redemption from the human condition — might be salvageable as allegorical vehicles of metaphysical, ethical and salvific truth. In the following chapter we examine Schopenhauer's evaluation of and philosophical assault on the transcendent dogmas of Christianity, which he regarded as an important preliminary to preserving the "true" and original part of the religion.

CHAPTER 3

THE DEATH OF GOD

I. The Problem with Theism

Schopenhauer thought that the death of God, or decline of the metaphysics of monotheism, was the immediate and natural corollary of Kant's exposure of the transcendental illusions of dogmatic metaphysics in the *Critique of Pure Reason*. As a result, he expected (or, rather, hoped) that the non-existence of God would become a generally acknowledged presupposition of European cultural and intellectual life once initial, unconscious resistance to the true, radical import of Kant's critical philosophy had receded. He acknowledged that many people might continue to believe in the existence of God on the basis of revelation, which, according to him, was and always had been theism's sole origin and support (PPI p. 106). However, he considered a revelation-based defence of theism to be insufficient warrant for extending into the future the intellectual and cultural privileges it had enjoyed in the past. There is, he claimed, "a boiling-point on the scale of culture where all faith, revelation and authorities evaporate", when people want "to be not only instructed but also convinced." (FR p. 180) The appearance of new forms of knowledge from the seventeenth century onwards had brought European culture to this boiling-point, and in this chapter we see how Schopenhauer applied his own form of heat to expedite theism's evaporation. But although Schopenhauer did not think that the dogmas of theism were true or otherwise worth preserving, he did observe their cultural marginalisation and imminent demise with a degree of trepidation, since in his view they had served the function of recommending and justifying the profound ethics and evaluations of the world and life of "genuine" Christianity.

In the Middle Ages the schoolmen had grounded the doctrines of theism in Aristotelian physics and its qualitative explanations of the being and actions of phenomena. However, in the modern age the combined effect of Copernican astronomy[1] and Descartes' revolutionary introduction of quantitative methods into natural philosophy, had progressively rendered

---

[1] Which, so Schopenhauer claimed, deprived God of a specific location in the cosmos (PPI p. 51).

the doctrines of God, his creation and providential care dispensable hypotheses, no longer necessary assumptions for the completion of knowledge and the unity of the European world-view.[2] The gradual retreat of the divine and the concomitant desacralisation of the natural realm produced a schism in the life of modern Europe. On the one hand it was committed to 'knowledge', referring to empirical phenomena and expressible in mathematical ratios: on the other it retained 'faith' in the system of theoretical dogmas that had provided a ground for value and satisfied the metaphysical needs of its forefathers, but which was becoming questionable and, for some, superfluous, as other forms of knowledge encroached onto its traditional domains. As Alasdair MacIntyre observes, in the context of an intellectual culture "where refutability is admitted", traditional theism has two options: it can

> acclimatise itself by being reformulated as deism. Or it can refuse to acclimatise itself; and in so doing it must clearly segregate itself from the secular intellectual disciplines. Theology then becomes a realm apart, a discipline which legislates for itself and which disowns the current badges of intellectual legitimation; its links with general culture are necessarily weakened.[3]

Schopenhauer affirmed this development in the intellectual history of modern Europe, remarking that faith ought to teach only what cannot be known, for it must yield when it comes into conflict with the "sterner stuff" of knowledge (PPII p. 360). However, theism's weaker links with the general culture had opened up a vacuum into which the 'theologians' of metaphysical naturalism, spurred on by the successes of the particular sciences, were threatening to step. Postulating atoms as the thing-in-itself, they attempted to explain all objects and events as manifestations of quantitative relations, presuming even to measure the moral worth of actions in accordance with whether they increase or decrease the quantum of worldly happiness (as in Bentham's late eighteenth-century Utilitarianism). Schopenhauer credited Kant with arresting this development with his distinction between the phenomenon and the thing-in-itself (WN p. 4), which provided theoretical justification for demarcating the quantitative and phenomenal realm from the qualitative and metaphysical. However, as a result of the strictures he placed on knowledge of the thing-in-itself, Kant had retreated into metaphysical agnosticism and

---

[2] Alasdair MacIntyre makes a similar point concerning the conceptual warrant that scholastic theology had obtained from association with Aristotelian physics, and also maintains that one of the results of the new cosmology's dissolution of this association was the desacralisation of the natural realm (MacIntyre (1966) p. 129).

[3] MacIntyre (1969) p. 11.

moral faith, which, given Schopenhauer's estimation of the strength of metaphysical need, could be little more than an interim solution (PPI p. 110). For Schopenhauer philosophy since Socrates had consistently attempted to combine metaphysics and ethics by demonstrating "a *moral* world-order as the basis of the *physical*" (WWRII p. 590). He considered his metaphysics of the will as the consummation of this quest, for by disclosing the character of the quality that objectifies itself with ever-increasing distinctness through the various grades of nature — from the inorganic forces presupposed by higher-level scientific explanations, through the various levels of organic life, up to the intellectual and ethical qualities of human beings — it had provided a metaphysical grounding for the researches of natural science, as well as a stable prop for the intuition-based, ethical doctrines of true and original Christianity.

Schopenhauer thought that the theoretical doctrines of Christianity had always been only a nominal rather than real ground and explanation of its ethics, and that an important propaedeutic to obtaining a clear image of the true spirit and essential tendency of the religion was to sever "the eternally insoluble Gordian knot on which most of the controversies of the Church turn" (WWRI p. 293) — namely, the forced and merely historical assimilation of Christian ethics to Hebrew theism. Christianity is "the child of two very heterogeneous parents", a compound of "*truth that is felt*" and "Jewish monotheism that is *ordained* and is essentially opposed to" the former (MRIV p. 389). The ethical and spiritual tendency of Christianity is based on experience and perception (*Anschauung*), but its transcendent dogmas are conceptual constructs of reason (*Vernunft*), the original source of which is revelation. Schopenhauer considered his discovery of an epistemological fault-line dividing the two parts of the religion to have axiological and historical parallels. Applying his typological opposition between optimistic and pessimistic *Weltanschauungen* to the latest research into the history of religion, Schopenhauer maintained that, originally, there were only two religions of opposite tendency, each with historical offshoots, and that what is now known as Christianity is an unwieldy combination of both. On the one side he placed Zoroastrianism, Judaism and Islam:

> All these agree in attributing to the phenomenon the highest reality and in regarding its laws as eternal. They explain the world in accordance with this and for this very reason also perpetuate individuals; they make existence an end in itself and, connected with this, have the character of optimism. But then they are forced to lay the blame for the evil and wickedness of the world on an Ahriman or Satan, who in the end will also reflect and be converted. They are monotheistic, abominate all idols and images, and assume a beginning and end of the world. — In accordance with my view, I must call this religion of realism, theism and optimism the religion of error.

On the other side he located the religious outlook of Hinduism, Buddhism and New Testament Christianity:

> it has the *avatār*, its character is knowledge of the world as mere phenomenon, of existence as an evil, of salvation therefrom as the goal, complete resignation as the path, and the *avatār* as the master of the path. — They have no theism proper, and they permit images. This latter is in my view the religion of truth. After the two religions had existed side by side for thousands of years and had divided the world between them, they finally encountered each other in Palestine, and the result of their conflict was that the followers of the former and cruder religion crucified the *avatār*. (MRIII pp. 337-338)

Having detected parallels between Christianity's intuition-based doctrines and those of the 'godless' religions that had satisfied metaphysical need in the east from ancient times to the present, Schopenhauer maintained that Christianity had been the allegorical vehicle by which Europeans had been introduced to the correct, pessimistic view of life and the human condition proclaimed by religious and philosophical geniuses throughout history, east and west (PPII p. 348). This true religion or *philosophia perennis* is, however, fundamentally at odds with the optimistic and realist metaphysics that Christianity inherited from its Jewish cultural milieu. Like a latter-day Marcion, therefore, Schopenhauer argued that theism's conflict with the culture of the age provided the occasion for correcting this erroneous association and for releasing the inner kernel of Christian feeling and practice from its alien, dogmatic shell.

Although this book is concerned mainly with the interpretative and contextual issues relevant to Schopenhauer's philosophy of religion in its two moments, in view of the Nazi regime's use of Indo-Aryan racial ideology as a pretext for attempting to annihilate the Jewish people in the Holocaust, it is important to clarify the nature of Schopenhauer's contrast between Judaism and the so-called 'Indic' religions of Christianity, Hinduism and Buddhism.

Initially, it is important to note that Schopenhauer's contrast between Judaism as a system of transcendent dogmas, and Christianity as essentially comprised of immanent doctrines concerning the nature of life and the world, is the reverse of what almost every present-day commentator says about the different tendencies of these religions. For example, Nicholas de Lange remarks that whereas "Christian creeds originated as tests of authentic Christian allegiance",[4] in Judaism

---

[4] de Lange (1986) p. 3.

abundant material in the form of institutions, public and private worship, ritual observances, and so forth…would be acknowledged by many Jews as being far more central to Judaism than religious beliefs or theological doctrines.[5]

Judaism is, therefore, the religion of immanence and ethical orthopraxy, of fulfilment of the law and ritual as prescribed by the Talmud, while Christianity is the religion of orthodoxy, of creedal statements concerning the nature of the transcendent Godhead and his relation to the world. Schopenhauer's false contrast was a consequence of his almost total disinterest in Judaism as actually practised by Jews, and he seemed to have obtained most of his knowledge about the religion from works of Christian theology and the Old Testament. He tended to use the terms 'Jewish' and 'Judaism' as rhetorical ciphers for the system of beliefs clustered around *Christian* monotheism, beliefs whose groundlessness Kant had exposed in the 'Transcendental Dialectic': in the existence of a personal creator, that the world is a created whole made for the happiness and well-being of creatures, and that God created the human person as a finite counterpart of himself, an integral reality set apart from nature by its freedom to observe a law other than the natural. Although Schopenhauer characterised these beliefs as specifically Jewish because they first appeared in the allegorical narrative of Genesis, he also knew that they had been systematically formulated as *sensu proprio* truths by Christians, and used to justify suppression of non-monotheistic philosophy.

Many writers and theorists of the eighteenth and nineteenth centuries presented this system of beliefs as the original and universal religion of primeval humanity. In Chapter 1 we saw that Friedrich Schlegel was disappointed to find that Sanskrit sources do not contain a pure system of monotheism combined with a doctrine of *creatio ex nihilo*: in a similar spirit, Sir Williams Jones remarked that the polytheistic pantheons of the Indian, Greek and Roman religions appeared when the "most distinguished inhabitants of the primitive world…deviated, as they did too early deviate, from the rational adoration of the only true God."[6] Schopenhauer reduced the supernatural portion of Christianity to Judaism to discredit the assumption that monotheism was the natural religion or perennial philosophy. He aimed to show that it was, in origin, a local, artificial and historically specific belief-system, having only one old-world representative in the provincial religious milieu of ancient Israel (FR p. 183). Its subsequent historical ascendancy in Europe and Asia

---

[5] Ibid. p. 5.
[6] Jones (1789a) p. 221.

through the religions of Christianity and Islam had lent it a spurious universality, artificially sustained by early education, social pressure, and the obliging efforts of philosophers to construct a theoretical prop for its doctrines. Schopenhauer maintained that the *Theodicy* of Leibniz was simply "Jewish mythology as philosophy" (WWRII p. 582), while the doctrine of the will's original indifference to either good or evil (*liberum arbitrium indifferentiae*) is a fiction invented to preserve "the fundamental dogma of Judaism" concerning the goodness of God and his creation (WWRII p. 604). He complained that modern-day Protestant-rationalists who "explain away by exegesis" the doctrine of original sin, thereby reduce Christianity to Judaism (WWRII p. 605), while Kant's doctrine of reason's erroneous but natural generation of the transcendent Ideas of God, world and soul reduces reason to Jewish mythology (WWRI p. 484).

But Schopenhauer's petition to separate Christian ethics from Jewish theism was also motivated by his conviction that "Christianity has Indian blood in its veins, and thus has a constant tendency to be rid of Judaism." (FR p. 187) This is a constant theme reiterated throughout his works — "it is not Judaism with its πάντα καλα λίαν, but Brahmanism and Buddhism that in spirit and ethical tendency are akin to Christianity" (WWRII p. 623) — and has been referred to as evidence that his interest in the Indian religions was motivated by anti-Semitism and support for programmes of social and political exclusion based on a myth of Indo-Germanic racial supremacy.[7] Of course, many nineteenth-century Germans attracted to Indian thought were motivated by such ideas, such as Julius Klaproth and Richard Wagner,[8] with the latter drawing on Schopenhauer's contrast between Christian ethics and Jewish theism in support of his anti-Semitism. And it is disturbing to learn that Hitler claimed to have carried *The World as Will and Representation* in his knapsack during the First World War.[9] Schopenhauer's opposition between the crude realism of Jewish mythology and the noble idealism of Hindu, Buddhist and Christian ethics, combined with the posthumous eminence and authority he attained as the 'Sage of Frankfurt', undoubtedly sanctified the political and social doctrines of anti-Semites such as Wagner. However, it is

---

[7] See Mack (2003) pp. 8-9.

[8] Klaproth, editor of *Das Asiatisches Magazin*, coined the term 'Indo-Germanic' in 1823 — see Schwab (1984) p. 184.

[9] Bullock (1993) p. 49.n. There is, however, no suggestion that Hitler studied the book, for had he done so he would have derived from it no theoretical justification for his racial or political doctrines.

important to separate the intention and meaning behind Schopenhauer's contrasts and the use they were put to in the pages of his self-proclaimed disciples, and to avoid projecting the latter onto Schopenhauer.[10] As stated above, Schopenhauer's conception of Judaism was ideological rather than racial, and reducible to the metaphysics of Christian monotheism. There is nothing in his published works or manuscripts to indicate that Schopenhauer himself harboured a personal grudge against Jews or Judaism. He was opposed only to the intellectual and cultural dominance of monotheism, which, as he knew, had gained ascendancy over European culture through Christianity. His contrast between Judaism and Christianity was therefore intended to discredit the metaphysical portion of the latter faith in the view of anti-Semitic Christians by emphasising its origin in a world-view they considered to be alien and abominable.

And the purely ideological intention governing Schopenhauer's rhetoric about Judaism can hardly be over-emphasised, for at no point does he make explicitly hostile remarks or construct scurrilous theories concerning the ritual practices, social, political and economic roles or racial characteristics of contemporary Jews. This is hardly surprising, given Schopenhauer's profoundly apolitical and ahistorical intellectual outlook. Contrary to Hegel and the philosophers of history, Schopenhauer remained faithful to the Kantian doctrine of the ideality of time. As a consequence, he considered the contingent events of history, by which groups of people form themselves into nations, philosophically irrelevant: nations are "in reality mere abstractions; only individuals actually exist." (WWRII p. 591) His works contain no discussions of biologically founded distinctions between races.[11] But even if Schopenhauer had thought it important

---

[10] Mack states that Wagner, Fichte and Schopenhauer "believed in an Aryan Christ" (Mack (2003) p70), but cites no text from Schopenhauer to support this claim. He refers readers instead to page 148 of Alfred Schmidt's book, where, he promises, they will discover a "discussion of the 'Aryan Christ' in Schopenhauer." (Mack (2003) p. 192) However, neither the page, nor Schmidt's entire book, contains any discussion of an Aryan Christ in Schopenhauer: page 148 contains mainly quotations from Schopenhauer's works relevant to his theory (discussed in the next chapter) that Jesus received Indian wisdom from Egyptian priests (Schmidt (1986) p. 148), which confirms my thesis that Schopenhauer's contrast between Judaism and Indian wisdom was purely ideological or ideational. If, however, Mack intends to present this as an implicit theory of an 'Aryan Christ' then this is clearly overkill, for — as Mack presents it — such a theory implies commitment to racial and biological doctrines, in which Schopenhauer had no interest.

[11] At one point only does Schopenhauer mention the concept of race, when he states that there are "three races of men, which on physiological as well as on linguistic grounds are not to be doubted and are equally original, namely the Caucasian, the Mongolian, and the Ethiopian." (WWRII p. 312) Yet this is referred to as evidence for the theory that human beings did not evolve on the continent of America, for all these races are, in his

to divide people into racial groups, denominating one as inferior and the other as superior, even a cursory perusal of his books shows that he would not have classified his fellow Germans in the latter category, and was very far from propounding a myth of Aryan-Germanic supremacy. He remarked that "[n]othing annoys me more than the expression *Indo-Germanic* languages, that is, the language of the *Vedas* brought into line with some jargon of the aforesaid idlers [i.e., Germans]." (PPII p. 578) His interest in Indian thought was as ideologically motivated as his opposition to Judaism, and was limited to appraisal of its metaphysical and ethical doctrines. Schopenhauer's occasional references to the theories of Jones, Herder and Friedrich Schlegel concerning India's formative relation to European civilisation and the western migrations of Asiatic peoples were external factors in his view, since the merits of Hinduism and Buddhism are proved by the allegorical truth of their doctrines rather than their antiquity or originality. His opposition between the optimistic monotheism of Judaism and the pessimistic monism of the Indic world-view was not, therefore, intended as an opposition traceable to biological or racial distinctions or 'thinking with the blood'. Instead, he attributed this opposition to a foundational but purely ideological error on the part of the ancient nation of Israel, an error that had subsequently led to the cultural and intellectual dominance of an erroneous metaphysic perpetuated by Christianity and Islam. One of the major benefits of Indology in Schopenhauer's estimation was that its disclosure of "the ancient wisdom of the *human race*" (WWRI p. 357 – emphasis added) provided the occasion for challenging monotheism's dominance over European culture and intellectual life.

Schopenhauer's critique of theism was mounted from as many directions as possible, for his ambition was total. He hoped to bring to an end the manner in which theism had, from Augustine onward, prescribed not only the horizon of philosophical questioning but also, in the majority of cases, its solutions. He also aimed to show that theism and its associated doctrines were not merely incompatible with modern philosophical and scientific knowledge, but also (and perhaps rather surprisingly) inessential to religion (PPI p. 115). Given the breadth of his ambition, it is hardly surprising to find Schopenhauer's critique advancing on every available front. He pursued the argumentative route of reiterating, with additions

phrase, "Old World". Hence, this discussion is not placed in the service of either racism or anti-Semitism.

of his own, Kant's critique of the arguments of natural theology, and supplemented this argumentative assault with a genetic strategy disclosing the non-rational causes of belief in God. Having dispensed with the cognitive grounds of theism, Schopenhauer set out to show that it fails to satisfy the criteria of metaphysical need — exemplified by its inability to account for suffering and evil, to explain moral responsibility, or sustain either a pure doctrine of virtue or viable doctrine of immortality. Given the breadth and ambition of Schopenhauer's critique and the variety of considerations and arguments he assembled in support of it, it is odd to find Douglas Berger stating that

> Schopenhauer gives no more justification for his rejection of theism than brief reference to the Kantian antinomy on the proofs for God's existence, which he took to be conclusive evidence that thinking about God's existence was unreasonable.[12]

Berger's claim is unequivocally and demonstrably false: not only did Schopenhauer reject Kant's theory that reason necessarily gives rise to antinomies, and accepted only the antitheses as true statements about the *apparent* world (WWRI pp. 493-4), as this chapter will show, he also built upon Kant's exposure of the deficiencies of natural theology by offering original objections of his own.

But if Berger's claim that Schopenhauer's works contain no independent critique of theism is palpably false, then David Berman draws attention to a rather more surprising omission when he asks "[w]here...does Schopenhauer deny the existence of God, or call himself an atheist, or explicitly argue against the existence of God — in the way that Baron d'Holbach, or Schopenhauer's near contemporary Shelley, did? I do not think that one can find any of this in his published writings."[13] Berman is not claiming that Schopenhauer was not an atheist in fact, for he acknowledges that Schopenhauer's metaphysics of the will is implicitly atheist, for if it is true "then theistic religions such as Christianity or Islam must be false."[14] Berman considers this omission to be the effect of social and political prudence, for early nineteenth-century German philosophers "felt the need to dissimulate or disguise their atheistic and irreligious statements".[15] Although Berman, like Berger, overstates the extent to which arguments against God's existence are absent from

---

[12] Berger (2004b) p. 144 n.3.
[13] Berman (1998) p. 178.
[14] Ibid. p. 179.
[15] Ibid. p. 178.

Schopenhauer's works, it is indeed true that he never made explicit proclamations of atheism in his publications. However, some of Schopenhauer's comments indicate that there are philosophical reasons for this oversight, in addition to Berman's identification of political causes. Initially, anticipating a line of thought made explicit by the Logical Positivists, Schopenhauer suggests that he avoided describing himself as an 'atheist' and his position as 'atheism' because to do so concedes too much to the opposite view, permitting theism to pose as the norm from which atheism has strayed: "What a cunning, underhanded and furtive insinuation is to be found in the word atheism! — as though the word theism were self-evident." (MRIV p. 12) A further reason is indicated when he notes that theism's entrenched position has led to the unquestioned but erroneous assumption that there is an intrinsic relation between morality and the concept of God, whereby terms such as 'atheist' and 'atheism' are used as "absurd and often spiteful" reproaches against a person's moral credentials. Contrary to this, Schopenhauer argued that "the necessary *credo* of all righteous and good men" is not exclusively 'I believe in God' but "I believe in a system of metaphysics." (WWRII p. 175) And, as if to underscore the merely local relevance of atheism's negative and immoral connotations, he consistently drew attention to the fact that Buddhism is not merely a religion without God, but one that specifically condemns belief in God, as a result of which 'atheist' and 'atheism' would connote religious orthodoxy in the languages of Buddhist nations (FR p. 184). This is sufficient to show that the concept of God is not merely specific to European philosophy, but also to its religion:

> to teach in philosophy that that fundamental theological idea is self-evident and that the faculty of reason is merely the ability directly to grasp it and to recognise it as true, is a bold and shameless pretence. Not only have we no right, without the most valid proof, to assume such an idea in philosophy, but it is by no means essential even to religion. This is attested by the religion that has the greatest number of followers on earth, Buddhism, which is very ancient and now numbers three hundred and seventy million followers. It is a highly moral and even ascetic religion and supports the most numerous body of clergy; yet it does not accept such an idea at all; on the contrary, it expressly rejects this out of hand and is thus according to our notions *ex professo* atheistic. (PPI p. 115)

However, some commentators have argued that Schopenhauer ought not to be characterised as a strict atheist.[16] Drawing attention to parallels between his philosophy and aspects of Christianity, they maintain that

---

[16] Most recently Gonzales (1992), Mannion (2003), and King (2005).

Schopenhauer's critique of theism was aimed only at rational demon-
strations of God's existence or crude, anthropomorphic conceptions of
his nature, and that he may have (albeit tacitly!) consented to a mystical conception of God beyond all knowledge and imagery. For example,
Gerard Mannion castigates the "textbook" account of Schopenhauer as
a "militant atheist" and states that his theory of metaphysical need and
its quest for extra-naturalistic meaning "both interprets and legitimates
theological enquiry".[17] Mannion's theological reading of Schopenhauer
proceeds by pointing out the many and undoubted parallels between
Christian and Schopenhauerian ethics, but seems to presuppose that
such parallels either do or ought to reflect metaphysical and even
theological parallels between the two systems. By so doing, Mannion
overlooks Schopenhauer's reiterated claim that the ethics of Christianity
are opposed to its theological dogmas, pays little attention to the theological implications of Schopenhauer's interest in the non-theist religions of the east, and seems to presuppose that questions of ethics,
mysticism and salvation resolve on or are identical to questions of God
and theology.[18] Mannion does explicitly state that he is not "suggesting
that there is a concept of God lurking somewhere behind Schopenhauer's thing-in-itself",[19] but rather surprisingly claims that there *ought
to be* and that "an acknowledgement of something analogous to a religious doctrine of God or ultimate reality would greatly increase the
overall coherence of his view."[20] However, this claim is simply inserted
without argument, for it is doubtful that the "overall coherence" of
Schopenhauer's philosophy would have been improved by incorporat-
ing a transcendent doctrine of God or ultimate reality. Indeed, commentators have usually accused Schopenhauer of inconsistency for
making any metaphysical claims at all, and for erecting an immanent
system on a Kantian framework:[21] Mannion is surely the first to claim
that Schopenhauer's inconsistency resides in a lack of metaphysical
hubris.

---

[17] Mannion (2003) p. 50.

[18] Mannion cites Schopenhauer's previously quoted tenet that "religion is related to
theism as the genus to a single species" (FR p. 187), and remarks that this statement
"should not be underestimated." (Mannion (2003) p. 63) However, he later ignores his
own counsel by stating that Schopenhauer's ethics and soteriology are paths to "the ultimate subject matter of theology, which he [Schopenhauer] really sought" (Ibid. p. 82).

[19] Ibid. p. 275.

[20] Ibid. p. 248.

[21] Copleston maintained that "the proper conclusion from Schopenhauer's epistemology, as from that of Kant, is agnosticism: a metaphysic is quite out of place." (Copleston
(1975) p. 65)

In Mannion's defence it might be stated that his interpretation is fairly typical of theological readings of extra-theological bodies of thought, which have persistently discovered God in the unlikeliest of locations.[22] Mannion's procedure finds a precedent in Christian claims that Buddhism is a veiled theology,[23] and also in the notorious 'God of the gaps', in which the tribal deity of Abraham, Isaac and Jacob is presented as the alpha and omega of scientific cosmology.[24] For the majority of theologians, God as universal spirit is such a fruitful hypothesis that he can be discovered anywhere or called upon to complete almost any speculative body of thought, but only on condition that he be placed at a convenient distance from the boundaries of human knowledge (and therefore criticism). Contrary to Mannion's theological reading, this chapter and the next illustrate the ruthlessness and comprehensiveness of Schopenhauer's critique of and opposition to theism, justifying Nietzsche's more than textbook statement that "[a]s a philosopher, Schopenhauer was the *first* admitted and inexorable atheist among us Germans".[25] Schopenhauer was, without doubt, the first major European *philosopher* in the modern period to announce the death of God.

Many of Schopenhauer's arguments against theism can be found in the works of precursors who set out to reinterpret the concept of God, such as Spinoza and Hume,[26] but he also anticipated criticisms now commonly associated with recognised anti-theists, such as Feuerbach, Nietzsche and Freud. As already stated, Schopenhauer's critique of theism was not mounted for the purpose of establishing naturalism, secularism or humanism, but for the religious end of preserving the 'essence' of Christianity by purging it of what he regarded as its false, harmful and supernatural

---

[22] Schopenhauer himself expressed despair at the hermeneutical persistence of commentators with a theist agenda. Quoting from an article in which it was stated that "'Kant's teaching was ordinary theism and contributed little or nothing to the changing of current opinions about God and his relation to the world'", Schopenhauer declaimed "in my opinion, universities are no longer the proper place even for the history of philosophy. In such places design and intention reign supreme." (WN p. 17) Oddly, Nietzsche tended to share this theological "design and intention" by discovering God thinly-veiled in locations not evidently reserved for him, as indicated by his notion of the "shadows of God" discussed in the Introduction.

[23] For example, Keith Ward's characterisation of the Buddhist path as a "quest for God" completely disregards Buddhist critiques of the concept of a First Cause or Supreme Being (Ward (1987) p. 74).

[24] Keith Ward again: "theism is the completion of that search for intelligibility which characterises the scientific enterprise" (Ward (1996) pp. 311-2).

[25] Nietzsche (1974) §357.

[26] That is, if one takes Hume's statement that "[t]he whole frame of nature bespeaks an intelligent author" at face value (Hume (1993b) p. 134).

elements. For most people in western countries, whether believers or not, the existence of God might seem to be the condition for the possibility of religion and spirituality. However, Schopenhauer's promotion of the godless religions of the east — "Brahmanism and Buddhism" — as substitutes for Christian theism, stemmed from his conviction that, whereas belief in God might be a sufficient condition for at least one species of religion, it is not a necessary condition for religion in general.

Schopenhauer's critique of theism has attracted little attention or response from constructive theologians and philosophers of religion. This is probably because many of the specifics of his critique are usually first encountered in Nietzsche's more widely read works, serving a purpose manifestly hostile to Christianity. However, as observed in the Introduction, Schopenhauer's critique of theism differs from Nietzsche's critique, insofar as Schopenhauer's project of releasing the Indic kernel of Christian feeling and practice from its historical shell of dogmatic belief was formulated in the interests of modernising Christianity. His project therefore has an aim in common with the efforts of late nineteenth and early twentieth-century Buddhist, Hindu and Muslim modernisers who similarly set out to restore the allegedly original and pristine core of their religions by dispensing with what they regarded as their superstitious and merely historical accretions.

II. The Nature and Origin of Theism

Schopenhauer's conception of theism accords with what is usually referred to as classical or objective theism, a species of belief advanced by, among others, Richard Swinburne. Swinburne defines a theist as

> a man who believes that there is a God. By a 'God' he understands something like a 'person without a body (i.e. a spirit) who is eternal, free, able to do anything, knows everything, is perfectly good, is the proper object of human worship and obedience, the creator and sustainer of the universe.' Christians, Jews, and Muslims are all in the above sense theists.[27]

Swinburne's definition may seem crude, anthropomorphic and burdened with an array of conceptual difficulties, but it represents the mainstream view among Anglophone theologians. One of its greatest merits is its comprehensibility; another is that it expresses the beliefs of the majority of Jews, Christians and Muslims. Schopenhauer defines philosophical theism in similar terms as

---

[27] Swinburne (1993) p. 1.

the doctrine of God, creator and ruler of the world, a personal and therefore an individual being endowed with understanding and will, who has produced the world out of nothing and rules it with the highest wisdom, power, and goodness. (FR p. 182)

His conception of theism can therefore be analysed into three separate but mutually supporting components:

(1) Theism is the belief in the existence of a supernatural, personal individual endowed with perfections — including intelligence and will — to the highest degree.
(2) It consists in the further belief that this individual used (or, more properly, uses, since God is not in time) his infinite power to create the world out of nothing.
(3) It incorporates the further belief that, as a personal being, God employs his power to arrange events in the world so that they lead up to an historical consummation compatible with wisdom and goodness.

In the light of these theological, cosmological and eschatological doctrines, Schopenhauer identified ontological realism and axiological optimism as theism's central and controlling assumptions (PPII p. 378). In other words, God's supreme power and benevolence entail that his creation is real (in the sense of being independent of the subject of knowledge) and good (in the sense that it was created for the happiness of individuals). Schopenhauer thought that this complex of beliefs had no foundation in human nature, experience or reason, and that theism's sole source is the Old Testament revelation. For him, therefore, Judaism is the sole historical instance of theism, historical Christianity and Islam being but sectarian tributaries flowing from this source (PPI p. 125; FR p. 183).

Many Christian theologians have confirmed Schopenhauer's claim by exclusively founding the doctrine of God's creation of the world out of nothing on scripture rather than reason or experience.[28] Schopenhauer tended to regard these doctrines as inseparable and mutually supporting, not because he perceived there to be a natural, logical or intuitive connection between them, but purely on account of their joint appearance in the Old Testament. For this reason, it never occurred to him that the God

---

[28] With reference to the theology of Philo of Alexandria, Janet Soskice states that philosophical reasoning "might disclose that there is a God, and even that God is One and Prime Mover, but philosophy alone could not arrive at the biblical Creator, or at *creatio ex nihilo*." (Soskice (2006) p. 153)

of monotheism might be compatible with an alternative metaphysical or religious cosmogony — such as the participationist or emanationist schemes found in Plotinus, the *Upaniṣads* and the *Bhagavad-Gītā*. Some recent theologians have found themselves increasingly attracted to a less disjunctive model of the relation between God and the world than creation out of nothing,[29] and might consider Schopenhauer guilty of trying to marginalise theism by identifying it exclusively with the biblical cosmogony, insofar as he thereby restricts the possibility of establishing points of comparison between monotheism and other religious or metaphysical systems. However, in support of his view, Schopenhauer could call on the testimony of innumerable Christian divines, as well as many scholars from the early period of European Indology, who in their expositions of heathen faiths similarly used the doctrine of creation as a criterion of distinction.[30]

Schopenhauer defined God as "a thinking, willing, commanding, and provident person" (PPI p. 54), the inseparable predicates of which are "supreme power and the highest wisdom." (PPII p. 101) He was as critical as Feuerbach of theological attempts to tamper with the traditional and anthropomorphic conception of God as individual personality,[31] arguing that an impersonal God is no God "but merely a word wrongly used, a misconception, a *contradictio in adjecto*, a shibboleth for professors of philosophy, who, having had to give up the thing, are anxious to slip through with the word." (PPI, p. 115) Many liberal theologians after Kant have attempted to revise the traditional concept of God, often depersonalising it in the process: once more, the objection may be raised that Schopenhauer's opposition to non-anthropomorphic conceptions of God is merely a ploy that permits him to ridicule and dispense with theism as rapidly as possible.

---

[29] For example, Charles Hartshorne's process theology — see Hartshorne (1962).

[30] In one of the first scholarly accounts of Buddhism, the author, Joseph Eudelin de Joinville, argued that it must have preceded Hinduism in India, on the grounds that its doctrines of "[a]n uncreated world and mortal souls" are primitive ideas which could not have supplanted the "fundamental articles" of true religion, adhered to by Hinduism, regarding "the creation of the world and the immortality of the soul." (de Joinville (1803) p. 400)

[31] Feuerbach regarded the concept of God as a contradictory compound of metaphysical and personal predicates. However since, for him, religion is founded on a projection of the human personality onto the cosmos, God's personal predicates are indispensable: "A God who is not as we are, who has not consciousness, not intelligence, *i.e.*, not a personal understanding, a personal consciousness (as, for example, the 'substance' of Spinoza), is no God." (Feuerbach (1957) p. 213)

However, in many ways Schopenhauer's veto on demythologisation seems justified. The traditional, objective God of classical theism, distinct from the world and discovered through external sources such as scripture or rational inference, may seem incompatible with modern attitudes and knowledge and therefore unworthy of belief, but it does have the merit of comprehensibility. By contrast, Paul Tillich's subjectivist conception of God as "ultimate concern" is deep, profound, and evocative, but completely obscure.[32] In the pre-modern era a prominent systematic theologian such as Tillich would have been an objective theist, constructing his theology with the Bible in one hand and Aristotle's *Metaphysics* in the other, all the while condemning the subjectivist, unfounded and obscure conceptions of the mystics. Only in the modern era have mainstream theologians begun to appropriate the subjective perspective and apophatic language of mysticism, in an effort to circumvent dependence upon the traditional sources, methods and conceptions of pre-Enlightenment theology. However, in the attempt, much of post-Kantian liberal theology seems to have sacrificed the substance of theism while retaining only its vocabulary. In their various efforts to reconcile belief to the secular culture that surrounds them, many theologians have evacuated theism of so much of its distinctive content that it is difficult to know what distinguishes it from atheism. Schopenhauer's opposition to demythologisation was motivated by similar lines of thought. He maintained that modernising, rationalist theologians achieve little more than a mean between a human being and a force of nature in their definitions of God's essence (PPII p. 391).[33] But the theology of the Absolute's votaries is an even sorrier affair, a matter of concealing God "behind a noisy edifice of words, so that hardly a sign of him is visible." (PPI p. 113) In opposition to the arcane formulations of professorial theology,

---

[32] Tillich (1957) p. 10.

[33] Schopenhauer seemed unaware that the same could be said of his concept of the world-will. He argued that "will" is the most appropriate term for Kant's thing-in-itself insofar as it denotes that with which every individual is "absolutely and immediately" acquainted as the innermost essence of their body: by contrast, concepts of force or energy are mediated by perceptual and conceptual forms. However, since "will" in ordinary use refers to "will guided by knowledge, strictly according to motives, indeed only to abstract motives" he said that it must be evacuated of these anthropomorphic connotations and reduced to its "innermost essence...known to us directly" before it can be transferred to natural phenomena, such as natural forces, plant and animal species (WWRI p. 111). But it is questionable whether these processes of evacuation and extension truly issue in the metaphysical concept that Schopenhauer tried to communicate, or whether what is left over is a centaur that is part human being, part natural force.

Schopenhauer remarked that only the "Synagogue, the Church and Islam use the word God in its proper and correct sense." (PPII p. 101) He may have thought that the spirit of the age had made the project of demythologising Christianity an imperative, but he considered it impossible to do the same for the concept of God:

> Those who attempt to clear theism of anthropomorphism, while imagining that they touch only the shell, really strike at its innermost core. In their efforts to conceive its object in the abstract, they sublimate it to a vague, hazy form whose outline gradually vanishes entirely in the endeavour to avoid the human figure. In this way, the fundamental childlike idea itself is finally evaporated to nothing. (PPI pp. 116-7)[34]

Schopenhauer considered theism essentially anthropomorphic not simply because some representations of God confine him to the limits of bodily shape, with hair and nails, nor because preachers occasionally represent God as prey to human passions and emotions such as jealousy and revenge. For Schopenhauer, even the spiritual conception of God as non-corporeal will guided by intellect is anthropomorphic, for such a phenomenon is known

> solely from the animal nature that exists on our small planet. It is so intimately associated with such nature that we are not only not justified in, but also not even capable of conceiving it as separate from, and independent of, that nature. But to assume a being of such a kind as the origin of nature herself, indeed of all existence generally, is a colossal and extremely bold idea. (PPI p. 115)

Schopenhauer here approaches Feuerbach's theory of projection, but whereas for Feuerbach man creates God by projecting the universal human attributes of reason, will and affection onto the backdrop of the cosmos,[35] for Schopenhauer the projection consists of man's *phenomenal* constitution alone, as will guided by intellect, and is therefore two removes from the truth. This is because, in opposition to the predominant tradition of philosophical anthropology in Europe, Schopenhauer maintained that the will

> as the thing-in-itself, constitutes the inner, true, and indestructible nature of man; yet in itself it is without consciousness. For consciousness is conditioned by the intellect, and the intellect is a mere accident of our being, for it is a function of the brain. (WWRII p. 201)

---

[34] This compares to Anthony Flew's objection that attempts to preserve the "fine brash hypothesis" of classical theism in the face of sceptical objections often amount to little more than "death by a thousand qualifications." (Flew (1964) p. 226)

[35] Feuerbach (1957) p. 3.

Schopenhauer's conception of the relation between intellect and will is an obvious precursor to Freud's contrast between ego and id, and his explanation of the causes of the projection that issues in theistic belief similarly anticipated Freud's theory of wish-fulfilment.[36] Schopenhauer maintained that faith in supernatural beings modelled on human nature does not arise from reflection on experience or any other operation of the intellect; it is, instead, a conjecture of the will, posited to satisfy the wishes of the heart for an all-powerful protector from the vicissitudes of existence:

> The constant need, now gravely oppressing then violently agitating man's heart (will), keeps him in a permanent state of fearing and hoping, whereas the things *about* which he hopes and fears are not in his power; indeed the connection of the causal chains whereon such things are produced can be traced by his knowledge for only a short distance. This need, this constant fearing and hoping, cause him to hypostasise personal beings on whom everything depends. Of such it may now be assumed that, like other persons, they will be susceptible to entreaty and flattery, service and gift, and will therefore be more tractable than the rigid necessity, the inexorable and unfeeling forces of nature, and the mysterious powers of the course of the world...in order that his heart (will) may have the relief of prayer and the consolation of hope, his intellect must create for him a God; but not conversely, that is, he does not pray because his intellect has correctly and logically deduced a God. Let him be without needs, desires, and requirements, a merely intellectual will-less being, then he needs no God and makes none. In its grave affliction the heart, i.e. the will, needs to call for almighty and consequently supernatural assistance. (PPI pp. 117-8)

Schopenhauer acknowledged that his genetic explanation of belief in God was not original, for he credited Hume with the discovery of the real ground of all popular theology — the *ceraunological* proof, "founded on man's feeling of need, distress, impotence, and dependence in face of natural forces infinitely superior, unfathomable, and for the most part ominous and portentous." (WWRI pp. 511-2) Theism from its inception was, therefore, intellectually indefensible, but the needs of the heart from within and the force of early education and the rules of the community from without have conspired against outright recognition of the paucity of its rational and experiential grounds. Whereas thinkers from Pascal to William James have claimed that humanity's wretched state constitutes not merely an explanation of belief in God but also, in some sense, a justification,[37] Schopenhauer thought that theism's origin in the will

---

[36] Freud (1985) pp. 198-9.
[37] Pascal (1995) p. 57; James (1979) p. 40.

warranted suspicion regarding the truth value of its doctrines. The will is not a cognitive faculty designed to acquaint us with the real constitution of objects, immanent or transcendent: it is, instead, the controlling element in human nature, colouring our judgement and perception to the extent that most acts of 'knowledge' are merely garments tailored to satisfy need and interest (WWRII p. 373). In Schopenhauer's view the condition for the possibility of true knowledge is the intellect's separation from the promptings of the will. In Freud's idiom, Schopenhauer considered belief in the gods to be an illusion posited by the pleasure principle, which, for that reason, needed to be curbed by the critical intellect and replaced by the reality principle.

However, Schopenhauer's genetic account of the gods as illusory projections satisfying the needs of the heart seems incompatible with his view, previously discussed, that theism has only one historical and contingent source in the Old Testament revelation. If theism is found only in Judaism and its offshoots, then it can be demoted to the status of an acquired or artificial belief easily dispensed with, but the theory of projection suggests that belief in God is natural, universal and therefore non-culturally specific, even if ultimately false. It may be that this contradiction is an indication of the extent to which Schopenhauer's aim to discredit theism tempted him to assemble as many considerations against it as he could, without care for their congruence. However, a resolution of the contradiction may lie in a distinction that Schopenhauer presupposed but never made explicit — between the monotheism of ancient Israel and popular systems of polytheism. He seems to have regarded polytheism as a natural and tolerable outgrowth of the needs of the will which, as unsystematic poesy, is easily assimilated to an esoteric or philosophical metaphysic and employed to convey its moods, values and insights through allegorical images of the gods. He considered this to have been the case in India, where the

> fantastic and sometimes strange Indian mythology, still constituting today as it did thousands of years ago the religion of the people, is only the teaching of the *Upaniṣads* which is symbolised, in other words, clad in images and thus personified or mythicised with due regard to the people's powers of comprehension. According to his powers and education, every Hindu traces, feels, surmises, or clearly sees through it or behind it; (PPII p. 225)

In opposition to polytheism, ancient Israelite monotheism is a competitive and intolerant world-view, incapable of co-existing with another species of metaphysics, whether religious or philosophical. Yahweh is a jealous God and his theologians hostile to dissent. In the Middle Ages Christians aped the language of philosophy in order to clothe the volatile figure of Yahweh in all sorts of metaphysical predicates, refashioning an originally popular and revelation-based belief in an anthropomorphic and jealous God into a version of the eternal doctrine of the One and the Many. Theism was thereby presented as monolithic truth, as an intellectually justifiable metaphysic with supports independent of revelation and justifiably enforced on all as officially sanctioned teaching. In its systematic and theological guise, therefore, Schopenhauer considered monotheism to be an artificial belief specific to ancient Israel and the Old Testament, whereas polytheism is natural and universal and satisfies the natural imagination of the non-philosophical without coming into conflict with other systems of metaphysics.

However, Schopenhauer thought that the long epoch of Europe's phenomenological immersion in a monotheist universe had, by the early nineteenth century, become a recognisable fiction. He identified three recent developments that had issued in the growing awareness of the intellectual indefensibility of Europe's hitherto dominant metaphysic:

> the influence of the *Kantian philosophy*, then the contemporary effect of the unparalleled progress in all the natural sciences, making every past age seem like one of childhood when compared with ours, and finally an acquaintance with Sanskrit literature, Brahmanism, and Buddhism. (BM p. 44)

Although Schopenhauer estimated that each of these movements had made their particular contribution to the decline of theistic Christianity, he also regarded the nineteenth-century's acquaintance with Sanskrit literature to be simultaneously cause of and remedy to the crisis of religious belief in Europe: in other words, the oriental renaissance provides the solution to the death of God.

III. Natural Theology

This section reviews Schopenhauer's account of the effects of Kant's critical philosophy on the traditional metaphysics of Europe, specifically on natural theology and the arguments for the existence of God. Many theologians have maintained that, prior to Kant, belief in God was as much a matter of personal and individual faith as it has become in the modern period. However, irrespective of the real grounds and supports of faith before Kant, the arguments for the existence of God also operated in defence of the claim that God is more than an esoteric object of faith and religious experience, but is, instead, a demonstrable and therefore public object of knowledge, denial of whose existence carried legal and political as well as theological consequences. These arguments thereby served as the intellectual justification for the establishment and ascendancy of Christian institutions in Europe, and for the proscription of alternative species of metaphysics.

Schopenhauer openly acknowledged that his critique of natural theology was heavily dependent on Kant, the "all-pulveriser" of transcendent metaphysics, but considered it necessary to reiterate and expand on Kant's critique. This is because, on the one hand, he saw that Kant's purely regulative use of the doctrines of God, freedom and immortality had unintentionally confirmed the common but erroneous assumption that ethical observance was dependent upon belief in God, whereas Schopenhauer thought that "a dogma that presumes to stamp as a rogue everyone who refuses to accept it deserves once for all to be seriously put to the test." (PPI p. 106) On the other hand he perceived how some of his contemporaries — especially the state's philosophical mouthpieces, Schopenhauer's despised 'professors' — were claiming Kant's mantle whilst simultaneously unravelling the achievements of the critical philosophy by making Kant's practical reason into a theoretical oracle, "a little window" admitting "us to the superlunal and even supernatural world." (FR p. 181) Schopenhauer primarily had Fichte, Schelling and Hegel in mind, who he accused of wilfully misinterpreting Kant's practical moral theology as "a real dogmatic theism, a new proof of the existence of God" (PPI p. 111), and of employing this misinterpretation to justify their retrograde step of redefining the 'love of wisdom' as "the service of God (Gottesdienst)".[38]

In opposition to his fellow post-Kantians, therefore, Schopenhauer regarded Kant's moral theology as the least significant part of the critical philosophy, the primary merits of which he located elsewhere and divided into three. The first and greatest of these was Kant's division between the phenomenon and the thing-in-itself (WWRI p. 417), a division that Fichte, Schelling and Hegel had, in various ways, endeavoured to overcome: the second primary merit of the critical philosophy was Kant's expulsion of *eudaemonism* from morals, achieved by showing that actions of genuine moral worth are paths upon which the virtuous and the saintly pass over the world and commune with the metaphysical (BM pp. 49-50).

---

[38] Hegel (1988) p. 79.

Schopenhauer regarded these merits of Kant's work as genuine philosophical insights, having universal and permanent value irrespective of time and place. By contrast, Schopenhauer considered the third merit of the critical philosophy to be of merely negative and local significance, consisting of Kant's "complete overthrow of the scholastic philosophy." (WWRI p. 422)

Schopenhauer thereby disputed the standard view in the history of philosophy of Descartes' role in bringing scholasticism to an end. Although he recognised that Descartes had dissolved the authority of the Bible and Aristotle in methodical doubt, Descartes' reconstruction of the cosmos on the far side of doubt remained dependent on scholastic models, such as soul-body dualism and the assumption that the forms and laws of the phenomenon are eternal verities independent of the subject (WWRI p. 421). Descartes did not therefore inaugurate an epoch of free philosophical investigation divested of theological assumptions, but had merely re-established the realist metaphysics of scholasticism on a novel, rationalist footing (WWRI p. 423). In Schopenhauer's view, not until Kant did the eternal verities of scholasticism (relations between substance and accident, cause and effect, and antecedent and consequent) become the focus rather than the presuppositions of philosophical investigation. Philosophers before Kant, such as Spinoza and Hume, may have succeeded in showing that the scholastic arguments for the existence of God admit of alternative conclusions, but Kant attacked their very foundations by showing that the forms and laws of objects are simultaneously forms and laws of the subject, and therefore invalid when applied beyond the bounds of sense. Schopenhauer thereby credited Kant with awaking western philosophy from the dream of realism (WWRI p. 420).

But irrespective of Schopenhauer's openly avowed dependence on Kant, his critique of natural theology does not merely reiterate the content of Kant's 'Transcendental Dialectic', but contains additional and original arguments of Schopenhauer's own making. This section will focus on those elements in Schopenhauer's critique that illustrate how his nominalist account of reason and concepts issued in a subtle shift away from Kantian transcendentalism towards an empiricist theory of language and meaning derived from Locke.[39] However, it needs to be emphasised

---

[39] Schopenhauer seemed generally unaware of the extent to which his conceptual nominalism was an unorthodox feature of his Kantianism. He claimed that whereas Kant's philosophy "had a decidedly polemical and destructive relation to the philosophy of Leibniz and Wolff", it confirmed and extended that of Locke and corrected and employed that of Hume (WWRI p. 418: see also Cartwright (2003)).

that this shift is very subtle indeed, since Schopenhauer's nominalist criticism of metaphysical concepts frequently betrays transcendental presuppositions that would be abhorrent to an empiricist (especially his derivation of the concepts of necessity and contingency from the transcendental law of the principle of sufficient reason). However, my exposition stresses the nominalist strain in Schopenhauer's critique of natural theology in order to illustrate how his epistemological distinction between intuitive perception and conception (of which his conceptual nominalism is a part), is the central presupposition for his rejection of the predominantly rationalist metaphysics and ethics of the west, and his concomitant appropriation of what he considered to be the superior ethical and metaphysical doctrines of India.

Another feature of Schopenhauer's critique of natural theological arguments for the existence of God is that it considers only those statements found in works of philosophy, and completely ignores their original formulations in works of medieval theology. For example, Schopenhauer claimed that Descartes was the true inventor of the ontological argument and that Anselm "had in a general way given merely an introduction to it." (FR p. 14)[40] This is partly a consequence of the way in which his critique presupposes that of Kant, who tended to do the same, but also reflects Schopenhauer's scant regard for systematic theology. We noted in the previous chapter how he thought that theological analyses of religion were of little value, since they are insufficiently free from interest to resist attempting to prove that the allegories of one specific tradition are literally and exclusively true. In his view, only the independent and disinterested perspective of philosophy is capable of investigating, analysing and explaining the inner significance and truth contained in religious doctrines without prejudice or interest.

Many recent theologians have taken the opposite course, favouring Anselm's statement of the ontological argument over those of Descartes and Leibniz, and Aquinas' cosmological arguments over those of Christian Wolff. These revisionist assessments of the theological heritage are unquestionably valid, insofar as they draw attention to the fact that a piece of discursive theological reasoning suffers distortion when transplanted to a philosophical context. However, they have often travelled

---

[40] Schopenhauer was not alone in taking the language of Descartes' premise as definitive. Hegel based his philosophy on a version of Anselm's ontological proof, but instead of using Anselm's negative definition of God as "something than which nothing greater can be conceived" (*aliquid quo nihil cogitari possit*) he attributed to Anselm Descartes' definition of God as the *ens perfectissimum* or most perfect being (Hegel (1988) p. 182).

too far in the opposite direction. Some seem to be obscurantist manoeu-
vres, conducted to shield the tradition from criticism by denying that
theology shares standards of rationality and evidence with other disciplines, all the time leaving the criteria of theological evaluation vague
and undefined: in the words of Alasdair MacIntyre quoted previously,
they make theology "a discipline which legislates for itself and which
disowns the current badges of intellectual legitimation", thereby weaken-
ing theology's links with the general culture of the age.[41]

This tendency is evident in Karl Barth's study of Anselm, where he
argues that Anselm's "Proof of the Existence of God" is mistakenly
called the ontological argument and that it has nothing in common with
"the well-known teaching of Descartes and Leibniz", and that nobody
"could seriously think that it is even remotely affected by what Kant put
forward against these doctrines — all that is so much nonsense on which
no more words ought to be wasted."[42] However Barth's statement of his
own understanding of the proof's status and abiding value is little more
than a eulogy to the glories of God, faith and theology. He contended that
Anselm's conception of proof was not that of

> a science that can be unravelled by the Church's faith and that establishes
> the Church's faith in a source outside of itself. It is a question of theology.
> It is a question of the proof of faith by faith which was already established
> in itself without proof. And both — faith that is proved and faith that proves
> — Anselm expressly understands not as presuppositions that can be achieved
> by man but as presuppositions that have been achieved by God...[43]

Barth's exegesis is hardly supported by Anselm's own commentary on
his procedure in the *Proslogion*, for Anselm clearly thought it was possible to comprehend the idea of God outside the life of faith. The atheist,
or fool who says "there is no God" in his heart, understands the definition of God, since "that which he understands is in his understanding,
even if he does not understand it to exist."[44] For Anselm, therefore, the
atheist entertains the *same idea* of God as the believer, so that the proof's
validity is non-contextual, appealing to the rational capacities of atheist
and theist alike. The ontological argument is used to show that the atheist *logically* contradicts himself when he entertains the *idea* of God as
"something than which nothing greater can be conceived" in his understanding, but denies that this idea has a referent in reality. It is proof at

---

[41] MacIntyre (1969) p. 11.
[42] Barth (1960) p. 171.
[43] Ibid. p. 170.
[44] Anselm (1990) Chapter II.

its most austere and compelling, mimicking the form of logical and mathematical demonstration in order to annihilate the possibility of non-belief. Barth's revisionist assessment of Anselm's understanding of proof seems to be predicated on a strategic disingenuousness that licenses him to read back into the works of a medieval thinker the embattled fears of a twentieth-century theologian at odds with the rebellious faithlessness of the surrounding culture.

Therefore, we begin our survey of Schopenhauer's critique of natural theology with his criticism of the *a priori* argument called by Kant the ontological, and presume that Schopenhauer had as his target genuine attitudes entertained by *some* theists concerning the demonstrative efficacy of this and other arguments for the existence of God. We have already mentioned that Schopenhauer combined his commitment to Kantian idealism with a nominalist theory of the origin and nature of concepts. Whereas Hegel thought that concepts acquaint us with a level of reality more adequate and richer than that encountered through undifferentiated sense, for Schopenhauer concepts are abstract simplifications of the empirically real, so that thinking in concepts always involves thinking *less* than is given through perception. He divided concepts into *concreta* such as "man" and "horse" and *abstracta* such as "relation" and "beginning", referring to the former as the "ground floor" and the latter as "the upper storeys of the edifice of reflection." (WWRI p. 41) Every concept has a horizon or sphere that circumscribes all that can be thought through or under it, but since this horizon is an extensive rather than intensive property, Schopenhauer maintained that "the content and extent of concepts are in inverse relation to each other, and thus the more that is thought *under* a concept, the less is thought *in* it" (WWRII p. 64). In other words, concepts on the lowest floor of the edifice of reflection will have the narrowest horizon but a more definite content, for they remain close to perception as the source of all thought. By contrast, concepts on the upper stories will be capable of subsuming a greater number of things under them, but for that reason they lack definition and border on being mere "words" without clear meaning.

These opposing evaluations of the nature of concepts with a broad horizon led to Schopenhauer's and Hegel's contrary assessments of the ontological argument. Whereas Hegel maintained that its assertion of the unity of thought and being means that it is "a necessary and true thought" in content, albeit faulty in form,[45] Schopenhauer thought that its major

---

[45] Hegel (1988) p. 187.

premise, the concept of a most perfect being or *ens perfectissimum*, has virtually no content at all. The concept of perfection "is entirely empty and void of content" when thought in isolation, for it derives meaning only in combination with another concept, when it indicates that its referent is a perfect or "numerically complete" instance of its species (WWRI p. 424). On this view, the concept of a 'most perfect horse' would denote an animal that possessed to the maximal degree qualities denoted by the concept of the species (height in hands, glossiness of coat, type and number of markings, gait, condition of teeth and gums, etc.). However, '*ens*' or 'being' is not a concept that stands for a species, but simply "the infinitive of the copula", used to conjoin concepts in judgements (such as in 'this horse *is* a perfect instance of its species'), and therefore "scarcely anything but a word." (WWRII p. 64) Since, therefore, every existent can be brought *under* the concept of 'being', virtually nothing is thought *through* or *in* it. As a result, even if we were to concede the possibility of demonstrating the existence of non-perceivable entities through concepts alone, on Schopenhauer's analysis the conjunction of 'most perfect' with 'being' is too thin to allow any purchase for thought, and is therefore an inadequate foundation for the belief system of theism.[46]

However, before we conclude that Schopenhauer's exposure of the slender content of the concept of an *ens perfectissimum* has completely dispensed with the ontological argument, it is worth hearkening to the arguments of those who have developed revisionist readings of Anselm's version. For example, Frederick Sontag draws attention to the fact that whereas Descartes, Leibniz and Spinoza used terms such as 'most perfect' and 'greatest' univocally, and presumed that they have an identical sense whether predicated of God or finite entities,[47] Anselm's approach is far more subtle. Contrary to Descartes' *via eminentiae*, or way of eminence, which defines God in positive terms and places him at the summit of being, Anselm's definition of God as not merely "something than which nothing greater can be conceived", but also "something greater than can be conceived",[48] situates his argument within the *via negationis*

---

[46] Schopenhauer distinguished his concept of will from the "word-formulations" of scholasticism by founding its content on *inner* perception: "when I say 'will,' 'will-to-live,' this is no *ens rationis*, no hypostasis made by me, nor is it an expression of vague and uncertain meaning. On the contrary, if anyone asks me what it is, I refer him to his own inner being, where he will find it complete, and indeed of colossal magnitude, as a true *ens realissimum*." (WN p. 142)

[47] Sontag (1967) p. 474.

[48] Anselm (1990) Chapter XV.

or way of negation. This is a method in western metaphysical speculation that stems from the Platonic Socrates' definition of the Good as "beyond being",[49] passes through the dialectical assertions and denials of Plotinus' sketch of the One, and received a Christian baptism in the fifth century from Dionysius the Areopagite. In accordance with this tradition, Anselm's negative conception locates God outside of rather than at the pinnacle of finite created entities, and therefore denies the possibility of enclosing God within a concept. Anselm's definition indicates that whatever we conceive God to be, he is always greater than that.

Schopenhauer was familiar with this negative tradition in western metaphysical speculation, and used negative or apophatic terms himself to formulate his theory of salvation as denial of the will. However, since he regarded theism as a world-view contrary to his own, having the essential characteristics of metaphysical realism and cosmic optimism, he thought that the negative way was inappropriate for theology. The Genesis narrative depicts God creating the world, judging it good, laying down laws and interacting with his people, but such a view of God's action towards and affirmation of the world indicates an uninterrupted communication of being and value from God to his creation, so that, in accordance with Descartes' way of eminence, terms used to describe the world ought to be univocally predicable of God. By contrast, Schopenhauer used negative terms to signify that which is in constitution and tendency diametrically opposed to the world. His comment on Dionysius the Areopagite's *Mystical Theology* indicates that, in his view, apophatic theology is tantamount to theological suicide, for it consists

> merely in the explanation that all the predicates of God can be denied, but not one can be affirmed, because he resides above and beyond all being and all knowledge, what Dionysius calls ἐπέκεινα, 'on yonder side' and describes as something wholly and entirely inaccessible to our knowledge. This theology is the only true one; but it has no substance at all. Admittedly it says and tells us nothing, and it consists merely in the declaration that it is well aware of this and cannot be otherwise. (MRIII p. 377)

However, Schopenhauer's interpretation of the purely negative achievement of Dionysius' theology conflicts with Denys Turner's presentation of the methods and aims of western apophatic theology from Dionysius onwards. Turner argues that Dionysius' apophaticism is not simple negation, but a dialectical process of negating negative terms in addition to 'cataphatic' or positive ones. He maintains that there

---

[49] Plato (1987) 509b (citations to Plato's works refer to the Burnet pagination).

is a very great difference between the strategy of *negative propositions* and the strategy of *negating the propositional*; between that of the *negative image* and that of the *negation of imagery*. The first of each of these pairs belongs to the cataphatic in theology, and only the second is the strategy of the apophatic.[50]

For Turner, therefore, apophaticism is a method that asserts the transcendence of God rather than his opposition to the world. Turner's study has stimulated a resurgence of interest in apophatic theology, including an article by Andrew King that identifies the apophatic elements in Schopenhauer as "a rich resource for those attempting to re-work the relationship between atheism and theism."[51] According to King, "if Schopenhauer can, by his own criteria, legitimately conclude his philosophy in Eckhartian-style mysticism, then what distinguishes his well-known atheism from Eckhart's Christian mysticism?"[52] King draws attention to the fact that Schopenhauer stated that "the mystic proceeds positively" beyond the negative knowledge of philosophy (WWRII p. 162), and that mystics have frequently described their experiences in positive terms, such as "ecstasy, rapture, illumination, union with God, and so on."[53] However, Schopenhauer qualified this observation in the following sentence by noting that the mystical state "cannot really be called knowledge, since it no longer has the form of subject and object" (WWRI p. 410). Since, for Schopenhauer, 'knowledge' depends on a knowing subject's encounter with an object, his recognition that "the mystic proceeds positively" beyond the negative knowledge of philosophy implies that they are hardly justified in doing so. Philosophically, the mystic's claim to have united with God is a shorthand expression for his liberation from the will, rather than experiential proof of the existence of an ultimate, ineffable reality. Schopenhauer often expressed admiration for the mystical works of medieval Christianity, but largely on account of their heterodoxy. He notes that whereas theism

> calculated with reference to the capacity of the crowd, places the primary source of existence outside us, as an object. All mysticism...draws this source gradually back into ourselves as the subject, and the adept at last recognises with wonder and delight that he himself is it. (WWRII p. 612)

Ultimately, however, Schopenhauer thought that the Buddhists had developed a more adequate language to describe the mystical state, since they

---

[50] Turner (1995) p. 35.
[51] King (2005) p. 253.
[52] Ibid. p. 265.
[53] Ibid. p. 263.

used nothing but negative terms such as *nirvāṇa* to indicate that which is "beyond all knowledge".[54]

And Schopenhauer's preference for the mystical language of Buddhism indicates a possible answer to King's question regarding the difference between Eckhart's Christian mysticism and Schopenhauerian atheism. Schopenhauer claimed that "[i]f we turn from the forms, produced by external circumstances, and go to the root of things" we find that the Buddha and Eckhart "teach the same thing". However, whereas the Buddha "dared to express his ideas plainly and positively" Eckhart was obliged to clothe his "in the garment of the Christian myth, and to adapt his expressions thereto. This goes to such lengths that with him the Christian myth is little more than a metaphorical language...he takes it throughout allegorically." (WWRII p. 614) This suggests that, in Schopenhauer's view at least, the difference between Eckhart's Christian mysticism and Buddhist (and Schopenhauerian) atheism consists of Eckhart's prudential resort to the language of theism to express his mystical transcendence of his nature as will.

Next we consider Schopenhauer's treatment of cosmological arguments. As previously noted, he never referred specifically to Aquinas, but his critique of the general procedure and form of cosmological arguments can be applied to the first three of Aquinas' Five Ways — the First, from motion to an Unmoved Mover; the Second, from efficient causation to a First Cause; and the Third, from contingency to a necessary being.

As a self-professed transcendental idealist, Schopenhauer thought that the law of causality (or principle of sufficient reason of becoming) is *a priori*, regulating the subject's interpretation of changes in material objects as effects of an antecedent cause (FR p. 53). It is therefore no surprise to find that one of Schopenhauer's main objections to cosmological arguments is that they use a principle which "has its roots in our intellect", and whose sole function is to connect one representation of perception with another, to explain "the totality of all existing things... including the intellect in which the world presents itself." (FR p. 232)

But despite Schopenhauer's idealist premises, his conception of causality does have some affinity with Aquinas' account of motion in the First Way. Their common source is Aristotle's account of change or

---

[54] Schopenhauer referred to I.J. Schmidt's writings on the *Prajñā-Pāramitā* literature of Mahāyāna Buddhism in support of his claim that knowledge necessarily ceases when the mystic has transcended the opposition between subject and object, so that mystical language proceeding positively beyond this point will be symbolic and expressive rather than literal and descriptive (WWRI p. 412; WWRII p. 275).

kinēsis as the movement from potentiality to actuality through the impetus of an external agent, although both modified this theory to suit their respective purposes. In agreement with Aristotle, Schopenhauer denied that the material part of objects is subject to causality, for matter is the eternal and indestructible substratum of objects, and for Schopenhauer the correlate of the subject's power of understanding. As a result, he maintained that "with causality we are obviously concerned only with changes in the form" of objects, for "a real genesis, a coming into existence, of that which previously never existed, is an impossibility." (FR p. 56) Causation therefore explains only the perceivable change of *state* of an object that occurs when a quality (i.e., heat) is communicated from one part of matter to another. However, whereas Aristotle posited a transcendent principle as the ultimate source of change or motion — the Unmoved Mover which, as magnetic force or supreme object of desire, initiates change in natural objects — Schopenhauer's metaphysics traces all change to one, non-causal and immanent principle, the will as the thing-in-itself. For Schopenhauer the relation between cause and effect is therefore merely the *occasion* for the will's manifestation in the phenomenon through natural forces such as gravity. Although in everyday language it is often said that gravity is the cause of a stone falling to the ground, Schopenhauer thought that this is strictly incorrect: the cause is particular rather than universal, being the stone's proximity to the earth, which provides the occasion for gravity's possession of a particular chunk of matter: "Take away the earth, and the stone will not fall, although gravity remains." (WWRI p. 131)

Aquinas took Aristotle's account in a different direction. Supplementing Aristotelian cosmology with ideas from revelation, Aquinas promoted Aristotle's Unmoved Mover to the position of absolute creator of time, space, form and matter. In the First Way Aquinas identified the Christian God as the ultimate explanation of changes in objects (or the movement from potentiality to actuality), and in the Second Way maintained that the series of efficient causes must terminate in a First Cause that causes but is not caused, and "to which everyone gives the name of God."[55] However, the extent to which Aquinas' metaphysical arguments presuppose revealed doctrines such as the creation of the world out of nothing (and, therefore, the non-eternity of motion) is a matter of debate. Frederick Copleston in particular maintains that Aquinas did not presuppose the temporal finitude of the world-process in the First and Second Ways,

---

[55] Aquinas (1911) S.T., Ia, 2,3.

stating that "when Aquinas talks about an 'order' of efficient causes he is not thinking of a series stretching back into the past, but of a hierarchy of causes, in which a subordinate member is here and now dependent on the causal activity of a higher member."[56]

If Copleston's interpretation is correct, then Schopenhauer's criticisms of cosmological arguments may be inapplicable to those of Aquinas, since they consistently employ temporal language, and therefore suggest that Schopenhauer envisaged a series stretching into the past rather than a hierarchy in the "here and now". For example, he objects that the conception of a First Cause acting prior to time is impossible, for if it became causal only at some point, "then something must have *changed* it at that time for its inactivity to have ceased", whereupon we find our-selves once more on the ladder of causality, enquiring after the cause that preceded and brought about this change also, *ad infinitum* (FR p. 58). He maintains that the chain of causes is "necessarily without beginning", for every change is brought about by a cause, which is in turn an effect of a cause preceding it and so on, for the understanding cannot conceive of a point at which the demand for causes might be annulled (FR p. 53). This implies that Schopenhauer had in mind a particular cause or deist God that gets the series going, rather than a providential God who, in accord-ance with Copleston's suggestion of a hierarchy, sustains motion and efficient causation in the "here and now."

However, in many ways Copleston's hierarchical interpretation of Aquinas' arguments makes them weaker as proofs, since it implies that the First Cause is a general cause, which for Schopenhauer is a completely superfluous hypothesis. This is clear in his objections to Kant's Idea of Reason, the unconditioned ground of the totality of conditions, recently resurfaced as the Absolute in the works of Schopenhauer's post-Kantian contemporaries. Contrary to the claim that the sufficient reason for finite conditions is an infinite unconditioned, Schopenhauer suggests that if we descend "from the indefinite generality of abstraction to the particular, definite reality", then we see that the understanding's search for *sufficient* reasons asks only after the cause of the nearest change, and is "extin-guished completely in each given sufficient reason or ground." (WWRI p. 483) In other words, sufficient reason has no interest in the cause of the whole, for the whole is merely a nominal description that groups together the particulars of the series. Schopenhauer's reasoning is similar to that of Philo in Hume's *Dialogues Concerning Natural Religion*:

---

[56] Copleston (1991) p. 122.

> Did I show you the particular causes of each individual in a collection of twenty particles of matter, I should think it very unreasonable, should you afterwards ask me, what was the cause of the whole twenty. This is sufficiently explained in explaining the cause of the parts.[57]

So, irrespective of whether the order of moved objects or causes is a series or a hierarchy, for Schopenhauer such arguments only arrive at their desired destination by presuming that the world exists as a whole, thereby justifying the assumption that an infinite regress of the series or hierarchy is impossible. In conclusion, Schopenhauer argued that it is contradictory to posit the extra-mental reality of processes such as motion and causality only to annul them in an Unmoved Mover or First Cause. The causal law is not a cab that can be dismissed on arrival at one's destination: a better illustration of its *modus operandi* is provided by the broom in Goethe's tale of the sorcerer's apprentice, which, once in motion, spreads itself throughout all parts of infinite time and space (FR pp. 58-9).

Schopenhauer contended that architects of cosmological arguments have tacitly acknowledged the understanding's presumption of the infinity of causal change, but to circumvent its demand for further causes they have resorted to the "trick" of resolving the series on a concept "problematical as to its reality" — namely, the conclusion of the ontological proof that God is a logically necessary being (FR p. 228-9). They have thereby set up the word-combination that asserts the identity of essence and existence in God as a satisfactory terminus for the world-process. Schopenhauer located the deficiency of this procedure in the fact that it confuses logical and real relations, to avoid which his doctoral dissertation had distinguished the principle of sufficient reason of becoming (regulating changes in material objects through the relation of cause and effect) from the principle of sufficient reason of knowing (validating judgements by resolving them on an appropriate reason or ground (*Grund*) of knowledge). He says that he distinguished these two laws for the purpose of advancing "towards greater lucidity and precision in philosophising", as well as guarding "against error and intentional deception" (FR p. 4). He alleged that several philosophical proofs, apart from cosmological arguments, have established spurious theses by eliding the important distinction between a real cause and a logical ground, such as when Descartes indiscriminately referred to God's immensity as the *cause* or *reason* why he requires no external cause of his existence (FR pp. 13-4),

---

[57] Hume (1993a) pp. 92-3.

and when Schelling hypostatised the logical distinction between antecedent and consequent by introducing it into the being of God itself (FR
p. 22).

But although Schopenhauer thought that his analysis of the understanding and causality demonstrated that the project of tracing relations
between phenomena is inexhaustible (PPI p. 78), he also recognised that
the prohibition on an infinite regress has some sort of intuitive force. For
him, however, this force is no more than local and psychological, being
the result of "early and deeply imprinted" prejudices given through
religious education, and an illustration of how judgement is easily paralysed through artificial means (WWRI p. 493). He maintained that the
Indian religions demonstrate the culture-specific origin of the ban on an
infinite regress, since neither consider it necessary to terminate the nexus
of causes in a First Cause that requires no explanation and is worthy of
worship (WWRI p. 495n.35); the Buddhists especially condem such a
belief as a religious heresy (FR pp. 184-5).

Schopenhauer's objections to the argument from contingency to necessity — Aquinas' Third Way — are, once more, a hybrid of transcendental-
ist and nominalist presuppositions. Contrary to the majority of analytical
philosophers, Schopenhauer did not regard the opposition between contingency and necessity as a logical criterion distinguishing different types
of proposition, but as a contrast grounded in the forms of thought, and
therefore applicable to experience. However, just as progress in philosophy had been retarded by the habit of confusing causes with reasons, so
he also claimed that it had suffered from the rationalist habit of applying
concepts too broadly without concern for the relation between their origin
and content (WWRII pp. 39-40). He detected this tendency in the cosmological argument from contingent beings to a necessary being, for it uses
these terms to distinguish different types of entity. For example, in the
Third Way Aquinas argues that the objects of experience are merely possible or contingent beings, for they are "found to be generated, and to be
corrupted, and consequently, it is possible for them to be and not to be."
He continues by stating that if the existence of everything were merely
possible in this way, then there would at one time have been nothing, and
therefore nothing now. But since experience informs us that possible or
contingent beings exist, "we cannot but admit the existence of some being
having of itself its own necessity...[t]his all men speak of as God."[58]

---

[58] Aquinas (1911) S.T., Ia, 2,3.

Schopenhauer objected to this on the grounds that contingency and necessity are not 'innate' properties at all, whether of beings or propositions. They merely characterise the relations between representations established by the principle of sufficient reason. This principle entails that just as an effect necessarily proceeds from its cause, so the truth of a judgement is necessitated by its ground of knowledge. For Schopenhauer, therefore, there is no metaphysical category of contingent being. Everything actual is necessary, since the generation and corruption of the particulars of experience are equally necessitated by causes. Necessity is therefore the original or positive concept, following directly from the transcendental laws of thought: contingency is a mere negation of necessity, or another way of saying that two objects are not related at all:

> every object, of whatever kind it be, e.g., every event in the actual world, is always at the same time both necessary and contingent; *necessary* in reference to the one thing that is its cause; *contingent* in reference to everything else...Therefore an absolute contingency is just as inconceivable as an absolute necessity, for the former would be just an object that did not stand to any other in the relation of consequent to ground. (WWRI p. 464)

Schopenhauer therefore claimed that *"to be necessary* can never mean anything but to follow from a given ground or reason", and that this is the only meaning attributable to the concept, insofar as it follows *a priori* from the transcendental forms of our faculty of knowledge. As a result, the metaphysical concept of an "ABSOLUTELY *necessary being"* is merely a contradictory combination of words, for if the word "absolute" is meant to denote "that which has no ground", then it contradicts the predicate of "following from a specific ground" by which the principle of sufficient reason gives sense to the concept of necessity (FR pp. 225-6).

It might be objected that Schopenhauer's rejection of the validity of the contrast between contingent and necessary being simply denies sense to the metaphysical question "why something rather than nothing", so that, like a positivist, Schopenhauer looked upon the world as a brute fact rather than as an object of wonder. However, Schopenhauer's response to the wonder expressed in the question "why something rather than nothing" was his metaphysics of the will as the thing-in-itself. Although, in his view, we do not have sufficient knowledge of the will to claim that it exists necessarily (and, moreover, actions of moral worth and ascetic salvation suggest that it does not), as the indestructible inner element that abides in the midst of change, the will as thing-in-itself suggests, contrary to Aquinas' Third Way, that there never was at one time nothing.

Schopenhauer's critical treatment of the argument *from* or *to* design (called by him, after Kant, the physico-theological argument) is more ambivalent than the outright hostility he showed towards the ontological and cosmological arguments. This argument, defended in embryonic form by Aquinas in the Fifth Way, had enjoyed something of a renaissance in the modern period, as empirical science's disclosure of the intricate order of nature was interpreted as decisive warrant for inferences to a designer God. However, Spinoza and Hume had criticised the teleological aspects of the argument for being based on anthropomorphic projection, which had led to Kant's theory that teleological judgement depends on our subjective awareness of our own conscious purposes.[59] Although Kant thought that teleological interpretations of organisms reflected a natural tendency of the mind, since we cannot show that they are justified he counselled that we regard them as regulative fictions, useful for guiding our investigations of nature but to be excluded from scientific explanations of nature's constitution.[60]

Schopenhauer surpassed Kant's cautiousness by (along with Schelling and Hegel) defending a *constitutive* rather than *regulative* theory of teleological judgement. He defended this move on the grounds that Kant's distinction between the phenomenon and the thing-in-itself had permitted a separation between teleology and theology (WWRI p. 513). For Schopenhauer, therefore, teleological explanation does not lead up to a transcendent designer or God, but is merely a matter of relating the suitability and fitness of nature's parts to the whole. In addition to this, he claimed that teleology, properly understood, provides *a posteriori* confirmation of his *a priori* metaphysical argument that nature is the visible expression of the "innermost essence" of every individual — the will (WWRII p. 329). An organism is the objective expression or visibility of the will of its species working blindly from within, so that every organism is at once thing-in-itself, or *natura naturans* (creative nature), and phenomenon, or *natura naturata* (created nature) (PPII p. 91).

In Schopenhauer's view, therefore, teleological interpretations of nature's fitness state no more than that it is a cosmos rather than a chaos, for the existence, sustenance and reproduction of nature's parts is accompanied by much suffering and brutality and with no final end in view. The will in its innermost essence is without knowledge, so that it wills

---

[59] Kant (1987) 360.
[60] Ibid. 379.

without any conception of a purpose to be attained by its objectification in the phenomenon. Schopenhauer regarded other teleological interpretations, such as the physico-theological proof, Schelling's *Naturphilosophie* and Hegel's metaphysics of process, as hopelessly anthropomorphic, insofar as they present the world as a stage for the fulfilment of moral or religious purposes and the final realisation of truth, beauty and goodness. Therefore, in agreement with Spinoza, Hume and Kant before him, Schopenhauer thought that the theistic argument from design was based on anthropomorphic projection, insofar as it represents a transcendent being acting on nature from the outside and in accordance with mental purposes, analogous to the way in which humans act on external objects. However, his constitutive teleological theory led him to argue that this projection is based on a genuine insight, albeit one obscured by allegorical wrappings. In lieu, therefore, of a wholesale rejection of the physico-theological proof, Schopenhauer recommended that it be demythologised:

> Even theism represents the world as proceeding from a *will*; the planets are represented as being guided in their orbits by a will, and a nature as being produced on their surface. But theism childishly puts this will outside the universe and causes it to act on things only indirectly, through the intervention of knowledge and matter, in human fashion. With me, on the other hand, the will acts not so much on things as in them; indeed they themselves are simply nothing but the very visibility of the will. However, in this agreement we see that we cannot conceive the original of things as anything but a *will*. (PPI p. 131)

This completes Schopenhauer's supplements to Kant's assault on the arguments of natural theology in the 'Transcendental Dialectic'. At this point it might be stated that Schopenhauer has shown no more than that metaphysical theism is incapable of rational justification, not that it is false or that it consists of unreasonable beliefs. However, Schopenhauer forestalled this conclusion by citing the principle *affirmanti incumbit probatio* ("proof is incumbent on he who asserts the positive"). In other words, the number of propositions incapable of being disproved is potentially infinite, but this does not entail that belief in any one of them is warranted in the absence of a demonstration of their falsehood (PPI p. 120).

Schopenhauer's argument that there is a logical asymmetry between positively proving a belief and demonstrating its falsehood seems substantially correct, even if, in practice, we take many beliefs on trust: this includes the belief that the external world exists independent of each individual (a belief supported by Schopenhauer's amalgamation of transcendental ideality and empirical reality), and that individuals generally mean well and are not out to destroy us (a belief at odds with Schopenhauer's doctrine of the unrestricted egoism of human nature). However, none of the components of metaphysical theism are beliefs of this kind. Instead, theism asserts the existence of something in addition to the furniture of the world which, if it does exist, has important consequences for the nature and meaning of life and the organisation of society. In the absence of a secure proof demonstrating the existence of this something, Schopenhauer thought that the cultural dominance of theism, and the institutional machinery by which it has been sustained, are unjustifiable. His examination of natural theology has put the central dogma of theism to the test and found it wanting, liberating anti-theists to deny the existence of God without fear of denunciation as moral rogues.

CHAPTER 4

TRUE AND ORIGINAL CHRISTIANITY

I. Evil, Freedom and Responsibility

At the close of the last chapter we saw how Schopenhauer thought that his critique of the metaphysical arguments of natural theology placed theism on the defensive, since it makes positive assertions that need to be supported by sound proofs. By contrast, atheism is not required to prove any particular position, but merely consists in rebutting the truth-value of theistic assertions. However, Schopenhauer supplemented his critique of natural theology with additional considerations, formulated to forbid even the sanctuary of belief in God through faith. In this part of his campaign he attempted to show that theism is contradicted by experience; that it fails to satisfy key criteria of metaphysical need; and that its doctrines are incompatible with those of "true and original Christianity". The latter strategy in particular may seem quixotic to many, insofar as Christianity is and always has been a monotheistic religion. However, as we shall see, Schopenhauer thought the opposite, and depicted "true" Christianity as essentially a non-theist religion that had become accidentally enmeshed with monotheistic doctrines. As a result, he thought that the death of God in the modern period provided an occasion for purifying the Christian faith of its contingent and merely historical accretions.

Schopenhauer thought it important to supplement his exposure of the weaknesses of natural theology with further criticisms because he regarded the doctrines of theism to be not merely wrong in fact but also harmful in effect. In his view, the cosmic optimism it sustains distorts our expectations by teaching that God bestowed life as a gift and created us to be happy and free of suffering. For Schopenhauer, cosmic optimism is like realism, a natural but erroneous view that flatters the will by shoring up its desire to attain final satisfaction through life (WWRII p. 584). This, however, is a metaphysical impossibility, since the will manifests itself as a plural world in a tragic bid to escape its inner emptiness by feeding on another, ignoring all the time that this other is in reality itself (WWRI p. 354). When, therefore, personal circumstances inevitably refute the belief that happiness is our birthright, we are prone to a sense of embitterment, which passes over into cosmic persecution when the inborn tendency to optimism is confirmed by the dogmas of theism (WWRII p. 634). In Schopenhauer's view, theism's tendency to support optimism merely succeeds in increasing man's psychic suffering, which is a greater burden than the merely physical pains he shares with the animals (WWRI p. 299). For this reason, Schopenhauer aimed to persuade his readers of the falsehood of the "palpably sophistical proofs of Leibniz that this is the best of all possible worlds", and set out to show that it is instead "the *worst* of all possible worlds." (WWRII p. 583)

Schopenhauer deduced three criteria for religious interpretations of exist-ence from the structure of metaphysical need: they must explain the ubiq-uity of evil and suffering; account for the otherwise merely felt moral significance of life; and, most importantly, provide consolation for death by supporting a viable doctrine of post-mortem existence (PPI pp. 121-2). Needless to say, he found metaphysical theism wanting on all three counts.

Monotheistic attempts to satisfy the first of the aforementioned criteria of metaphysical need has given rise to a dilemma quite as old as belief in God itself, referred to by Hume's Philo as "Epicurus' old questions... yet unanswered" and summarised as "Is [God] willing to prevent evil, but not able? then is he impotent. Is he able, but not willing? then is he malevolent. Is he both able and willing? whence then is evil?"[1] As *the* philosopher of pessimism, Schopenhauer's works are peppered with vividly emotive accounts of the wretchedness and sufferings of existence conditioned by the will, and his estimation of the world's natural and moral evil is equalled perhaps only by Augustine, whose *Confessions* narrate a personal quest to comprehend the existence of evil.[2] Schopenhauer similarly considered "wickedness, evil, and death" to be the main source of man's need for metaphysics, arguing that it is not merely the existence of the world that gives rise to metaphysical need, "but still more that it is such a miserable and melancholy world" (WWRII p. 172). The ultimate point of disagreement between Augustine and Schopenhauer consists in the Church Father's monotheism, from which he derived solace and a ground for hope in the belief that existence proceeds from and is ruled by an omnipotent, morally perfect personal Lord. However, Schopenhauer

---

[1] Hume (1993a) p. 100.

[2] However, Augustine's most condensed statement of the horrors of existence is con-tained in his *City of God* (Augustine (1972) XIX.4. Citations from Augustine's works refer to chapter and section rather than page number).

maintained that Augustine had purchased his solace and hope at the cost of both logical consistency and agreement with experience (FW p. 59), and that this contradiction was especially manifest in Augustinian theodicy, by which the Church Father attempted to answer Epicurus' questions by explaining the existence of evil.

Schopenhauer was generally contemptuous of theodicy. This is partly because, as we have seen, he had already examined the theoretical arguments for the existence of God and found them wanting. He also thought that, even when we grant God's existence on faith, the opposition between his goodness and the misery of the world is like "an arithmetical sum which never comes right, but the remainder of which appears now in one place, now in another, after it has been concealed elsewhere" (WWRI p. 407n): this is because the theistic view that the world is "the successful work of an all-wise, all-benevolent, and moreover almighty Being is too flagrantly contradicted" by its "misery and wretchedness" (PPII p. 301). In relation to this point, Matthew Alun Ray claims that Schopenhauer "does not bother to provide an account of the main trends of thought regarding theodicy; much less does he offer anything in the way of a head-on argument against them."[3] But although Ray is correct to state that Schopenhauer offers no "head-on" argument against theodicy, his philosophy of nature and ethics can be interpreted as *indirect* ripostes to Christian theodicy. Moreover, Ray identifies as theodicy's "main trends of thought" its theologically-based defences, such as Augustine's doctrines that "we are in fact all more or less sinful and so every one of us is deserving of some punishment, as scripture testifies in the story of the flood", and "that natural disasters are sent from God to test man's piety, like the appalling afflictions in the book of Job."[4] However, with regard to the first of the "main trends" of theodicy enumerated by Ray, Schopenhauer in fact concurred with Augustine on the relation between punishment and desert. His doctrine of *"eternal justice"* states that the "world itself is the tribunal of the world" (WWRI p. 352), and that "tormentor and tormented are one. The former is mistaken in thinking he does not share the torment, the latter in thinking he does not share the guilt." (WWRI p. 354) This is because he who suffers and he who inflicts suffering are equally led astray by space and time as the principles of

---

[3] Ray (2003) p. 60.

[4] Ibid: p. 61. Alvin Plantinga offers a similarly audacious, wholly infra-theological account of evil with his argument that it is *possible* that natural evil stems from an abuse of freedom on the part of Satan and other non-human agents (Plantinga (1977) p. 58).

individuation (*principium individuationis*) or "veil of *māyā*", as a result of which they interpret the spatial distance between their bodies as a real quantity and thus fail to recognise that individuality is an illusion of the phenomenon. Schopenhauer maintained that the Christian doctrines of the Fall and original sin are, properly understood, myths that communicate the same insight concerning the equality of punishment and desert (WWRI p. 354). However, he also thought that the communicative power of these myths is distorted when combined with the belief in a perfectly benevolent and omnipotent creator God, as a result of which they assume a repugnant air (PPII pp. 301-2).

As for Ray's suggestion that Schopenhauer unjustifiably neglects Augustine's explanation that natural disasters are sent by God to test man's piety, this seems to be little more than a theological extravagance. Schopenhauer clearly neglected to formulate a rejoinder to this explanation of evil since it transgresses his maxim that atheism is a presupposition of philosophical procedure by presupposing the existence of that which, for Schopenhauer, evil puts in doubt — namely, the existence of God.[5] The claim that God sends suffering to punish evil is not really an explanation but a saving hypothesis, a ruse by which belief reconciles itself to belief, tolerable in a pastoral context but unlikely to persuade a philosophical combatant out to challenge the coherence of theism. Moreover, it is questionable whether even modern theologians would countenance such an 'explanation' of evil, and Ray seems to be indulging in a sort of strategic folly when he represents it as one of the "main strands" of Augustinian theodicy. Most commentators on Augustine, not to mention most theologians and philosophers of religion, have considered his doctrines of the privation of the good (*privatio boni*) and the freedom of the will to be the strongest buttresses of his theodicy. Schopenhauer's system has counter-arguments against both, although, as Ray comments, they are not offered as "head-on" refutations, but arise directly from his elaboration of his metaphysics of will.

We turn first to Augustine's privative theory of evil, a top-down explanation that presupposes the *ex nihilo* creation of the world by an omnipotent and perfectly benevolent God. Without these *a priori* premises Augustine would have no motive for constructing a theoretical explanation

---

[5] The maxim that atheism is a presupposition of philosophical procedure, irrespective of whether the philosopher is a theist or not, has been asserted in one form by Flew (Flew (1976) pp. 13-4), and in another by Heidegger (Heidegger (2000) pp. 7-8). I interpret Schopenhauer's maxim *affirmanti incumbit probatio* as implying the same methodological principle.

of evil, and his definition of it as non-being or the privation of the good would be counter-intuitive. Augustine's monotheistic premises support his further premise that everything to which God gave the gift of being must, like God himself, be good (at least after its own kind): together they lead up to Augustine's conclusion that evil has no substantial foundation in God's creation, and that our experience and perception of it is an effect of the parts of the good substance of created nature setting themselves "at variance with other things."[6] Evil is therefore parasitic and irrational, for the extent to which it takes possession of any created thing threatens the existence of its host, and thereby also its own 'existence'.[7]

Schopenhauer's ontology of suffering and evil is developed in the opposite direction, from the 'bottom-up', and departs from a phenomenological analysis of the relation between pleasure and pain. He argues that all pleasure or satisfaction is merely the cessation of an antecedent state of longing or want (which, in Schopenhauer's view, are instances of suffering and pain). But this relation suggests that the phenomenological states subsumed under the word 'good' — such as pleasure, happiness, satisfaction — are the parasitic elements, being mere privations of a suffering that "proclaims itself immediately." As a result, the feeling of happiness that arises on attainment of the object of one's will

> is only of a negative, not a positive nature, and that for this reason it cannot be lasting satisfaction and gratification, but always delivers us only from a pain or want that must be followed either by a new pain or by languor, empty longing, and boredom. (WWRI p. 320)

As a result, for Schopenhauer evil is not a privation of the good, but the good a privation of evil. It is debatable whether his account of the phenomenological priority of want over satisfaction confirms or presupposes his metaphysical thesis that nature is the objectification of an insatiable will striving without end or aim. If it is a presupposition, then an Augustinian theologian might issue the rejoinder *tu quoque*, for if the presuppositions of theism are to be discounted prior to analysis of the nature of suffering and evil, then why not also Schopenhauer's metaphysics of will? Schopenhauer thought that his view was preferable because his metaphysics is immanent and "thought out in the presence of perceived reality", so that the mutual confirmation of its separable parts is merely a reflex of reality's agreement with itself (WWRII p. 184). By contrast, the metaphysics of theism consists of a number of dogmas

---

[6] Augustine (1961) VII.13.
[7] Ibid. VII.12.

dubiously culled from ancient documents and systematised into a transcendent metaphysical system. Its groundlessness is shown by the fact
that the theologian is obliged to construct further hypotheses to reconcile
his abstract system of beliefs with his pre-cognitive experience of the
ubiquity of evil and suffering. Hence, for Schopenhauer, his view is not
merely favourable, but tends to derive extra confirmation from the true
and original sense of the immanent doctrines of Christian theodicy, once
they have been separated from their theistic presuppositions.

If Augustine's privative theory is his account of the ontological status
of evil, then the free-will defence constitutes his explanation of evil's
origin. Augustine considers evil in both its natural and moral forms as
the consequence of sin, which is the perverse movement of a creaturely
will that, in its pride and folly, seeks to find satisfaction through itself
and other things created out of nothing rather than through the supreme,
uncreated and immutable good.[8] Augustine's voluntarist account of the
genesis of sin and evil is consistent with his doctrine of *privatio boni*,
insofar as it avoids the implication that the created substance to which
the sinful will turns is itself evil or the efficient cause of evil. Augustine
stated that sin resides not in created substance but in the will's movement
itself, which "becomes bad not because the thing to which it turns is bad,
but because the turning itself is perverse."[9] He seems to have envisaged
the *ex nihilo* appearance of evil from the sinful will of creatures as some
sort of burlesque parody of the creative activity of God, for this turning
of the will does not create anything substantial but, in its aversion from
God, upsets his ordained order. Augustine therefore interposed the power
of finite choice between the goodness of God and the evil of the world,
making the will the efficient 'first cause' of man's turning from God and
subsequent bondage to sin:

> what cause of willing can there be which is prior to willing? Either it is a
> will, in which case we have not got beyond the root of evil will. Or it is not
> a will, and in that case there is no sin in it. Either, then, will is itself the first
> cause of sin, or the first cause is without sin. Now sin is rightly imputed only
> to that which sins, nor is it rightly imputed unless it sins voluntarily.[10]

It might be objected that Augustine's account of the appearance of sin
and evil is overly abstract, insofar as it completely discounts tempera-
mental, biographical or environmental factors working on choice. His

---

[8] Augustine (1957) II, xix.53.
[9] Augustine (1972) XII.6.
[10] Augustine (1957) III, xvii.49.

notion of an innate metaphysical power to will either good or evil seems like a fissure in the fabric of creation, a sort of Sartrean void or nothingness unrelated to the good substance of an individual. We might enquire as to why a creaturely will allied to a nature created good and enjoying the intimate fellowship of Supreme Goodness chose to do evil, for such a will ought to have a very strong inclination to do only good. Without such an explanation, sin and evil remain enigmatic. However, Augustine seems to have grown unsatisfied with his early defence of the freedom of the will, for in a later work (most of which was written during the controversy with Pelagius), he argues that the will by itself is not an efficient cause of sin, but that its fall from God was the consequence of deficient causation:

> The truth is that one should not try to find an efficient cause for a wrong choice. It is not a matter of efficiency, but of deficiency; the evil will itself is not effective but defective. For to defect from him who is the Supreme Existence, to something of less reality, this is to begin to have an evil will. To try to discover the causes of such defection — deficient, not efficient causes — is like trying to see darkness or to hear silence.[11]

It is difficult to know what to make of this notion of deficient causation. It seems to denote the absence of any power, and therefore an attempt to depict that which cannot be depicted, or think the unthinkable — or as Augustine says, to "see darkness" or "hear silence." Augustine frequently acknowledged that he was at a loss for imaginative or conceptual resources when trying to account for the mystery of the will's freedom:

> no one therefore must try to get to know from me what I know that I do not know, unless, it may be, in order to learn not to know what must be known to be incapable of being known! For of course when we know things not by perception but by its absence, we know them, in a sense, but not-knowing, so that they are not-known by being known — if that is a possible or intelligible statement![12]

Compared to this obscurity, Augustine's illustrations of the will's servitude and bondage to pride, folly and sin are vivid and comprehensible and supported by innumerable instances taken from his own life and observations. In his view, this is no contradiction, since he thought that the finite freedom to choose either good or evil in the absence of determining causes presupposed an original condition now lost. Only Adam in his innocent and newly-created state before the Fall had the power to

---

[11] Augustine (1972) XII.7.
[12] Ibid.

choose good over evil: "When we speak of the freedom of the will to do right, we are speaking of the freedom wherein man was created."[13] Subsequent to Adam's Fall humanity has lost "the freedom of the will to do right" originally conferred by God. The guilt accruing from Adam's transgression has corrupted the nature of his descendants, who can now do only evil and therefore deserve God's punishment and death. Having surrendered their freedom, the restoration of the original condition of humanity is beyond the power of individuals, and is contingent upon the gift of God's freely bestowed grace, the decision to award or withhold which God predestined in eternity through inscrutable decree.

Schopenhauer's longest and most systematic examination of the doctrine of the freedom of the will is contained in a treatise for which he was awarded a prize by the Royal Norwegian Society of Sciences in 1839. Opening with some definitions of key terms, he introduces his doctrine of the necessity of the actual encountered previously, according to which *"necessary is that which follows from a given sufficient ground."* (FW p. 6) If we negate this primary concept we attain that of the *"absolutely contingent"*, which he describes as an "extremely problematical" concept which "nevertheless coincides in a curious way with the concept of *freedom.*" (FW p. 7) If we were to imagine a human will that is either contingent or freely operating, then it would be one that is "determined by nothing at all", and whose individual acts "proceed absolutely and quite originally from itself" (FW p. 8). In other words, a free will would be one that has the power to be the "first cause" in a series of changes, in accordance with the concept of will implied by Augustine's rhetorical question "what cause of willing can there be which is prior to willing?"[14] However since, for Schopenhauer, necessity is the primary concept, the notion of an action or event for which there is no explanation marks the point at which "clear thinking is at an end because the principle of sufficient reason in all its meanings is the essential form of our whole faculty of cognition, yet here it is supposed to be given up." (FW p. 8) There is a resonance here with Augustine's admission that no positive illustration of original freedom can be given, for it is akin to the attempt to "see darkness" or "hear silence". Yet if, as mainstream theology argues, Adam's fall from freedom into sin took place under spatio-temporal and embodied conditions,[15] then finite freedom ought to be

---

[13] Augustine (1957) III, xviii.52.

[14] Ibid. III, xvii.49.

[15] It is, however, debatable whether the view that the Fall occurred within rather than prior to history is now as theologically mainstream as previously, since, in the words of a

conceivable in positive rather than negative terms. This is because the metaphysical tradition has generally resorted to negations for the purpose of signifying or sketching the outlines of the transcendent or transcendental realm beyond human experience or knowledge. At this point we have arrived at Schopenhauer's conception of transcendental freedom.

However, before we discuss this doctrine, we need to outline the steps and arguments by which Schopenhauer led up to it, beginning with his theory — taken from Kant — of the empirical character and its role in explaining action or the causality of the human body.

For Schopenhauer causal explanation involves three elements — the sufficient cause, its effect, and a quality or force presupposed by explanation that is neither cause nor effect, but which lends potency to the cause and uses the occasion of causality for its manifestation in the phenomenon. We touched on this earlier with the example of a stone falling, whereby its proximity to the ground is the cause and the occasion for the operation of the universal force of gravity. Etiological sciences, such as physics and chemistry, refer to natural forces such as gravity, electricity and impenetrability to explain change by connecting causes with their effects (WWRI pp. 96-7). For example, we might say that the illumination of a room is a change, called the effect, brought about by a prior change or cause, such as the tripping of a light-switch. Although electricity is the crucial factor in this event, it is neither cause nor effect, but one of the ever-present forces that manifest themselves in the changes connected by the law of causality. And, according to Schopenhauer, explanation in the human sciences, such as moral psychology, jurisprudence and history, proceeds in a similar way, connecting the motive or cause with the action or effect by presupposing a third element which is neither, but which lends efficacy to the motive — namely the disposition of the human will or character. But if we think that explanation in the human or moral sciences advances knowledge, then the disposition of the will must be more determinate than the notion implied by the doctrine of its freedom or original indifference towards either good or evil (*liberum arbitrium indifferentiae*). This disposition must be capable of accounting for patterns of behaviour, or why "different individuals act in very different ways when prompted by similar observable motives", as well as

---

contemporary theologian "we are fallen, we are not as we were created to be, we have stepped out of the garden of nature into the open and boundless plain of history. Leaving behind a world and a life at one with itself, a life lived just as it came, in and for the moment and with no care for the morrow, human beings found themselves exposed to all the contingency and uncertainty of life in time" (Pattison (2005a) p. 75).

why "any individual in exactly the same circumstances acts in exactly the same way." (FR1 p. 55)

Schopenhauer called this additional element that connects motive and action the empirical character, which he regarded as both identical and different. In other words, although the universal features of the human species are common to every individual, each person also belongs to its own unique species, because every agent responds to identical circumstances in slightly different ways. The universal and regular operations of the lowest grades of the will — natural forces such as gravity, electricity and cohesion — mean that we can deduce knowledge of their particular manifestations through general concepts or laws, but the individuality of character entails that we cannot deduce or predict an individual agent's behaviour from an Idea of human nature in the abstract. As a result, before we can understand an individual's fundamental traits, including our own, we must build a general picture through observation of particular acts over time (FW p. 42). But this difference between the manifestations of character and those of natural force relates only to our knowledge, since Schopenhauer thought that character determines the connection between motive and action in the same way that forces determine the relation between cause and effect: just as the effect necessarily follows from the appearance of a sufficient cause, so character necessitates action on the appearance of a sufficient motive. The explanatory analogy between the two is therefore significant, and an indication that character shares fundamental properties with forces such as electricity, gravity, cohesion and impenetrability: like these, character reveals itself completely in each of its actions; is original and inborn (in the sense of not being the effect of an individual's early circumstances); and is immutable (FW p. 46). For Schopenhauer, therefore, character is a person's concrete and foundational element, by which he or she has

> fundamental essential qualities that…require only occasioning from without in order to come forth. Consequently, to expect a human being on the same occasion to act at one time in one way and at another in an entirely different way would be like expecting the same tree which bears cherries this summer to bear pears the next. Closely considered, the freedom of the will means an *existentia* without *essentia*; this is equivalent to saying that something *is* and yet at the same time *is nothing*, which again means that it *is not* and thus is a contradiction. (FW p. 51)

And in support of his rejection of the doctrine of the freedom of the will in favour of character-determinism, Schopenhauer referred to the "original and evangelical" doctrines of Augustinian and Lutheran Christianity, such as the Fall, original sin, the post-paradisial servitude of the will and predestination (FW pp. 59-60; WWRI p. 406). He preferred these "profound mysteries" to the minimalist version of Christianity served up by modernising theologians, who, with their "homely, Pelagian intellects" have rejected mystery and reduced Christianity to the realist, optimistic and supposedly demonstrable doctrines of God, the immortal soul and its freedom to work out its own salvation (PPII p. 35). However, Schopenhauer commended Augustinian and Lutheran Christianity as nothing more than *sensu allegorico* equivalents of philosophical truth. Predestination might be seen as equivalent to his teaching that an action is externally necessitated by the law of motivation, while the Fall and original sin communicate in the form of allegory his doctrine of character and its corollary that a person's moral qualities are coeval with his or her existence. However, he complained that when these mysteries are interpreted literally and in alliance with the Old Testament teaching that God created humans out of nothing, they assume an "offensive and absurd" air by implying that God "had summoned into existence a feeble race subject to sin in order then to hand it over to endless torture." (PPII pp. 364-5) Such a scheme inevitably elicits moral disgust and the criticisms of theological rationalists. However, as we saw in Chapter 2, Schopenhauer thought that the dispute between theological rationalists and theological supernaturalists was pointless, insofar as it turned on the erroneous assumption, common to both, that religious doctrines are or ought to consist of literally true propositions about human nature, the world and the events of history. To resolve this dispute, he proposed the middle way of interpreting Christianity's mysteries as allegorical vehicles of a higher truth that finds direct conceptual expression in his own philosophy (PPII p. 389).

One might have expected that Schopenhauer's determinist theory of action would have prompted him to reject the moral world-order and defend a version of Nietzsche's principle of "the innocence of becoming".[16] It is a surprise, therefore, to find him arguing that the sting of conscience, or feelings of regret for what we have done, ought to be taken at face value. This is because our actions inform us that, as the *doers of*

---

[16] Nietzsche (1976a) VII.7. Schopenhauer described the view that the events of life have a physical rather than moral significance "the real *perversity* of mind…that which faith has personified as antichrist." (PPII p. 201) He seems to have thereby supplied Nietzsche with a book title.

our deeds, we are accountable for them, irrespective of the fact that they could not have been otherwise (FW p. 83). However, Schopenhauer acknowledged that there is a seeming contradiction in experiencing regret over actions that we know could not have been otherwise, but offered a transcendental resolution to it by heavily modifying Kant's distinction between the empirical and intelligible character. He maintained that Kant's separation between phenomenon and thing-in-itself had not only secured the compatibility of empirical reality and transcendental ideality, but also explained the possibility of the coexistence of strict empirical necessity with transcendental freedom (FW p. 86). On this view, the intelligible character is the ground of the "I will" by which I identify all of my deeds as my own. It is therefore the *a priori* unity of the agent, indicating a transcendental act of self-constitution, or "indivisible act of will that is outside time." (WWRI p. 156) The empirical character is the multiplication, spread out in space and time, of this transcendental unity, its particular acts of will unfailingly expressing, according to circumstance and motivation, the fixed law of the intelligible character (WWRI p. 289). Since this 'act' of self-constitution is transcendental and prior to time, Schopenhauer maintained that it is free from the necessity that characterises phenomenal events governed by the principle of sufficient reason. And in a move that is both audacious and ingenious, he claimed that since this act of self-constitution is free of necessitating grounds, it is a choice for which the empirical individual is responsible. As a result, Schopenhauer thought that regret over deeds that could not have been otherwise is not as quixotic as it seems, for such actions announce to us not merely what we have done, but who we are or what sort of character we have, for our actions unfailingly display our inner nature. And, although what we have done was necessitated by our nature meeting with external circumstances, what we are was freely chosen before our individuality appeared in the phenomenon, and is therefore the ultimate object of our feelings of accountability.

In Schopenhauer's view, his doctrine that our empirical existence is the product, or more properly the visibility in space and time, of a pre-phenomenal and individual 'Platonic Idea' or intelligible essence, was the only theory able to combine conscience and regret over what we have done with act-determinism. By contrast, he argued that the doctrine of God's creation out of nothing undermines the moral world-order and responsibility for what we have done with its teaching that the creator determined the nature or essence of each character when he called it out of an original nothingness. But theism thereby contradicts itself insofar as it depicts our nature as conditioned by another and our acts as free. But, in accordance with the maxim *operari sequitur esse* ('action follows from being'), if the creator determined what we are, then any putative freedom ascribed to the creature is annulled by the omnipotent freedom of the creator, so that theism actually negates moral responsibility by attributing our nature, and thus ultimately our actions, to God:

> the concept of a *moral freedom* is inseparable from that of *primordial orig-*
> *inality.* For that a being is the work of another but is nevertheless *free* as
> regards his willing and acting, is something that may be said in words but
> cannot be conceived in thought. Thus whoever called him into existence out
> of nothing at the same time created and determined his true nature, that is
> to say, all his attributes and qualities...so theism and man's moral respon-
> sibility are incompatible because such responsibility always comes home to
> a man's author and originator who is really the centre of gravity of that
> responsibility...The *free* being must also be the *original*. If our will is *free*,
> so too is the *primary and fundamental nature*; and conversely. (PPII
> pp. 235-6)

However, Schopenhauer's doctrine that individual existence is the result of a Fall from transcendental freedom is not merely audacious and ingenious, but equally vulnerable to some of the objections he brings against cosmological arguments. For example, if the notion of a cause beginning to act without a preceding change is inconceivable to the understanding, so is the notion of a will acting outside spatio-temporal conditions. And apart from the difficulties raised in obtaining a clear conception of this notion, Schopenhauer's doctrine of character also seems incompatible with his metaphysics of the will. Character for him is individual, so that whereas his other Platonic Ideas include many particulars under them, he claims that "every person is to be regarded...as a special Idea", and as the sole member of their own unique species (WWRI p. 132). But this seems to import the plurality of the phenomenon (and therefore space and time) into the thing-in-itself by reintroducing transcendental objects or "things-in-themselves", which Schopenhauer criticised Kant for not clearing from his system (WWRI p. 444). On a few occasions Schopenhauer did acknowledge the possibility that his doctrine of the transcendental individuality of character contradicted the monism of his metaphysics of the will. However, he raised the issue only to pass over it, stating that the metaphysical roots of individuality "is one of those questions I do not undertake to answer." (PPII p. 227)

Schopenhauer's defence of his doctrines of intelligible character and transcendental freedom tended to rely more on anecdote and appeal to putative precursors than on proof or argument. He cited the first two of

Kant's critical works as his main source for the distinction, but Kant's use of it to explain the radical evil in human nature in his late work, *Religion within the Limits of Reason Alone*, comes closer to Schopenhauer's version. Kant referred to a subjective ground or "disposition" (*Gesinnung*) that determines every empirical deed, a disposition that proceeds from a pre-temporal "deed of freedom" for which the individual rather than nature must bear either the credit or the blame (*Schuld*).[17] Schopenhauer maintained that a dim presentiment of the same truth inspired Plato's picture of pre-natal souls choosing the circumstances of their future lives in the *Myth of Er*.[18] However, he claimed that Plato's ignorance of transcendental idealism led him to present this insight mythically, "in the form of time...and in connection with metempsychosis." (BM p. 113) He speculated that Plato may have learnt this doctrine from Egyptian priests, whose religion was of Indian origin (PPI p. 60), for Schopenhauer detected the same basic insight in the doctrine common to all Indian religions, that of *karma* and rebirth. On his understanding, this doctrine communicates the philosophical doctrine of transcendental freedom in the form of allegory by teaching that every individual inherits an immutable, *a priori* constitution that is the residue, or fruit, of actions performed in a previous life (WWRI p. 355).

Lastly, Schopenhauer claimed that the Platonic-Christian doctrine of Adam as the symbolic Form of fallen humanity, in whose guilt and suffering we participate, was a further allegorical support for his doctrine of the intelligible character's fall from transcendental freedom into empirical necessity (WWRII p. 628).[19] As different as the Indian and Christian doctrines appear on the surface, Schopenhauer stated that "both identify, and indeed with a moral tendency, the existing person with one who has existed previously; transmigration of souls does this directly, original sin indirectly", since Adam is represented as the ancestor of the human race rather than as man in the universal (WWRII pp. 506-7). Schopenhauer commended these religious doctrines insofar as they indicate in different ways that we have inherited our present constitution from a previous existence, and that moral judgement refers to what we are, indeed to our

---

[17] Kant (1960) 6:21.

[18] Plato (1987) 617d-619e.

[19] Schopenhauer seemed unaware that his metaphysical interpretation of the Fall was pre-empted by Origen and other theologians from the Alexandrian school, who tended to interpret the Bible as a repository of Platonic allegories. There is, however, a great difference between a third-century Christian Platonist for whom all things are signs and allegories, and a nineteenth-century philosopher who thinks that religious doctrines are 'mere allegory'.

very existence, rather than what we do, in agreement with the maxim *operari sequitur esse* ('action follows from being'). However, he thought that the various forms in which they present this insight was literally false, for they commit what Kant called the *"fallacy of subreption"*[20] insofar as they represent space, time and causality as real, transcendent qualities, and thus paradoxically assign a temporal and causal origin for a transcendental, perduring state of the subject. For this reason, Schopenhauer thought that an *explicit* recognition of their allegorical nature would preserve their integrity and future influence, whereas insisting on their literal, *sensu proprio* truth would invite rationalist criticism. However, he was pleased to discover that the inner meaning of religious doctrines formulated in different times and in remote places is in fundamental agreement with the conceptual truths of his own system, for this confirmed his conviction that his philosophy is no invented fable or eccentric construction, but the conceptual and systematic presentation of the pre-understandings about the world and life that humans have entertained for millennia (WWRI p. 383).

II. Ethics and Immortality

In the previous section we saw that Schopenhauer's doctrines of the ontological primacy of suffering and evil and the necessity of the acts of the will can be interpreted as indirect rather than head-on responses to the best defences of theodicy — the privation of the good and the freedom of the will. Yet, we have also seen how Schopenhauer enlisted certain Christian doctrines in support of some of his positions, such as the Fall of Adam, which indicates that "existence is certainly to be regarded as an error or mistake" (WWRII p. 605); the doctrine of the will's bondage to evil through original sin, which proclaims that "since we are what we ought *not* to be, we also necessarily do what we ought *not* to do" (WWRII p. 604); and the doctrine that suffering and death are the wages of sin, which confirms the maxim of eternal justice that "it is the great *sin of the world* which produces the many and great *sufferings of the world*" (PPII p. 302). Schopenhauer identified these immanent and pessimistic teachings as the core of Augustinian and Lutheran Christianity, and annexed them as weighty allies against the optimism and rationalism of modern "Pelagianism" (WWRII pp. 167-8). He thought that if the

---

[20] Kant (1987) 257.

sublime mysteries of Augustinian and Lutheran Christianity were to endure the critical outlook of the age and continue to cater to the spiritual needs of Europe, they needed to be separated from the doctrines of God and creation, since these are not merely contradicted by experience, but undermine eternal justice and divest human beings of responsibility by teaching that they have received their nature from another.

But Schopenhauer's objections to theism did not end there, for he laid down two further criteria for religio-metaphysical schemes: they must give an intellectually viable explanation of the phenomenon of virtue, as embodied in the lives of philanthropists and the great saints of the world's religions, and — most important of all — they must offer consolation for the certainty of death (PPI p. 121). According to Schopenhauer, Judaeo-Christianity fails on both counts, and — again — on account of the doctrines of God and creation out of nothing.

Most nineteenth-century Europeans (and perhaps still many today) considered it an axiom that God is the only sufficient support for morality and atheism a morally and socially disastrous position. In the words commonly (albeit erroneously) attributed to Ivan Karamazov, "if God is dead, then everything is permitted".[21] We have already seen that Schopenhauer rejected this reasoning, defining the *credo* of every good man as "I believe in a system of metaphysics" rather than 'I believe in God' (WWRII p. 175). However, he not only thought that the existence of God was an unnecessary condition for morality, but that the history of theism also showed that it had frequently been insufficient. Theologians have constructed the content of God's will from "the exceedingly hazardous medium of dubious documents and of their interpretation by the priestly caste" (MRIII p. 483), with the result that it is just as common to find God legislating acts of pure virtue as those of malicious cruelty.

Ultimately, Schopenhauer thought that abstract maxims and commandments could never be the ground of an action's ethical worth. This is because reflective reason is simply the medium rather than the agent of choice. Its function is limited to presenting possible maxims of action to the real sovereign — the inner character or will — to register which maxims are most pleasing to it, and to calculate the shortest route to their satisfaction. As a result, action in accordance with virtue does not

---

[21] Ivan actually says "[t]here is no virtue if there's no immortality" (Dostoyevsky (1982) p. 78), which tends to confirm Schopenhauer's argument that theological morality represents individual immortality as a *reward* for moral observance (BM p. 55). It therefore appeals to egoism and the will-to-live by promising the continued existence of the individual.

proceed from concepts or depend on holding certain beliefs, but is a manifestation of the inner disposition or will of the individual agent. Maxims or commandments can therefore do no more than guide the will or set it in a new direction. When, therefore, the will of God is presented as a motive for virtue, in most cases it has to appeal to egoism and self-love to be efficacious, enforcing morality in the same way that the state enforces its laws, through sanctions backed up by threats of punishment and promises of reward (BM p. 137). Theological morality, therefore, appeals to prudence rather than sanctity, and operates in a similar fashion to Hegel's cunning of reason, being a ruse by which egoists are duped into behaving *as if* virtuous.

Schopenhauer acknowledged that pure, disinterested virtue, which for him was stimulated by compassionate identification with the sufferings of another and manifested in acts to remove their source (BM pp. 145-6), may be drawn out and encouraged by theological doctrines. However, ultimately he thought that dogmas, concepts and beliefs were incapable of producing virtue or removing primary egoism. A compassionate person or saint who believes in monotheistic doctrines may attribute his or her sainthood to this system of beliefs, but Schopenhauer commented that a "saint may be full of the most absurd superstition, or, on the other hand, may be a philosopher; it is all the same." (WWRI p. 383) Sainthood and virtue do not depend upon logical proficiency in deducing valid maxims from religious dogmas. They spring instead "from intuitively appre-hended, immediate knowledge of the world and of its inner nature" (Ibid), and the impact that this species of non-rational knowledge (*Erkennt-nis*) exerts on the saint's inner character or will. As a consequence, reli-gious dogmas are merely epiphenomenal. They are occasionally useful insofar as they enable a saint to explain his actions to himself, but they more often conceal their true origin (WWRI p. 368). As for those mono-theists whose character does not dispose them towards compassion or sainthood and whose religious life consists merely in believing and per-forming rituals, Schopenhauer thought that their religious affiliation is equally likely to discourage acts of compassion and kindness as to encour-age them. In the case of many, their monotheism is simply an extra motive for enmity against infidels and non-believers, while concentration on performance of ritual duties can often assume the status of a substitute for love shown to humanity (PPII p. 354).

Schopenhauer also thought that the dominance of theological morality had distorted philosophical reflection on ethics in the same way, and for the same reason, that the officially sanctioned dogmatic theism had impeded the progress of philosophical metaphysics. The source of these errors was an anthropology which presented the human being as God's analogue, a purely spiritual, rational and thinking substance that transcends the material realm. Presupposing this model, the metaphysical speculations of scholasticism "feasted only on formulas and words" (WWRI p. 48) or consisted of a *"continued misuse of universal concepts"* (WWRII p. 40), while philosophical ethics has constructed "artificial concept-combinations" in the vain hope that they might place "bridle and bit on the impulse of strong desires, the storm of passion, and the gigantic stature of egoism." (BM p. 62) Schopenhauer cited Kant's legislative ethics as the most recent and spectacular instance of a rationalist morality dependent on and corrupted by theological paradigms. Although Kant had extricated himself from dogmatic metaphysics in the *Critique of Pure Reason*, and was the first to demonstrate that "the undeniable moral significance of human conduct" is "quite different from, and not dependent on, the laws of the phenomenon" and "not even capable of explanation according to them" (WWR I p. 422), Schopenhauer claimed that Kant had banished self-love and the doctrines of theology from ethics more in appearance than reality (BM p. 49). He thought this was especially evident in Kant's justification of the categorical imperative, for Kant's notions of respect, command, duty and obligation to the moral law are denuded of all logical sense and moral weight when divorced from the context of belief in God (BM p. 55). Kant's ethical theory is therefore philosophically unverifiable and has external grounds for its justification, such as faith in authority, its true paradigm being the Mosaic Decalogue (BM p. 54). As a result, Schopenhauer maintained that it is no surprise to find Kant shoring up his categorical imperative with theological doctrines — the practical postulates of God, freedom and immortality — since theology was always the unacknowledged basis of Kant's ethics (BM p. 57). And with the introduction of the postulates, Kant made every categorical imperative into a hypothetical one in reality, and therefore, like the theological ethics that preceded him, appealed to and confirmed the propriety of egoism and self-love as the real bases of virtue (BM p. 103).

Schopenhauer maintained that the legislative form of both theological and Kantian ethics is fundamentally at odds with the spirit of "true and original" (as opposed to merely historical) Christianity. He found this spirit manifested in the compassionate actions and self-renunciation of the great saints of Christendom, whose self-denial testifies to the Christian insight that all striving for justification along the path of the principle of sufficient reason of acting is religiously impotent, in agreement with the maxim "since we are what we ought *not* to be, we also necessarily do what we ought *not* to do." (WWRII p. 604) For this reason, he affirmed the Augustinian and Lutheran doctrine of justification by faith, since it teaches that

> works according to law and precept, i.e., according to motives, can never satisfy justice or save us, but salvation is to be gained only through faith, in other words, through a changed way of knowledge. (WWRI p. 407)

He regarded this teaching of salvation through faith, or through a "changed way of knowledge", as an allegorical counterpart of his explanation that actions of genuine moral worth spring not from concepts operating as motives, but from the impact of inarticulate, intuitive knowledge of the inner identity of all things on the disposition of character or will (WWRI p. 408).

In Schopenhauer's view, therefore, Christianity is not in origin and essence a communal religion of divine commandments and rituals praising and glorifying God. This is merely what it became over time and through the accidents of history. It is, instead, a purely soteriological religion. Commandments acting as motives and the performance of religious rituals for personal gain merely appeal to natural man represented by the Idea of Adam, the symbol of the affirmation of the will, while Christianity insists on salvation through "a complete transformation of our nature and disposition" (WWRII p. 604), represented allegorically as rebirth and participation in the Idea of Christ the redeemer, the symbol of the denial of the will-to-live (WWRI p. 405). While theological ethics legislates the impossible by commanding us to change our conduct while our essential nature remains unchanged, the superior wisdom of Christianity (in agreement with "Brahmanism and Buddhism") is shown by the fact that it states that salvation requires us to "become something quite different from, indeed the very opposite of, what we are." (WWRII p. 604) This superior ethical outlook was what enabled Christianity to supplant the shallow optimism and purely civic morality of Greco-Roman paganism, as a result of which it rescued Europe from a "crude, shallow identification of itself with an ephemeral, uncertain, and hollow existence" (PPII pp. 347-8). According to Schopenhauer, the curve of Christian ethics describes a loosening of the bonds first to self-centred action, then to all attachment to natural existence:

> Christianity preached not merely justice, but loving kindness, sympathy, compassion, benevolence, forgiveness, love of one's enemy, patience,

humility, renunciation, faith, and hope. In fact it went further; it taught that the world is evil and that we need salvation. Accordingly, it preached a contempt for the world, self-denial, chastity, giving up of one's own will, that is, turning away from life and its delusive pleasures. Indeed, it taught one to recognise the sanctifying force of suffering; an instrument of torture is the symbol of Christianity. (PPII p. 348)

Such an anti-natural ethics is, argued Schopenhauer, inconsistent with theoretical theism and its doctrines of God's good creation and ethics of obedience to the divine law. Disinterested compassion (*Mitleid*) — and self-renunciation as an intensification of its inner tendency — finds its true metaphysical explanation not in theism, but in the age-old monist doctrine of One in All, which asserts the identity of all beings through their inner essence. Schopenhauer maintained that this was why the Old Testament God reappeared "tacitly allegorised" in the New as a symbol of love (PPII p. 363; PPI p. 142). But whereas other versions of the metaphysical doctrine of the One in All might be capable of accounting for compassion or actions directed towards another, an ascetic morality of self-mortification and voluntary acceptance of suffering is explicable only on the presupposition that virtue is purchased at the cost of the inner essence of the world, as taught by Schopenhauer's principle of the denial of the world-will. For this reason, he claimed that his teaching "could be called Christian philosophy proper, paradoxical as this may seem to those who do not go to the root of the matter, but merely stick to the surface." (PPII p. 315) He detected the same moral and ascetic tendencies in the ancient religions of India, Brahmanism and Buddhism, and claimed that such uniformity, manifested in vastly separated times and places, shows that the inner springs of religion are not dogmas but inner intuitions. Their agreement also shows that his philosophical ethics of compassion and asceticism is

> not some philosophical fable, invented by myself and only of today. No, it was the enviable life of so many saints and great souls among the Christians, and even more among the Hindus and Buddhists, and also among the believers of other religions. Different as were the dogmas that were impressed on their faculty of reason, the inner, direct, and intuitive knowledge from which alone all virtue and holiness can come is nevertheless expressed in precisely the same way in the conduct of life. (WWRI p. 383)

The last of Schopenhauer's objections to theism consists of his accusation that it is incapable of sustaining a viable doctrine of a future life, which he regarded as "the strongest and essential point" of any metaphysical interpretation (WWRII p. 161). A religio-metaphysical interpretation stands or falls with its doctrine of immortality on account of the fact that the knowledge and the fear of death are central to human consciousness. Whereas an "animal learns to know death only when he dies", the reflective capacities of human beings means that every individual "consciously draws every hour nearer his death" (WWRI p. 37). Theistic religions may pretend that the existence of God or the gods is the main point, but if

> continued existence after death could also be proved to be incompatible with the existence of gods, because, let us say, it presupposed originality of mode of existence, they would soon sacrifice these gods to their own immortality, and be eager for atheism. (WWRII pp. 161-2)

In many ways this quotation expresses the nub of Schopenhauer's prediction of the decline of Judaeo-Christian monotheism, for its doctrine that God created humans out of nothing denies "originality of mode of existence", and thereby renders God not merely superfluous to but also incompatible with the central criterion of metaphysical need. The absence of a doctrine of immortality in the Old Testament is therefore consistent, since the "assumption that man is created out of nothing necessarily leads to the assumption that death is his absolute end." (WWRII p. 488) The other two monotheist religions, Christianity and Islam, have affixed a doctrine of immortality to creation out of nothing by teaching that every appearance from original nothingness on the occasion of an individual's birth (or conception) is the beginning of an eternal existence. But such a teaching is fit only for belief, since its attempt to combine radical contingency with continued existence renders it unlikely. Schopenhauer traced the clamour for political reform among nineteenth-century English factory workers and Young Hegelians in Germany to the shakiness of combining creation out of nothing with the expectation of personal immortality. Having had such doctrines impressed on their minds at an early age and later realising their incompatibility, he claimed that Europeans have been rendered unreceptive to alternative metaphysical pictures, and have as a result sunk to the "absolutely physical viewpoint." (WWRII p. 464)

However, in opposition to the doctrine of creation out of nothing Schopenhauer advanced the scholastic maxim "*Ex nihilo nihil fit, et in nihilum nihil potest reverti* [Nothing comes out of nothing, and nothing can again become nothing]" (WWRII p. 487). In other words, just as moral responsibility implies freedom and therefore "originality of mode of existence", so does immortality, which leaves us free to dispense with the services of the gods (WWRII p. 161). Schopenhauer erected a doctrine of post-mortem survival on his metaphysics, but preferred to speak of the "timelessness" or "indestructibility" of our inner nature rather than its immortality, probably because he thought that the latter notion had been too closely associated with dogmas of the individual's survival after death (WWRI p. 282). He offered two different theories of post-mortem existence, both of which ultimately lead back to or presuppose metaphysical originality. The first of these is a hybrid of naturalism and transcendentalism. As mentioned previously, Schopenhauer's conception of causality maintains that only the forms of objects arise and perish, while matter and the forces of nature (of which matter is the visibility), are imperishable:

> Because the strong arm that three thousand years ago bent the bow of Ulysses no longer exists, no reflective and well-regulated understanding will look upon the force that acted so energetically in it as entirely annihilated. Therefore, on further reflection, it will not be assumed that the force that bends the bow today, first began to exist with that arm. (WWRII p. 471)

This theory of the eternity of matter and natural force is supported by further considerations taken from Kant's doctrine of the ideality of time and Schopenhauer's metaphysics. Schopenhauer maintained that he who has truly absorbed the "higher" view afforded by philosophy will realise that birth and death are only mutually conditioning events of the phenomenon, which do not disturb the content compressed into the present, the will, and its mirror or reflection, the subject of knowledge. Buoyed up by the certainty that the separation of that which exists into past, present and future is merely phenomenal, Schopenhauer stated that he who affirms the will in its objectification as a world

> would look with indifference at death hastening towards him on the wing of time. He would consider it as a false illusion, an impotent spectre, frightening to the weak but having no power over him who knows that he himself is that will of which the whole world is the objectification or copy, to which therefore life and also the present always remain certain and sure. (WWRI p. 284)[22]

Schopenhauer acknowledged that these considerations are unlikely to appear consoling to all those who have been educated to think that humanity is set apart from animals and the rest of nature, and who imagine that "under the boastful name of immortality" their individual personality, or soul, will endure for eternity (WWRII p. 482). However, he

---

[22] Providing Nietzsche with materials for thought, Schopenhauer comments that he who attains this perspective might wish that the course of his life be of "endless duration or of constant recurrence [endloser Dauer, oder von immer neuer Wiederkehr];" (WWRI p. 284).

thought that the anthropomorphic perspectives of theism, of which the immortality of the soul is a corollary, needed to be rooted out before the doctrine of the indestructibility of our inner nature, the only view capable of offering metaphysical consolation for death in a critical age, would become acceptable. He referred to the Indian religions as evidence that an impersonal account of continued existence is capable of offering consolation for death, for in the subcontinent we see "contempt for death of which we in Europe have no conception." (WWRII pp. 463-4) He discovered two accounts of post-mortem existence in the Indian religions, both of which presuppose "originality of mode of existence". On the one side is the popular allegory of the transmigration of the soul, and on the other the *sensu proprio* explanation of this found in the *Upaniṣads* concerning the Self's identity with all things. With regard to the latter doctrine, Schopenhauer commented that he who dies "with the words of the sacred *Upaniṣads* on his lips or even in his heart: *hae omnes creaturae in totum ego sum, et praetor me aliud ens non est* [I am all these creatures, every one of them, and besides me no other being exists]" will accept death "calmly and serenely." (PPI p. 125)

As we have seen, Schopenhauer maintained that Islam and Christianity were inconsistent in this regard, insofar as they took their theories of immortality from "other and better doctrines, and yet retained the God creator." (PPI p. 125) He does not specify which "other and better doctrines" he has in mind, but it would not be a surprise to find that he was referring to those of Brahmanism and Buddhism. Subsequent to his early encounter with the religions of India and his discovery of their opposition to the metaphysics of the Old Testament, Schopenhauer soon developed the habit of tracing everything he found good or favourable in other religions to Indian wisdom. This often encouraged him to assert some rather arbitrary associations which might, on first sight, appear to be intuitive, but which dissolve under closer scrutiny. If I am right to suspect that Schopenhauer meant to convey that Christianity and Islam derived their doctrines of immortality from the "better doctrines" of Hinduism and Buddhism, then this would be another manifestation of his uncritical enthusiasm for everything Indian. This is so because there is no clear passage from either transmigration or Upaniṣadic union to the New Testament doctrine of the resurrection of the body, the Qur'anic picture of paradise, and the theological doctrine common to both religions of the immortality of the soul in heaven. In fact, the only feature common to all is that, in one way or another, they are all doctrines of continued existence.

However, Schopenhauer would have known that Islam and Christianity obtained their conception of the soul from Greek philosophers such as Pythagoras and Plato, whose theories of a transmigrating intellect were, perhaps, the "other and better doctrines" to which he refers. These philosophers would therefore be the link connecting Islamic and Christian conceptions of immortality to India, since Schopenhauer claimed that Pythagoras and Plato obtained their doctrines of metempsychosis from Egypt (WWRII p. 505), and that the religion of Egyptian priests originated in India (PPII p. 383). However, it seems that he thought that the Christian and Islamic doctrines had transformed the Indian, Egyptian and Greek conception of the soul by assimilating it to the anthropomorphic outlook he associated with Jewish theism, and which he regarded as a metaphysical elaboration of the Genesis narrative in which God distinguishes Adam by appointing him lord and master over nature (BM pp. 177-8; PPII p. 370). As a result, Islam and Christianity teach that the individual personality, or "transcendent hypostasis called soul" (WWRII p. 198) survives death, whereas neither Hinduism nor Buddhism hypostatise the human personality, but

> faithful to truth, definitely recognise the evident kinship of man with the whole of nature in general and the animals in particular and represent him, by metempsychosis and otherwise, as being closely connected with the animal world. (PPII p. 370)[23]

This is because Schopenhauer knew that the transmigrating element in Indian metempsychosis was not the human personality, but a more refined element that is united with a new nature at every rebirth. The difference, therefore, between Christian and Islamic conceptions of the immortality of the soul in heaven and the Indian doctrine of metempsychosis consists in the fact that the theistic version not only lifts human beings out of the natural cycle by making heaven a terminal state, but, more importantly, depicts the soul as personal rather than non-personal. It seems, then, that Schopenhauer thought that Christianity and Islam had reconciled the "better doctrine" of metempsychosis to the anthropomorphic perspectives of theism by denying transmigration and retaining only the notion of the soul, upon which was affixed one, inalienable personality at the moment of its creation out of nothing, and with which it must learn to get along for an eternity thereafter.

---

[23] We saw in Chapter 1 that one of Herder's main objections to transmigration was its tendency to dissolve the unity of humanity (*Humanität*) into the natural world (see p. 34).

Schopenhauer offered his previous theory of post-mortem survival as a *consolation* for death, which therefore presupposes the affirmation of the will-to-live, or humanity's participation in the Idea of Adam (WWRII p. 628). Schopenhauer's second theory view is soteriological, relevant to those who want to die actually rather than apparently, and in whom knowledge (*Erkenntnis*) has quietened the will and brought about the realisation that liberation from existence rather than reconstitution as a new individual is the most desirable state, since "individuality is no perfection but a limitation, and that to be rid of it is, therefore, no loss, but rather a gain." (PPII p. 282) In Schopenhauer's view, such an individual finds consolation not in the prospect of the eternity of natural force or the ideality of time, but in the denial of his inner essence as will.

Schopenhauer's doctrine of the denial of the will-to-live has frequently been interpreted as annihilationist.[24] However, whether or not Schopenhauer meant it to be annihilationist or mystical is a fruitless debate, since his Kantian strictures on transcendent knowledge prohibits him from saying what becomes of the will after it has turned and denied itself. His descriptions of the ascetic are fairly ambiguous, for while at one point he is said to be "poor, cheerless and full of privation", he is also "full of inner cheerfulness and true heavenly peace...an unshakeable peace, a deep calm and inward serenity, a state that we cannot behold without the greatest longing" (WWRI pp. 389-90). However, on a Schopenhauerian view, terms such as "peace", "calm" and "serenity" may seem to bear a positive meaning, but are in fact simply negations of "the restless pressure and effort...the constant transition from desire to apprehension and from joy to sorrow" that characterises life conditioned by the will (WWRI p. 411). And herein lies the central difficulty in deciding whether Schopenhauer's soteriological scheme of the denial of the will is annihilationist or not, since "we lack image, concept, and word" to describe the condition of the ascetic saint, because thought and language presuppose the construction of the world, the objectification and affirmation of the will-to-live, in relation to which its opposite appears as a "mere negation." (WWRII p. 609)

---

[24] This interpretation, enunciated recently by Roger Pol-Droit (Pol-Droit (2003) p. 92), gained credence from Schopenhauer's first disciples. For example, Philip Mainländer interpreted the denial of the will as a death-wish and duly committed suicide on completion of his book, *Die Philosophie der Erlösung*, in 1876. Nietzsche also promulgated the annihilationist interpretation of Schopenhauer, but also considered Mainländer to be one of Schopenhauer's crankier followers (Nietzsche (1974) §357).

We touched on the problem of Schopenhauer's use of negative terminology in the last chapter, where we drew a distinction between Denys
Turner's theory of dialectical apophaticism in Dionysius the Areopagite
and others, and Schopenhauer's far more severe employment of negative
language. Whereas Turner's theory has it that apophatic language
establishes God's transcendence of human thought and language, for
Schopenhauer negative terms do not assert the transcendence of the
thing-in-itself as will but its denial, and since the will is the essence of
the phenomenon, it is questionable whether there can be anything left
over when the body of the ascetic, in whom the will has turned and
denied itself, finally perishes. Schopenhauer acknowledged that his
account of salvation seems, from the ordinary perspective, to augur
annihilation and an entry into nothingness, but argued that the concept of
nothing is necessarily relative to that which it negates. In the case of
salvation, therefore, what is negated is the world or the phenomenon, so
that the denial of the will indicates not an absolute nothingness (*nihil
negativum*), but a relative nothingness (*nihil privativum*) (WWRI p. 409).
However, it is not clear whether this argument is meant to be consoling,
since it could be interpreted as a logician's version of the wisdom of
Silenus. On this reading, the absolute nothingness (*nihil negativum*)
would refer to Silenus' best state of all — never to have existed — and
the relative nothingness (*nihil privativum*) to the second best state available to all those who have the misfortune of having fallen into existence
— to die very soon. If this is so, then Schopenhauer's soteriology of the
denial of the will might be described as decidedly annihilationist.

However, the recent resurgence of interest in Schopenhauer among
theologians has led to a different interpretation of Schopenhauer's contrast
between a relative and absolute nothingness. In the previously mentioned
works of Mannion, Gonzales and King, the former notion has been
baptised as a species of God, while Schopenhauer appears as a descend-
ant of Rhineland mysticism, whose doctrine of the denial of the will
appears as the negative expression for a mystical state of union with a
being known as "relative nothingness". For example, Gerard Mannion
states that

> Schopenhauer's 'relative nothing' which confronts the person who has
> denied the will is like the God who, for Rahner, remains incomprehensible,
> in a sense, *even in* the beatific vision because it is then that the one behold-
> ing that 'vision' realises their own true relation to that which has given them
> their own very being.[25]

[25] Mannion (2003) p. 277.

Although there is a very definite strain of mysticism in Schopenhauer's soteriology of the denial of the will, Mannion has erroneously hypostatised Schopenhauer's conception of a relative nothing and raised it to the level of an ineffable reality, for Schopenhauer nowhere states that it is something that "confronts the person who has denied the will". He was very cautious to avoid making transcendent statements about the state of the mystic who has denied his nature as will, but also kept open the possibility that it was not simply annihilationist. For example, he maintains that, from the contrary perspective of mysticism, the contrast between the world as the positive factor and salvation as its negation is reversed, so that what "exists for us" appears as nothing, "and this nothing as that which exists." (WWRI p. 410) However, Schopenhauer was consistently critical of the rationalist habit of making words such as "nothing" into things or realities, and ultimately thought that what the will might be or become in its denial is beyond our ability to know. If, however, these abstract considerations are not sufficient to "banish the dark impression of that nothingness…which we fear as children fear darkness" (WWRI p. 411), Schopenhauer recommended that we supplement our reliance on negations stemming from constraints on knowledge by reading the positive (but necessarily figurative) soteriological accounts contained in religious literature. He especially valued the writings of Christians such as Meister Eckhart, Tauler and the anonymous author of the *German Theology*, of the Sufis of Islam, but in his opinion best of all the mysticism of the Indian religions, of the *Upaniṣads* and of Buddhism.[26] Irrespective of the fact that these mystics have expressed themselves using different and contradictory conceptual schemes, such as union with God, reabsorption in *Brahman* and *nirvāṇa*, Schopenhauer claimed that they all proceed from an identical experiential base (WWRII p. 614). We may take some sort of solace from their unanimous testimony to the positive bliss and rapture to be gained through liberation from the pressure to will, but insofar as they attempt to communicate knowledge of transcendent states, they are "unable to convince." (WWRII p. 614)

It might be asked whether Schopenhauer's theories of continued existence and soteriology really do offer *consolation* in the face of suffering and death, for the indestructibility of the force in my arm and of the metaphysical essence of the phenomenon, or the possibility that the will may become something else in its denial, seem equally irrelevant to my

---

[26] In keeping with his general lack of interest in Judaism, Schopenhauer was unaware of the historical importance of its mystical tradition. For an account of mystical Judaism, see de Lange (1986) Chapter 7.

fears about *my* death. As Antony Flew remarks, "the news of the immortality of my soul would be of no more concern to me than the news that my appendix would be preserved eternally in a bottle",[27] and this objection applies *a fortiori* to Schopenhauer's theory of continued existence, insofar as it is distinctly non-personal. However, Schopenhauer's theory of continued existence seems to have offered consolation to at least one reader, albeit a fictional one. Having read the chapter 'On Death and its Relation to the Indestructibility of Our Inner Nature' in the second edition of *The World as Will and Representation*, Thomas Buddenbrook derives solace from the reflection that he is more than simply a link in the chain of a family in decline, but is instead

> the seed, the tendency, the possibility of all capacity and all achievement. Where should I be were I not here? Who, what, how could I be, if I were not I — if this my eternal self, my consciousness, did not cut me off from those who are not I? Organism! Blind, thoughtless, pitiful eruption of the urging will! Better, indeed, for the will to float free in spaceless, timeless night than for it to languish in prison, illuminated by the feeble, flickering light of the intellect.[28]

Subsequent to Mann, this view that an impersonal portion of each individual lives on as some sort of generalised life-force has frequently been offered as a consolation for death.[29] It might be said that the posthumous triumph of Schopenhauer's theory of continued existence is an indication of how far western thought has traversed from the personalist assumptions of its central metaphysical tradition, assumptions whose incipient decline prompted Hamlet to grieve at the reflection that the 'stuff' of Alexander the Great's body might now stop up a beer-barrel.[30]

III. Indian Christianity

In this chapter and the last we have observed how Schopenhauer traced theism to the will rather than the intellect; followed his supplement to Kant's refutation of natural theology; seen him measure the central doctrines of theism against the testimony of experience, only to find them

---

[27] Flew (1955) p. 270.
[28] Mann (1996) pp. 526-7.
[29] Paul Harrison, Founder and President of the World Pantheist Movement, maintains that many pantheists "find great comfort in the idea that when they die, their elements and energy will melt and merge into the nature that they love and will enable new life to emerge." (Harrison (1999) p. 103)
[30] Shakespeare, *Hamlet*, V.i, 209-214.

wanting; and learnt why he thought these doctrines fail to satisfy the requirements of metaphysical need. But although we have witnessed Schopenhauer dispensing with doctrines that, from an historical perspective, seem intrinsic to Christianity — the existence of God, creation out of nothing, the goodness of creation, the freedom of the will, and the immortality of the soul — we have also seen how he constructed non-Christian and non-theological arguments to vindicate the doctrines of the Fall, original sin, the equality of suffering and desert, predestination, and the need for salvation from the human condition through self-sacrifice and asceticism. It is clear that Schopenhauer looked upon Christianity as a complex of contradictory doctrines that falls apart under critical examination. His critique of theism was mounted to separate the genuine pre-cognitive categories of authentic Christian existence from the metaphysics that had previously served as their justification, but which had come into conflict with "the advanced spirit of the times". He stated that if, "as has often been feared, and especially at the present time", Christianity's conflict with the general culture should issue in its decline, the main cause would be that "it does not consist of one simple element, but of two originally heterogeneous elements, brought into combination only by means of world events." Yet, even if the religion should disappear, he predicted that its "purely ethical part would still be bound always to remain intact, because it is indestructible." (WWRI p. 388)

Schopenhauer's project of modernising Christianity by releasing its kernel from a merely historical shell has many points in common with Rudolf Bultmann's demythologisation of the New Testament in the 1920s. As George Pattison states, in a technological age Bultmann maintained "that we cannot use the electric light and believe in the New Testament world of demons and miracles."[31] Under the guidance of Heidegger's existential analytic, Bultmann sought to recover the basic existential structures of original Christian existence, concealed within the ontico-mythical cosmology of first century Palestine and recorded in the New Testament. However, ultimately, any comparison between Schopenhauer and Bultmann on Christianity can be no more than formal or methodological, insofar as Bultmann did not consider the existence of God to number among Christianity's outmoded beliefs.[32]

Schopenhauer drew on several criteria in defence of his particular conception of the distinction between the kernel and shell in historical

---

[31] Pattison (2005b) p. 19.
[32] Bultmann (1984) p. 155.

Christianity. The first of these was founded on his epistemological distinction between intuition and reason, according to which the true essence of Christianity consists of those doctrines that communicate in the medium of allegory insights about the world and life, while its expendable portion consists of the transcendent doctrines of God and the soul, both of which are merely abstract concept-combinations that support metaphysical anthropomorphism. The next criterion derives from his axiological distinction between optimistic and pessimistic world-views, and leads to Schopenhauer's detection of an identical fault-line dividing the pessimistic tenor of Christianity's immanent teachings from the optimistic outlook communicated by its transcendent doctrines. In addition, he found that these epistemological and axiological criteria of distinction were confirmed by a historically-based contrast, according to which the transcendent and optimistic complex of doctrines stem from the Old Testament and the religious milieu in which Christianity was founded, while the immanent and pessimistic doctrines founded on intuition belong to Christianity proper. Since he thought that the transcendent doctrines had come into conflict with modern knowledge, but that the immanent doctrines were salvageable when reinterpreted as allegorical equivalents of his philosophical theories, he recommended that we make "the whole of dogmatics...rational" by removing the Jewish portion from Christianity (WWRI p. 406).

And Schopenhauer called upon a further criterion for distinguishing the exclusively Christian kernel from the Jewish shell in Church Christianity, a criterion unique to the nineteenth century and provided by its acquaintance with "the ancient religions of the human race", Brahmanism and Buddhism (WWRI p. 357). He maintained that just as comparative linguists such as Franz Bopp[33] had been using Sanskrit to reconstruct the origin and development of Greek and Latin, so philosophers of religion should use knowledge of Brahmanism and Buddhism to elucidate the origin and descent of Christianity (PPII p. 381). The result of such a comparative enquiry is a very different image of the religion from that encountered in works of theology. Instead of the traditional drama of Creation, Fall, Atonement and Redemption through eschatological fulfilment, Christianity is a doctrine of Fall and Redemption, with Christ as the *avatār* (PPII p. 380), or docetic epiphany with "a phantom body"

---

[33] Author of the 1816 work, *Über das Conjugationssystem der Sanskritsprache in Vergleichung mit jenem der griechischen, perischen und germanischen Sprache*, which methodically confirmed Friedrich Schlegel's thesis concerning the descent of Indo-European languages from Sanskrit — see Schwab (1984) pp. 177-180.

(WWRI p. 405), who shows us the way to salvation through self-denial and voluntary acceptance of suffering. The New Testament is therefore "diametrically opposed" to the Old, but identical in spirit to Brahmanism and Buddhism (PPII p. 380). Whereas Genesis depicts God's seven-day creation and judgement that all he made was very good, the New Testament presents an *avatār* descending into a world ruled by the devil (PPII p. 381).

In the interests of accounting for these similarities between the ancient religions of India and the New Testament, as well as their mutual opposition to Hebrew theism, Schopenhauer states that if "we wished to indulge in conjectures of all kinds", we might assume

> that the gospel note on the flight to Egypt was based on something historical; that Jesus was educated by Egyptian priests whose religion was of Indian origin and from whom he had accepted Indian ethics and the notion of an *avatār*; and that he subsequently had endeavoured to adapt these to the Jewish dogmas in his own native land and to graft them on to the ancient stem. (PPII p. 383)

Schopenhauer speculates that the only point of contact that Jesus could find in the Old Testament for the pessimistic wisdom of India was the story of the Fall, "not further utilised" in Judaism (WWRII p. 620). He also maintains that, for Jesus, this process of adaptation and accommodation was only partly conscious (WWRI p. 387). Schopenhauer's presentation of Jesus implies that he was a saint rather than a metaphysician philosophising to escape wonder, like the *ṛṣis* or Kant. Jesus taught no "false doctrines", and was

> careful not to dogmatise, because he felt the worthlessness of every false teaching. He merely moralised, but he knew that the foundation of morality was too exalted for the people; he was concerned merely with the people and not with the one learned man among thousands. (MRIV pp. 143-4)

Jesus' morality was of the ascetic type found in all religions, issuing in acts of selflessness and renunciation: he was "a Buddha who teaches salvation of the world through self-denial" (MRIV p. 193). However, whereas the Buddha had supported his ethical precepts of renunciation with theoretical doctrines, Jesus' avoidance of dogma permitted the assimilation of his pessimistic ethics to the optimistic metaphysical scheme prevailing in his environment. Schopenhauer thought that Jesus' subsequent disciples have erred by almost unanimously taking the latter, dispensable part as his main teaching.

Schopenhauer's historical "conjectures" on Jesus and his relation to Judaism and the eastern religions situates him as the first modern figure to have promulgated a thesis that has since gained a dubious popularity — the theory of the Indian genesis of the religion of Jesus. Schopenhauer's theory was the origin for Nietzsche's description of primitive Christianity as "a new, an entirely original basis for a Buddhistic peace movement, for an actual, *not* merely promised, *happiness on earth*",[34] and has since been surpassed by a growing body of scholarly works aiming to *demonstrate* the Indian origin of Christianity.[35]

But irrespective of his thesis of Christianity's descent from the true religions of Brahmanism and Buddhism, Schopenhauer seems to have thought that the modern crisis of European spirituality and the threat it posed to metaphysical need would not be resolved by merely stripping Christianity of its transcendent doctrines. Christianity may be in origin "a reflected splendour of the primordial light of India from the ruins of Egypt" (BM p. 178), but over the course of the centuries it has grown into an alien shell, one that is "thicker than is often supposed" (WWRII p. 625) and therefore likely to resist the processes of demythologisation necessary for Christianity's survival. In addition to this, Schopenhauer thought that the nascent discipline of Indology had not merely disclosed Christianity's descent from the religions of India, but also Christianity in its pure and original form, for "[e]verything that is true in Christianity is found also in Brahmanism and Buddhism." (PPII p. 381) Europeans may send "English clergymen and evangelical linen-weavers" to the Indians to teach them that they are created out of nothing and ought to be grateful for it, but they thereby make a mockery of themselves by preaching a distorted version of the original faith of India. It is, says Schopenhauer,

> as if we fired a bullet at a cliff. In India our religions will never at any time take root; the ancient wisdom of the human race will not be supplanted by the events in Galilee. On the contrary, Indian wisdom flows back to Europe, and will produce a fundamental change in our knowledge and thought. (WWRI pp. 356-7)

It seems, then, that Schopenhauer regarded Jesus' mission and fate, whereby a saint promulgating the *philosophia perennis* was crucified for contradicting the dogmas of a religion with opposite evaluations (WWRII p. 620), as a merely peripheral event in the history and expansion of the 'true religion'. Christianity's axiological, ethical and salvific doctrines may be in essential agreement with the truth-claims of the *philosophia perennis*, but they conceal its content under a greater number of allegorical

---

[34] Nietzsche (1976b) §42.
[35] Recent examples include Gruber & Kersten (1995) and Thundy (1993). For a non-scholarly, speculative defence, closer to Schopenhauer's own, see Wynne-Tyson (1970).

veils than either Brahmanism or Buddhism. For example, Christianity communicates the two ways taught by philosophy as affirmation and denial of the will through the allegorical figures of Adam and Christ. But since it presents these figures as historical individuals rather than universal symbols, its ability to satisfy metaphysical need is dependent on the integrity of its historical records, and acceptance of its central teachings of original sin and salvation is tied up with beliefs concerning the possibility of biological inheritance of metaphysical guilt and mechanical theories of the transmission of grace. When positivism's superior knowledge of the operations of the phenomenon refutes these beliefs, Christianity's ability to inculcate moods and evaluations and guide conduct will be eradicated. As a result, Schopenhauer thought that Buddhism had an advantage over Christianity insofar as it is a pure doctrine rather than an historical narrative (PPII p. 369). It represents the two ways of affirmation and denial without historical admixture, as a conceptual contrast between *saṃsāra* and *nirvāṇa*, and thus in a form more suited to an age of critical and scientific culture, such as the nineteenth century.

CHAPTER 5

THE ORIGINAL *WELTANSCHAUUNG*

We have already encountered Schopenhauer's theory of the need for metaphysics, that it is "strong and ineradicable", following close on the satisfaction of physical needs (WWRII p. 162). Since, in his view, the death of God had discredited true and original Christianity through association, it was imperative to set up an alternative scheme to explain life, guide conduct and offer consolation for death. In his own case estrangement from the prevailing metaphysic of Judaeo-Christianity was not a conclusion attained through reasoning alone, but the effect of experience when, at seventeen and "affected by the *misery and wretchedness of life*," he concluded that

> this world could not be the work of an all-bountiful, infinitely good being, but rather of a devil who had summoned into existence creatures in order to gloat over the sight of their anguish and agony. (MRIV p. 119)

When, four years later in 1809, he embarked on a study of the natural sciences in combination with Kant's philosophy at Göttingen, his early impression of optimistic monotheism's falsehood received theoretical confirmation as well as the materials necessary for its articulation. By 1813 he was claiming that the doctrines of a religion need to be equal "to the degree of each nation's mental training", and that the cultural and intellectual advances of modernity had brought about the need for a new system of religious metaphysics (MRI p. 38). When, later in the same year, Friedrich Majer directed him to the scriptures of classical India, Schopenhauer discovered therein the outlines of a system of religious metaphysics he considered compatible with (or "more or less" adaptable to — MRIII p. 694) the intellectual outlook of the age.

Several features of the Indian religions seemed modern and attractive to Schopenhauer, but one above all made a very strong impact on his imagination. This was the opposition articulated alternatively as *māyā* and *Brahman* or *saṃsāra* and *nirvāṇa*, which he interpreted as equivalent to the "greatest merit" of Kant's critical philosophy, the distinction between phenomenon and thing-in-itself (WWRI p. 417). He took this as an indication that Hinduism and Buddhism sensibly observe the boundary demarcating metaphysics from physics, and therefore entertain no conception of a First Cause that originates the phenomenal series (WWRI p. 484, 495n.35). For that reason they are improvements on cosmological theism, the realist presuppositions of which had set it in opposition to natural scientific realism, to its eventual detriment. His conviction that Hinduism and Buddhism adhered to a version of the distinction between phenomenon and thing-in-itself suggested to Schopenhauer that they shared his own view of the central problem of sound metaphysical enquiry, which is to investigate the inner nature, or *what*, of that which appears in the phenomenon, rather than ask causal questions regarding the *whence*, the *how* or the *why* of individual phenomena, answers to which are inadequate since they refer to the principle of sufficient reason in one of its forms (WWRII p. 612).

In addition to discovering a correct conception of metaphysics in Hinduism and Buddhism, Schopenhauer found that many of their determinate doctrines seemed to be independent anticipations of his own philosophical positions, communicating his insights in the medium of allegory, inculcating its moods and guiding conduct in agreement with his ethics. In 1835, twenty-two years after his initial encounter with the thought-world of ancient India, Schopenhauer wrote a small treatise entitled *On the Will in Nature*, for the purpose of drawing attention to the "corroborations" his philosophy had obtained from "unprejudiced empiricists who are not familiar with it", and to demonstrate how his "metaphysics and the sciences meet of their own accord and without collusion at the same point." (WN p. 19) The chapter entitled 'Sinology' was written to illustrate the further corroborations his philosophy obtained from the doctrines of Buddhism and the religions of China. It suggests that Schopenhauer expected empirical science, Buddhism and his own philosophy to serve as separate components of a unified *Weltanschauung*, co-operating in the same way that Aristotelian cosmology, the metaphysics of the scholastics and popular Christianity had during the Middle Ages. Together they would restore unity to European culture after the death of God and Kant's unsatisfactory separation of the realms of fact and value.

In this chapter we look at Schopenhauer's conception of the origin and nature of Indian religion, and its historical relations to other systems of thought. However, we begin with a brief survey of his encounter with the productions of early European Indology; partly to place the subsequent reconstruction of his Indian interpretation in its proper context, but more immediately to evaluate the thesis, defended by some commentators, that

Schopenhauer's philosophical positions were originally and substantially derived from Indian texts. A discussion of whether or not Schopenhauer was influenced by Indological works is pertinent to his philosophy of religion since, if indeed he was, then his distinction between philosophy as a self-sufficient, demonstrative science, and religion as a venerable tradition with external, authoritative supports, would be refuted in his own case. His assimilation of Hinduism and Buddhism as religio-allegorical and popular equivalents of his own philosophical metaphysics would therefore be fraudulent. For this reason, we begin this chapter with the much-debated question of influence.

I. The Question of Influence

As mentioned previously, Schopenhauer's first significant encounter with the thought-world of classical India came through Anquetil-Duperron's Latin translation of the *Upaniṣads* — the *Oupnek'hat* — on the recommendation of Friedrich Majer. Schopenhauer met Majer at his mother's house in Weimar at some point in the winter of 1813-14, a few months after submitting his doctoral dissertation to the University of Jena. Schopenhauer's subsequent manuscript notes testify to the immediate impression made upon him by the doctrines of the *Oupnek'hat*, as he experimented with speculative parallels between some of its main ideas and those of his own developing system (MRI p. 181, p. 247, p. 286, p. 332, p. 449). From this period to his death in 1860 Schopenhauer read as many works as he could find on classical India, especially its religious and philosophical thought. During the first period of his encounter — from his meeting with Majer up to the completion of the first edition of *The World as Will and Representation* in late 1818 — Schopenhauer's main sources included the first nine volumes of *Asiatick Researches* (the journal for the proceedings of the Asiatic Society of Bengal), Mme de Polier's *Mythologie des Indous*, Julius Klaproth's journal *Das Asiatisches Magazin* (which contained Majer's German translation of Charles Wilkins' English *Bhagavad-Gītā*) and Friedrich Schlegel's *On the Language and Wisdom of the Indians*. In summary, it might be said that Schopenhauer's early sources were small in number and of uneven quality. Many — such as Klaproth's journal and Schlegel's treatise — were written in the interests of supporting an emphatic cultural agenda, such as Indo-Germanism or Romanticism. Moreover, apart from three brief articles on Buddhism (one published in *Das Asiatisches Magazin*, the other two in early editions of *Asiatick Researches*) all of Schopenhauer's pre-1818 Indian sources were either scriptures from or expositions of the main ideas and practices of various Hindu schools.

Irrespective of the paucity and inadequacy of Schopenhauer's early sources, Dorothea Dauer,[1] Urs App,[2] and most recently and comprehensively Douglas Berger,[3] have all argued that the simultaneity of Schopenhauer's immersion in Indian texts and the development of his system is a sufficient indicator that the form and content of his philosophy was somehow indebted to Indian ideas. Schopenhauer's own comments have simply confused the issue. He usually portrayed his thought as the outcome of the occidental tradition of philosophical reflection, and that it only fortuitously converged with the unsystematic religious thought of India working from this ground (PVI p. 106). However, some of his comments seem to indicate a vague indebtedness to Hindu sources such as the *Oupnek'hat*. We have already encountered the manuscript note from 1816 in which Schopenhauer remarked "I do not believe my doctrine could have come before the *Upaniṣads*, Plato and Kant could cast their rays simultaneously into the mind of one man" (MRI p. 467), while in the Appendix of his main work of 1818 he stated that "next to the impression of the world of perception, I owe what is best in my own development to the impression made by Kant's works, the sacred writings of the Hindus, and Plato." (WWRI p. 417) These quotes suggest that, up to 1818 at least, Schopenhauer considered his philosophy to be partly dependent on ideas he found in the *Upaniṣads*. However, in the Preface to his main work he complicates this by asserting an asymmetry between the world-view of the *Upaniṣads* and his philosophy, an asymmetry which effectively denies the possibility of historical dependence or influence:

> did it not sound too conceited, I might assert that each of the individual and disconnected utterances that make up the *Upaniṣads* could be derived as a consequence from the thought I am to impart, although conversely my thought is by no means to be found in the *Upaniṣads*. (WWRI pp. xv-xvi)

The implication is that Schopenhauer arrived at the same point as Indian wisdom on the independent route of argumentation, and that the conceptual form of his system establishes and confirms the experientially-based and "disconnected" insights of the *ṛṣis* conveyed in the *Upaniṣads*. This account is consistent with the later distinction he made between the

---

[1] Dauer (1969) pp. 7-9.
[2] App (1998a) p. 13n.4; App (2003) p. 14.
[3] Berger (2004a) p. xv.

conceptual and argumentative form of philosophy and the non-systematic nature of religion, which, as different responses to metaphysical need, can — and are even likely to — agree on the substantial level of truth.

Schopenhauer unequivocally regarded Kant as the most influential — because most philosophical — of his three attested sources. Although he thought that Kant, Plato and the Hindus had equally promulgated the doctrine of the merely relative existence of the phenomenal world, he maintained that Plato and the Hindus had arrived at this insight through "a universal perception of the world; they produced them as the direct utterance of their consciousness, and presented them mythically and poetically rather than philosophically and distinctly", while Kant "not only expressed the same doctrine in an entirely new and original way, but made of it a proved and incontestable truth through the most calm and dispassionate presentation." (WWRI p. 419) But Schopenhauer's conception of the relative importance of Kant over his other sources has been contested. The Soviet scholar Bernard Bykhovsky, who favoured a proto-Marxist and materialist reading of Kant, argued that Schopenhauer's system owed more to the Indian religions than to his avowed European forerunners:

> Kant and Plato were not the real inspirations of Schopenhauer. They did not lead him to the summit of philosophical extravagance, and the cult of nothing. In the age of classical German philosophy, which served as the spring of creative philosophical thought, which reached for the future, Schopenhauer turned philosophy to the past, the ancient religious past, having revived in philosophical incrustation the antiquarian mysticism of Brahmanism and Buddhism, erecting a philosophical altar to *nirvāṇa*.[4]

However, Bykhovsky's assertion that Kant and Plato were not the "real inspirations" of Schopenhauer's philosophy and that, by implication, the Indian religions were, seems fairly nebulous, and might mean nothing more than that Hinduism and Buddhism encouraged him in reflections he developed on other grounds. Douglas Berger has defended the stronger and more rigorously argued thesis that Schopenhauer's interpretation of Kant's idealism as a doctrine of illusion was unthinkable without the impetus of the Hindu doctrine of *māyā*, which became the "linking concept" for his account of the world as representation, monist metaphysics of will and ethics of compassionate identification. Berger maintains that, before the first edition of *The World as Will and Representation*, Schopenhauer's

---

[4] Bykhovsky (1984) p. 173.

philosophical writings concentrated on theories of perception and judgement which were influenced by Kant, Hume and Goethe. His concern with ethics had not yet been awakened and his attitude towards metaphysics was sceptical and almost non-existent…his philosophical outlook changes dramatically after his reading of Duperron's translations and commentaries on the *Upaniṣads*. He appropriates Duperron's material and therewith reassesses Kant to include within idealism a falsification theory, which in Kant's philosophy as well as in places of Schopenhauer's own writings originally was not to be found. He followed this up with an understanding of ethics and asceticism which he thought were demanded by the falsification thesis, not to mention to have precedents in Indian religion. Schopenhauer's metaphysics and ethics are made possible by the aepistemological falsification theory inspired by his understanding of the concept of *māyā*.[5]

In support of this theory, Berger refers to the fact that whereas Schopenhauer's favoured term for the phenomenon in his 1813 doctoral dissertation was "the principle of sufficient reason", by 1818 — and under the stimulus of the *Oupnek'hat* — it had become "*māyā*, the veil of deception [*Maja, der Schleier des Truges*]".[6]

Berger's thesis is a controversial but interesting one, and for this reason it is a pity that his study does not do more to substantiate it. Apart from opening and closing with chapters that outline his interpretation and illustrate its main points and implications, the bulk of Berger's book is devoted to a fairly standard exposition of Schopenhauer's epistemology, metaphysics and ethics, tailored to support his hypothesis that *māyā* functions as the "linking concept" between them. Although Berger investigates the relevance of Schopenhauer's 1813 doctoral dissertation and pre-1818 *Nachlass* to his thesis, he ignores the many passages that challenge it. He also completely neglects to enquire into whether the metaphysical and ethical directions in which Schopenhauer took Kant's critical philosophy might not have taken its stimulus from quarters other than Anquetil-Duperron's scholarly appendices to the *Oupnek'hat*.

Taking the second point first, Berger's implication that Kant's critical philosophy was exclusively devoted to epistemological questions concerning perception and judgement (the problem of synthetic *a priori* propositions) is highly dubious, for Kant consistently drew attention to the metaphysical and ethical consequences of his theories. In Chapter 2 we noted how he had used his theory of judgment to introduce the regulative notion of a "supersensible substrate" as the common source of the theoretical and practical powers of the subject, nature and freedom,

---

[5] Berger (2004a) p. xxi.
[6] Ibid. p. xvi.

phenomena and noumena, and how this move had stimulated his successors to develop systems of metaphysical monism at odds with the prevailing dualism of pre-Kantian metaphysics.

Fichte was the first of Kant's successors to expand on the metaphysical and ethical implications of the critical philosophy. In his popular work of 1800, *The Vocation of Man,* he anticipated Schopenhauer's description of the phenomenon as *"māyā,* the veil of deception [*Maja, der Schleier des Truges*]" when he referred to the series of representations known to the theoretical understanding as "empty pictures"[7] and a "deceptive show [*trugendes Bild*]".[8] He also anticipated Schopenhauer's argument that only a metaphysical turn can endow the system of representations with "an interest that engrosses our whole nature" (WWRI p. 95), by stating that pictures which appear empty to the understanding acquire substantial reality when viewed within the perspective of practical faith, wherein they take on the aspect of "Infinite Will" expressed through the moral agency of individuals.[9] Schopenhauer's early exposure to Fichte's particular brand of post-Kantianism is well-documented in his manuscript notes, and pre-dated his knowledge of the Indian traditions.[10]

However, if Schopenhauer's abusive references to Fichte as the "father of *sham philosophy*" (WWRII p. 12) are taken at face-value, then passages from his 1813 doctoral dissertation show that he had already made a correlation between the principle of sufficient reason and the insubstantiality of phenomena before his encounter with the doctrine of *māyā* in Anquetil's *Oupnek'hat.* At one point he states that the "common root" of the four forms of the principle of sufficient reason is the "innermost seed of all the dependency, relativity, instability and finite character of the objects of our consciousness", and cites Plato's characterisation of the world as "that which is for ever coming into being and perishing and never really existing at all" and the Christian teaching that temporality is the "schema and the prototype of all that is finite" as further confirmations of this view (FR1 p. 68). In the first edition of *The World as Will*

---

[7] Fichte (1956) p. 92.

[8] Ibid. p. 83.

[9] Ibid. p. 134.

[10] Schopenhauer attended two lecture courses given by Fichte in Berlin, 'On the Facts of Consciousness' in the autumn term of 1811 and 'On the Doctrine of Science' in the winter of 1811-12. His notes record his growing disillusion with Fichte (MRII pp. 16-233), and he later commented that "in 1811 I moved to Berlin in the expectation that in Fichte I should become acquainted with a genuine philosopher and a great mind. But this *a priori* veneration was soon changed into disdain and derision." (MRII p. xiv)

and Representation completed five years later, the Upaniṣadic phrase "the veil of *māyā*" appears as further confirmation of this universal doctrine of the instability of the phenomenon, a teaching that Schopenhauer considered common to genuine metaphysicians in all ages and circumstances:

> Heraclitus lamented the eternal flux of things; Plato spoke with contempt of its object as that which for ever becomes, but never is; Spinoza called it mere accidents of the sole substance that alone is and endures; Kant opposed to the thing-in-itself that which is known as mere phenomenon; finally, the ancient wisdom of the Indians declares that 'it is *māyā*, the veil of deception, which covers the eyes of mortals, and causes them to see a world of which one cannot say either that it is or that it is not; for it is like a dream, like the sunshine on the sand which the traveller from a distance takes to be water, or like the piece of rope on the ground which he regards as a snake.'
> (WWRI pp. 7-8)

Schopenhauer's pre-1813 manuscript notes constitute further evidence that he interpreted Kant's idealism as a doctrine of illusion with metaphysical and ethical implications before reading the *Oupnek'hat*. In 1811 he described the temporal divisions of past and present as "illusions" (MRI p. 15), and in subsequent notes elaborated on this with a Platonic contrast between the "rational" consciousness that perceives and thinks in accordance with the forms and laws of the phenomenon, and the "better" consciousness that transcends these forms and therefore eludes positive description (MRI p. 23). By early 1813 Schopenhauer was explicitly associating the better consciousness with an ethics of virtue and asceticism. Its disclosure that one is in essence "an extra-temporal, supersensuous, free and absolutely blissful being" leads to virtue, or "affirmation of the extra-temporal existence", and asceticism or "intentional negation, the formal denial and rejection of anything temporal as such." (MRI pp. 39-40) These passages contradict Berger's thesis that without the *Oupnek'hat* Schopenhauer would have remained an epistemologist solely concerned with theories of perception and judgement, and confirm Arthur Hübscher's contrary opinion that Schopenhauer's encounter with the *Oupnek'hat* was not "the start of a new core of experience, but an ever new, intellectually related influx of ideas, received with yearning readiness, illuminated by what was already his own, and assembled into a brilliantly outlined design."[11]

Moira Nicholls has formulated an alternative thesis concerning the impact of Indian texts on Schopenhauer's philosophy, one in which the

---

[11] Hübscher (1989) p. 67.

influence is gradual rather than immediate and develops over time as better and more sources became available to him. Nicholls maintains that "three significant shifts that occurred in Schopenhauer's doctrine of the thing-in-itself after 1818...can be plausibly explained, at least in part, by his increasing familiarity with and appreciation of Eastern thought."[12] These shifts are the limitations that Schopenhauer placed on knowledge of the thing-in-itself in the second, 1844 edition of *The World as Will and Representation*; his recognition that the thing-in-itself apart from its appearance in the phenomenon might be something other than will; and his attempts to assimilate what can be said of the thing-in-itself with concepts and doctrines from the eastern religions.

While it is difficult to identify with any certainty the traces of a particular source on a creative thinker such as Schopenhauer, Nicholls' thesis of growing influence does have greater historical and textual support than Berger's thesis of original influence. It seems especially significant that the academic study of Buddhism emerged from Indology between the publication of the first, 1818 edition of *The World as Will and Representation* and the second in 1844, since the majority of the shifts identified by Nicholls have a close conceptual relation to Buddhist doctrines.

The European study of Buddhist languages and scriptures was inaugurated by a group of French scholars led by Eugène Burnouf at the Collège de France in Paris. In 1826 Burnouf collaborated with Christian Lassen to produce the first scholarly study of Buddhism based on original sources, the *Essai sur le pâli*. Its title notwithstanding, this work was not based on a study of the early scriptures of Buddhism, but on Sanskrit, Mahāyāna sources sent to Europe from Nepal. Independent of Burnouf and each other, the Hungarian amateur Buddhologist Alexander Csoma Körösi, and the German scholar of the St. Petersburg Academy I.J. Schmidt had, by the late 1820s and early 1830s, begun to translate scriptures from and publish studies of two further Mahāyāna traditions, Tibetan and Mongolian Buddhism respectively. The impact of the newest of seams to be mined by academic Indology on Schopenhauer is evident in his 1835 work *On the Will in Nature*. In the chapter 'Sinology' he not only established parallels between his own ideas and those belonging to Buddhism and Daoism, but summarised and evaluated the latest European scholarship on these venerable systems of thought. In a long footnote he recommended some recent European publications on Buddhism, including those by Burnouf, Körösi and Schmidt (WN p. 130n.2).

---

[12] Nicholls (1999) p. 171.

Several commentators apart from Nicholls have remarked on the discontinuities between Schopenhauer's 1818 statement of his *Willensmetaphysik* and that of 1844.[13] Whereas in the first edition of *The World as Will and Representation* he tended to state that knowledge of our body's inner nature as will constitutes unmediated, non-representational acquaintance with Kant's thing-in-itself (WWRI p. 110, p. 112, p. 501), in the second edition this claim is generally accompanied by a gloss that explains and qualifies it. Willing is still "the one thing known to us *immediately*, and not given to us merely in the representation, as all else is", and therefore the sole datum "capable of becoming the key to everything else...the only narrow gateway to truth" (WWRII p. 196), but this insight does not "furnish an exhaustive and adequate knowledge of the thing-in-itself." This is because inner apprehension (*Wahrnehmung*) of the will dispenses with only two forms of outer perception (*Anschauung*) — space and causality — while remaining mediated by the form fundamental to all knowledge — the division between subject and object — as well as appearing successively, under the form of time. As a result, every individual becomes acquainted with his or her will over time, through individual acts, rather than all at once and as a whole. Inner apprehension of the body as will is therefore "only the nearest and clearest *phenomenon* of the thing-in-itself", or the thing-in-itself known "under the lightest of veils" but not "quite naked." Schopenhauer remarked that only in this sense does he "teach that the inner nature of every thing is *will*" or "call the will the thing-in-itself" (WWRII p. 197). If someone were to enquire into the nature of the thing-in-itself "ultimately and absolutely in-itself", apart from its objective and temporal manifestation as will to the knowing subject, then "[t]his question can *never* be answered": however

> the possibility of this question shows that the thing-in-itself, which we know most immediately in the will, may have, entirely outside all possible phenomena, determinations, qualities, and modes of existence which for us are absolutely unknowable and incomprehensible, and which then remain as the inner nature of the thing-in-itself, when this, as explained in the fourth book [on ethics and asceticism], has freely abolished itself as *will*, has thus stepped out of the phenomenon entirely, and as regards our knowledge, that is to say as regards the world of phenomena, has passed over into empty nothingness. If the will were positively and absolutely the thing-in-itself, then this nothing would be *absolute*, instead of which it expressly appears to us there only as a *relative* nothing. (WWRII p. 198)

---

[13] Gardiner (1963) pp. 172-3; Hamlyn (1980) pp. 84-5; Janaway (1989) p. 196; Atwell (1995) pp. 111-2; Young (2005) pp. 89ff.

In the last chapter we touched on Schopenhauer's metaphysics of the will in relation to his soteriology and the problem of whether his doctrine of its denial is mystical or annihilationist. If, as he suggests here, it is *possible* that the thing-in-itself is will only in relation to the phenomenon, and *may* have additional "determinations, qualities, and modes of existence" unknowable to us, then this provides some sanction for a mystical rather than annihilationist interpretation of the denial of the will. Ultimately, however, as Schopenhauer says, this question "can *never* be answered", for it is transcendent. Knowledge of the thing-in-itself presupposes its objectification as will, and the only consideration leading to the concession that it may have other "modes of existence" is that we observe its limitation and denial in the lives of philanthropists and saints. However, Schopenhauer was cautious enough to offer this as no more than an explanatory inference, since he thought that, ultimately, we cannot know the true and certain explanation of the possibility of virtue and asceticism.[14]

Schopenhauer's acknowledgement of a possible distinction between the thing-in-itself manifesting itself as will and the thing-in-itself apart from this manifestation points to a resolution of an alleged contradiction between his metaphysics and his soteriology. Several commentators have agreed with Luis Navia when he objects that Schopenhauer's "*Erlösung* lacks any practical applicability and its value is mostly rhetorical", since it is inconceivable that an ascetic could deny his essence as will.[15] However if, as we have seen Schopenhauer concede, it is possible that the thing-in-itself is will only in relation to appearance and may have other modes of existence unknowable to us, then this points to a possible solution to Navia's antinomy. Ultimately the contradiction stems from the fact that commentators such as Navia (as well as the Thomist Frededrick Copleston[16]) have conceived Schopenhauer's will to be some sort of

---

[14] The section entitled 'The Sceptical View' in *On the Basis of Morality* shows that Schopenhauer thought that philosophical ethics consisted of interpretations of external behaviour and inferences to their probable motives, as opposed to direct knowledge of the operations of the will (BM pp. 128-30). His distinction between the thing-in-itself appearing as will and the thing-in-itself apart from this appearance was similarly conjectural and interpretative, and suggested by his theories of the possibility of virtue and ascetic denial. But whereas Schopenhauer tended to be agnostic about this contrast and emphasised only its probability, theological interpreters such as Mannion, King and Gonzales have tended to present him as stating it as a fact or item of transcendent knowledge, or proof of a metaphysical something 'beyond' the will.

[15] Navia (1980) p. 175.

[16] Copleston (1975) p. 195.

unchanging Absolute or substance, similar to the God of the Aristotelian scholastics. But since Schopenhauer thought that we never observe the will directly and as a whole, but know it only through successive acts of the body, we cannot attribute to it substantive or metaphysical properties such as immutability, or distinguish states that are possible for it from those that are not. Our conceptual knowledge of the will is indirect and consists mainly of negative statements, so while we might say that it is radically free from morality, purpose, dependence or categorial description, we have no grounds for stating that it necessarily affirms and objectifies itself as will in the phenomenon, for in-itself it is free from sufficient reason as the principle of all necessity (WWRII p. 629). In many ways, Schopenhauer's concept of the thing-in-itself as will has more metaphysical properties in common with the radically free God of the nominalists than the substantial form or *actus purus* of Aquinas. Schopenhauer himself explicitly stated that his will is not a substance or necessary existent:

> Contrary to certain silly objections, I observe that the *denial of the will-to-live* does not in any way assert the annihilation of a substance, but the mere act of not-willing; that which hitherto *willed* no longer *wills*. As we know this being, this essence, the *will*, as thing-in-itself merely in and through the act of *willing*, we are incapable of saying or comprehending what it still is or does after it has given up that act. And so *for us* who are the phenomenon of willing, this denial is a passing over into nothing. (PPII p. 312)

Given that Schopenhauer's later qualifications of the *Willensmetaphysik* have an intimate relation to his doctrine of salvation, it is significant, as Nicholls argues, that they are paralleled by a raised assessment of the philosophical possibilities of certain Indian and Asian doctrines, in particular the Buddhist concept of *nirvāṇa*. Whereas in 1818 Schopenhauer seems to have thought that Buddhists use *nirvāṇa* to designate some sort of being or higher reality, and therefore counselled that "we" (i.e., philosophers) avoid seeking refuge from "the dark impression of that nothingness, which as the final goal hovers behind all virtue and holiness" in religious "myths and meaningless words, such as reabsorption in *Brahman*, or the *nirvāṇa* of the Buddhists" (WWRI p. 411), by 1844 his appreciation of the term had changed markedly. He no longer presents *nirvāṇa* as a myth or religious allegory veiling a hard philosophical truth, but as a negative term signifying the mystic's liberation from the will. He distinguishes it from Hindu soteriology by commenting that whereas the *Vedas* (by which he meant the *Upaniṣads*) use the mythological formula "reunion with *Brahman*" to refer to this state of liberation, the

Buddhists "with complete frankness describe the matter only negatively as *nirvāṇa*, which is the negation of this world or of *saṃsāra*." (WWRII p. 608)

Schopenhauer's explanation of the meaning of *nirvāṇa* was highly sophisticated for his time, and suggests that he gave the matter far more attention and thought than virtually all of his contemporaries, including the Buddhologists. Whereas Eugène Burnouf's studies contained lengthy discussions of the possibility that *nirvāṇa's* literal meaning of "extinction" might signify absolute annihilation,[17] Schopenhauer's approach was far more agnostic and philosophical. According to him, Buddhists avoid positive descriptions of the soteriological state on account of the inadequacy of language, the purpose of which is to delimit and describe features of the phenomenon. They therefore use the negative term *nirvāṇa* because "*saṃsāra* contains no single element that could serve to define or construct" an accurate image of salvation (WWRII p. 608). Schopenhauer's later distinction between the thing-in-itself and the will clearly assisted his renewed appreciation of Buddhist terminology, for just as we lack concepts for positive descriptions of the denial of the will, so we similarly lack concepts for positive descriptions of *nirvāṇa*. In Schopenhauer's later view the denial of the will and *nirvāṇa* together indicate transcendence of or liberation from the will, the point at which the opposition between knower and known has vanished, and which therefore "remains for ever inaccessible to all human knowledge precisely as such." (WWRII p. 560)[18]

Nicholls' gradualist thesis of the influence of Indian sources on Schopenhauer is therefore very useful, since it not only accounts for his revised evaluation of the concept of *nirvāṇa*, but identifies a possible cause of changes of emphasis in his metaphysics between 1818 and 1844. However, as Nicholls rightly states,[19] the revisions in the *Willensmetaphysik* are only partly explained by Schopenhauer's growing acquaintance with Indian thought, and are likely to have a wider number of causes. These might include Schopenhauer's gradual extrication from transcendentalism and turn towards a more naturalistic presentation of his

---

[17] Welbon (1968) p. 59.

[18] Regarding Schopenhauer's interpretation of *nirvāṇa*, Guy Welbon states "[s]eldom during the century and a half since those words were written have the meaning of *nirvāṇa* and the motive forces undergirding classical Indian speculation been approached more closely by Westerners. The parallels between this creative philosophical effort and much of the Indian *mokṣa* literature are remarkable." (Welbon (1968) pp. 165-6)

[19] Nicholls (1999) p. 171.

doctrines; greater critical reflection on the contradictions in the initial statement of his system, specifically between his metaphysics and ethics; and, most importantly, the rise of the spectre of Hegel, and Schopenhauer's eagerness to distinguish his concept of the will from the Absolute Idea.[20] However, Nicholls' thesis does highlight an important feature of Schopenhauer's relation to his Indian sources, since his re-evaluation of the philosophical possibilities of *nirvāṇa* shows that his engagement with them was dialectical and left room for revision, in agreement with Gadamer's account of understanding.

Schopenhauer's reappraisal of the meaning and philosophical possibilities of *nirvāṇa* also complicates his binary opposition between the allegories of religion and the literal, *sensu proprio* truths of philosophy, displacing it for a multi-layered scheme in which truth appears under veils of varying transparency. At the densest allegorical level we might find palpably figurative religious doctrines, such as those which recommend virtuous actions as causes of future rewards, whether through the causality of the will of God or the impersonal mechanics of *karma* and rebirth. At a more refined level there is the Buddhist opposition between *saṃsāra* and *nirvāṇa*, with the latter term being almost indistinguishable from Schopenhauer's philosophical notion of the denial of the will, insofar as both derive content from what they negate.[21] In Chapter 2 we noted Schopenhauer's theory of why "all religions at their highest point end in mysticism and mysteries", for they signify the blank spot where the division between subject and object has been eradicated and all knowledge necessarily ceases (WWRII p. 610). For this reason he affirmed the religious resort to symbols and signs, such as dim light and silence in temples, as means for evoking the limits of knowledge and, in Wittgenstein's idiom, for showing what cannot be said.[22] However, Schopenhauer thought that the most adequate method for running up against the limits of knowledge and transcending the distinction between subject and

---

[20] See especially Schopenhauer's letter of 21ˢᵗ August 1853 to his disciple Frauenstädt, where he explained that by *will* he does not mean "the supersensuous, the divinity, the unending, the unthinkable, or most prettily, with Hegel, '*die Uedäh*' [a parody of Hegel's pronunciation of *die Idee*]." Schopenhauer went on to explain that the will is within things as their very essence, rather than external to them as their cause or ground (GB p. 280).

[21] See Schopenhauer's discussion of various etymological definitions of *nirvāṇa* in which, to take just one example, he notes Spence Hardy's explanation that it is derived "from *vana*, 'sinful desires,' with the negative *nir*." (WWRII p. 508n.34; Hardy (1850) p. 295)

[22] Wittgenstein (2000) 4.1212 (citations to Wittgenstein's *Tractatus* follow the standard practice of referring to proposition rather than page number).

object had been developed by the mystical yogis of Brahmanism, who cultivated techniques to arrest the flow of thoughts and perceptions, "for the purpose of entering into the deepest communion with one's own self, by mentally uttering the mysterious *Om.*" (WWRII p. 611)

Although Schopenhauer acknowledged the power of mysteries and mysticism to signify and achieve states beyond the distinction of subject-object and the limitations of knowledge, he never claimed that mysteries signify an ineffable reality or that mystics attain union with a transcendent being, and was consistently agnostic about what might lie 'beyond' liberation from the will. In his view, the *ṛṣis* and yogis of the Indian traditions may have enjoyed 'knowledge by acquaintance' of the metaphysical identity of all phenomena, and preached it on their personal authority in the Upaniṣadic phrase "*tat tvam asi*" (that art thou), but they are "unable to convince", because their views reside on private experience (WWRII p. 611). By contrast, post-Kantian philosophy has obtained knowledge of the same thesis concerning the metaphysical identity of all beings through reasoning on inter-communal and quotidian facts of inner and outer experience available to all, and can therefore give a persuasive account of its doctrines, as 'knowledge by description'. However, neither philosophy nor mysticism can know what becomes of the will when it has turned and denied itself. Although Schopenhauer remarked that "the mystic proceeds positively" beyond the negative knowledge of philosophy expressed through the denial of the will, and recommended that anyone desiring a poetic or figurative supplement to this should seek it in mystical literature (WWRII p. 612), he did not think that the positive claims of mysticism were justifiable. His epistemology and nominalist account of concept-formation entail that the content of phrases such as "union with God" or "reabsorption in *Brahman*" is ultimately negative, for they refer primarily to the feeling of freedom that follows the denial of the will. The "pantheistic consciousness, essential to all mysticism" appears only secondarily, "in consequence of the giving up of all willing, as union with God." (WWRII pp. 612-3) The positive claims of mysticism are therefore analogous to the concept of happiness, being positive in connotation but negative in origin and content. Just as happiness describes a temporary state of the will's satisfaction, the language of mystical union has as its primary referent the mystic's feeling of liberation from the pressure to will. We noted earlier Schopenhauer's suggestion that Meister Eckhart had knowingly used the allegories of Christianity as a vehicle for signifying his transcendence of his inner nature (WWRII p. 614).

It would seem, therefore, that the mystical and annihilationist interpretations of Schopenhauer's soteriology assert too much, insofar as they make transcendent claims about the nature of the thing-in-itself after it has turned and denied itself as will. The former pretends to know that the thing-in-itself attains to a different kind of existence, while the latter pretends to know that it is extinguished without remainder. But, as I have argued, Schopenhauer's admission that the thing-in-itself may have "determinations, qualities, and modes of existence" apart from its objectification as will was introduced to avert the conclusion that our perceptions of virtuous and ascetic acts are apparent, and that they are in reality indirect expressions of egoism (or, as Nietzsche claimed, subterranean forms of the will-to-power). It was not intended to provide materials for a positive theory of a mystical afterlife or "union with God". Schopenhauer's commitment to Kantian premises necessitated agnosticism on this issue, and he would have concurred with Wittgenstein's maxim that "[w]hat we cannot speak about we must pass over in silence."[23] However, the greatest analogy with Schopenhauer's soteriology, as he himself realised, was with the Buddha. Like his Indian precursor, Schopenhauer taught the two ways of suffering through affirmation (or *saṃsāra*) and release through denial (or *nirvāṇa*), and thereby adhered to a 'middle way' that avoids the extremes of either eternalism (*śāśvatavāda*) or annihilationism (*ucchedavāda*).[24]

II. India and its Wisdom in History

As noted previously, Schopenhauer more often praised the profundity and nobility of India, its peoples and their wisdom, than stated explicitly and systematically his reasons for pronouncing all things Indian profound and noble. In accordance with the theories of Herder and Friedrich Schlegel, he proclaimed India as the "fatherland of the human race" (PPII p. 222), whose natural environment, "endowed with life in quite a different degree"

[23] Wittgenstein (2000) 7.
[24] These Sanskrit terms refer to the contrary extremes rejected by Buddhism as the 'middle way'. The Buddha refused to give an answer to ten questions (*avyākṛta*), on account of the fact that they draw their assumptions from either one of these positions. One pair of questions asks whether the Tathāgata, or Enlightened One, exists or does not exist after death: the former thesis presupposes the eternalist view, the latter the annihilationist. Buddhism's doctrine of no-Self avoids either position by teaching that the Enlightened One is not a substantial entity that will exist for eternity or pass out of existence. Some scholars have compared the *avyākṛta* to Kant's antinomies (see Murti (1974) p. 38).

from northern lands, greatly facilitated the *ṛṣis'* quest to discern the inner principle or One animating nature's Many forms (WWRII p. 475). Although Schopenhauer never learnt Sanskrit, he extolled the benefits of doing so, remarking that a comparison between "lofty Sanskrit" and "English jargon" is proof of the greater perfection of ancient languages (PPII p. 565). The Indians are "the noblest and oldest" of peoples (WWRI p. 356), their mild and inclusive temperament appearing even in their religious doctrines: we have seen that Schopenhauer commended the doctrine of metempsychosis for including animal species within the cycle of rebirths. According to him, such religious imagery instils forbearance and compassion for all creatures, while simultaneously avoiding the anthropocentrism by which the monotheistic faiths have flattered the human species (PPII pp. 370-1). The histories of the Indian religions, though obscure and incomplete, are less marked by the bloodshed and cruelty of monotheistic history, with the annals of Buddhism containing fewer instances of persecution than those of any other religion (PPII p. 358).

Although Schopenhauer shared Hegel's opinion that the original genius of the Hindus is now "depressed" (PPII p. 401), and contemporary Indians "degenerate...in many respects" (WWRI p. 356),[25] he diverged from Hegel by attributing this not to the effects of the outmoded and debilitating ethics of "Brahmanism and Buddhism" on the peoples of India,[26] but to monotheism which, under the guise of the "detestable doctrine of Islam", had attempted to eradicate "with fire and sword the ancient and profound religions of humanity" (WN p. 143). However, even the aggressive spirit of Islam (in Schopenhauer's view, the "saddest and poorest form of theism" — WWRII p. 162) was tempered in the subcontinent through association with the indigenous religions, eventually flowering under their influence into the mysticism of the Sufis (WWRII p. 605). Rejecting the monotheistic dualism of creation out of nothing, Sufism has embraced Indic monism, and professes that "we ourselves are the kernel of the world and the source of all existence, to which everything returns." (WWRII pp. 612-3)[27]

---

[25] A claim often found in histories and travellers' reports of the time, such as James Mill's 1818 *History of British India*, written to justify British presence in the subcontinent — see Mill (1858) pp. 303-342.

[26] Hegel thought that the absence of mediation between universal and particular in Hinduism had exerted a malign influence on the ethical life of the nation: "Deceit and cunning are the fundamental characteristics of the Hindoo. Cheating, stealing, robbing, murdering are with him habitual." (Hegel (1956) p. 158)

[27] Schopenhauer's theory that Sufism was originally non-Islamic and developed through association with the Indian religions was common in the nineteenth century.

Schopenhauer claimed that the mythology of the Indian religions, albeit "fantastic and sometimes strange" (PPII p. 225), was "the wisest of all mythologies" (WWRI p. 275), its inner meaning "transparent" to philosophical interpretation (PPI p. 62). He thought that Buddhism was the most excellent of the religions, containing "deeper ethical and meta-physical views" than any other (PPII p. 203). Its "sublime and loving doctrine" and "intrinsic excellence and truth" have made it into the larg-est religion on earth (WN pp. 130-1), and it "speaks greatly" in its favour that it sustains itself in civilised nations such as China through the assent and devotion of the people alone (WN p. 132). This distinguishes it from Judaeo-Christianity, which has been kept afloat in European nations through imposition by state law and compulsory education, and lent philosophical respectability through the collusion of time-serving profes-sors (PPI pp. 140f). If agreement with Schopenhauer's system be accepted as a criterion of philosophical truth, then of all religions Buddhism com-municates the greatest quantity of truth under the lightest of allegorical veils (WWRII p. 169). Some scholars have alleged that Schopenhauer's philosophical sponsorship of the Indian religions is patronising.[28] How-ever, if he sought to validate Buddhism through association with his own system, then the reverse is also true, insofar as he considered the quality and authority of his own doctrines to be demonstrated through their agreement with those of "the oldest of all world-views." (PVI p. 105)

Schopenhauer tended to detect either direct historical dependence upon or, alternatively, fortuitous convergence with the metaphysics and ethics of the Indian religions in all periods of western intellectual history, phil-osophical and religious. The "same fundamental wisdom" that underlies "Brahmanism and Buddhism" and "true Christianity" was also taught by Pythagoras, Empedocles and Plato, all of whom portrayed individual existence as a state of guilt and therefore suffering, and the path to lib-eration as a discipline of self-denial (PPI p. 35). He speculated that Pythagoras and Plato probably received their pessimism and doctrines of transmigration and asceticism from the Egyptians (WWRI p. 356), whose religion was of Indian origin (PPI pp. 60), while Empedocles received

---

Contemporary scholars now generally dispute this, and argue for Sufism's purely Islamic integrity and origin — see Schimmel (1975) pp. 8-11, p. 345.

[28] Douglas Berger goes as far as to argue that Schopenhauer's characterisation of India manifests "ethnocentricity" in crude "racial terms" (Berger (2004a) p. 230). And this is only one of the many moral objections that Berger assembles against the "evidentiary value" that Schopenhauer invested in the doctrines of Hinduism and Buddhism (Ibid. p. 233).

his doctrines from Pythagoras (PPI p. 35), and therefore promulgated a third-hand version of Indian wisdom. Schopenhauer also denied philosophical creativity to the Neo-Platonists: they were neither "original thinkers" nor "philosophers in the proper sense", since their sole achievement was to transcribe "Indo-Egyptian wisdom" into the language of Greek philosophy. Plotinus' All-One doctrine "undeniably testifies to this Indian origin, through Egypt, of the Neo-Platonic dogmas" (PPI p. 58), while the doctrine of the ideality of time appeared "probably for the first time in western philosophy" in Plotinus, but had "long been current in the east" (PPI p. 59). Schopenhauer inferred from Porphyry's report of Plotinus' aspiration to accompany Gordian's armies to Persia and India that his intention was to encounter the Indian wisdom he received from his teacher, Ammonius Saccus, in its original context (PPI p. 60).

In addition to being a source for ancient western philosophy, we saw at the close of the last chapter that Schopenhauer also thought that Indian wisdom had been the original source of western religion. Jesus was alternatively an *avatār* or a Buddha who attempted to graft the immanent, ethical doctrines of Indo-Egyptian wisdom onto an opposing and incompatible theoretical scheme, the result being the contradictory complex of dogmas that make up Christianity. With the descent of the Dark Ages and the termination of intellectual exchange with the east, Schopenhauer speculated that Dionysius the Areopagite, "who probably lived in Alexandria" during the last period of ideological fermentation at the close of the fifth century, had been the conduit for the "drop of Indian wisdom" that occasionally seeped into Christian doctrine during this period (PPI p. 64). He cites Scotus Erigena as an example, whose "Indian mildness" was the motivation for his refusal to consign sinners to an eternity in hell (PPI p. 62). And, notwithstanding theism's consolidation during the Middle Ages and the state privileges bestowed upon it up to the nineteenth century in Europe, Schopenhauer maintained that several philosophers during this period converged with Indian wisdom independent of historical transmission. Giordano Bruno and Spinoza would have escaped the persecution they suffered for their heterodox monism had they philosophised in their spiritual homeland on the banks of the Ganges (WWRI p. 422n.2), while Kant's *Critique of Pure Reason* would have been received as a "salutary confirmation of the orthodox doctrine of idealism" in Buddhist countries (FR p. 187). Even the surreptitious pantheism of his professorial contemporaries was, according to Schopenhauer, a sub-standard version of Indian pantheism, "which is also destined later to pass into the popular creed. *Ex oriente lux* [Out of the east comes light]." (PPI p. 54)

Schopenhauer's potted history of the various ways in which oriental ideas have both fructified and supplied a standard of adequacy for western metaphysics and ethics subverts Douglas Berger's argument that there is "something highly suspect" about Schopenhauer's "sharp dichotomisation of the 'philosophical' and 'religious' approaches to metaphysics".[29] This is especially evident in Schopenhauer's evaluation of Neo-Platonism's contribution to philosophy, which he considered unoriginal and formal and limited to translating the substance of Indian wisdom into the abstract concepts of Greek philosophy. As mentioned previously, whereas Hegel and Husserl used the distinction between allegorical and conceptual form to assert the superiority of western over eastern thought, Schopenhauer's preference for intuitive perception over reason led him to elevate the allegories of Indian religion over the abstractions of mainstream western metaphysics.

We also noted previously that Schopenhauer combined his doctrine of the irrelevance of history to philosophy with a fascination for the antiquity of the Indian religions, which he saw as an additional consideration confirming their intrinsic authenticity and excellence. In the notes he took from *Asiatick Researches* between November 1815 and May 1816 he methodically transcribed estimations of the dates of the Indian scriptures, such as Sir William Jones' comment that three of the *Vedas* are "more than 3000 years old" (MRAR p. 208).[30] Such broad timelines not only demonstrated that Indian wisdom was older and more original than either Moses or the Greeks, but gave the impression that it was pre-historical, primordial truth itself. This gave Schopenhauer confidence that it was a suitable candidate for the satisfaction of metaphysical need: conscious that his enthusiastic prediction of the decline of Judaeo-Christian monotheism amounted to an upheaval of fifteen centuries of continuous metaphysical reflection and spiritual practice in Europe, he recommended the Indian religions as palliatives for this rupture, for they were, as he thought, the original *Weltanschauung* of the forefathers of present-day Europeans:

> We may therefore hope that one day even Europe will be purified of all Jewish mythology. Perhaps the century has come in which all the peoples of the Japhetic group of languages coming from Asia will again receive the

---

[29] Berger (2004a) p. 242.
[30] Schopenhauer is quoting from Jones (1790) pp. 305-6.

sacred religions of their native country; for they have again become ripe
for these after having long gone astray. (PPII p. 226)

A consequence of Schopenhauer's rejection of the philosophy of history
and its belief in progress was that he did not consider the originality and
antiquity of the Indian religions to be proofs of their childlike simplicity,
or that they were products of an infant state of civilisation since superseded.
He thought that the Indians had established the basis for a refined culture
from the earliest times, as testified by the "highest human wisdom" contained in the *Upaniṣads* (PPII p. 398). As a result, he did not expect Indian
culture to benefit greatly from colonisation by Europeans. Colonialism
might bring the fruits of European technical know-how and facility with
concepts — such as science, technological innovation and more effective
means of social and political organisation — but Schopenhauer thought that
neither "constitutions, legal systems, steam-engines, nor telegraphs can
ever make anything that is essentially better." (WWRII p. 443) For him,
real culture consisted of metaphysical and ethical wisdom, in which "the
ancients are still our teachers" (WWRII p. 187). In opposition, therefore,
to apologists of the English presence in India, Schopenhauer feared that
colonial facilitation of missionary activity might bring about Indian cultural
decline. Anglican missionaries were using colonial power as a tool for per-
suading Indians to convert to a distorted form of their original faith, teaching them that they are made out of nothing and that Jesus is the sole and
exclusive *avatār*. Schopenhauer considered it fortunate that their sermons
had so far met "with such pathetically little success" (PPII p. 222), and he
frequently and gleefully drew attention to evidence or reports of the failure
of Christian missions in India, mischievously suggesting that the greatest
value of evangelists such as Spence Hardy consisted in their having "fur-
nished us with admirable and complete accounts of Brahmanism and Buddhism and with faithful and accurate translations of sacred books" (PPII
p. 226). Since he thought that the religions of India represented a more
mature and advanced stage of metaphysical and moral insight than Christian theism, Schopenhauer (with a heavy dose of mischief) recommended
that missionaries redirect their efforts and seek to convert those whose
religious culture was genuinely inferior to their own, such as the "Hotten-
tots, Kaffirs, South Sea Islanders, and others", because "the Brahmins treat
the discourses of the missionaries with condescending smiles of approbation or with a shrug of the shoulders" (PPII p. 328).

Unlike almost all of his contemporaries writing on India, Schopenhauer exhibited little concrete interest in its social or political life, or in

the communal rituals of Hinduism or Buddhism. This indifference reflects his more general lack of interest in communal or institutional affairs, in favour of questions of metaphysical meaning, ethics and soteriology addressed to the individual. In his published works he referred to the institution of caste only once, and in the context of noting that the Buddha had cleansed Indian wisdom of some of its extrinsic forms, such as the myths and stories of Hinduism and the mythical institution of Vedic authority by which Brahmins had sustained their privileged position (WWRI p. 356). However, he offers this observation without further comment, and his remarks on caste differ radically from the fulminations on its pernicious social consequences found in the works of Herder, Frie-drich Schlegel and Hegel. Indeed, at one point Schopenhauer seemed to affirm the rationale of caste divisions, albeit on intellectual rather than social grounds. He maintained that the division between the twice-born castes who have the right to read the *Vedas*, and the masses who have to make do with folk versions of its teachings, was an Indic parallel of his contrast between those whose metaphysical need is satisfied by exoteric or allegorical systems of metaphysics, and the intellectual elite whose need is nurtured by esoteric or philosophical metaphysics (WWRI p. 355).

III. Sources and Nature of Indian Wisdom

Schopenhauer regarded the metaphysical and ethical insights of Indian culture as products of genius, possession of which distinguishes its bearer from ordinary mortals through the power of his intellect which, exceed-ing the demands of his will, is capable of obtaining an objective view of things. However, in Schopenhauer's view the intellectual power of genius is not necessarily or originally a facility for conceptual thought, for the latter is mere "talent". The condition for genius lies instead "in the com-pleteness and energy of the knowledge of *perception* [*der Vollkommen-heit und Energie der anschauenden Erkenntniß*]" (WWRII p. 376), which facilitates apprehension of the universal aspect of things within particular objects, their essence or Platonic Idea divested of relations, especially the relations they have to the body and its needs and purposes as the visible expression of individual will (WWRII p. 377). Schopenhauer maintained that this ability to perceive the universal in the particular was "extremely lively in those sublime authors of the *Upaniṣads* of the *Vedas*" (WWRII p. 475), whose "almost superhuman conceptions" is testimony to their possession of "greater energy of the intuitive faculty of knowledge [*größere Energie der intuitiven Erkenntnißkräfte*]" (WWRII p. 162).

In addition to greater energy of the faculty of perception, Schopenhauer also attributed to the *ṛṣis* a greater capacity for rational thought. This was a consequence of their standing "considerably nearer to the beginning of the human race and to the original source of organic nature than we do", which entailed that they possessed "a more genuine disposition of mind [*eine richtigere Stimmung des Geistes*]." (WWRII p. 162) In other words, the reasoning faculty of the *ṛṣis* was uncorrupted by the erroneous metaphysical pictures or occluding concepts of an existing tradition, which enabled them to grasp (*auffassen*) "the inner essence of things more clearly and profoundly" than succeeding generations, and to portray this inner essence in adequate and truly representative imagery (WWRII p. 475). These twofold mental properties of perceptive power and rational clarity placed the *ṛṣis* "in a position to satisfy the need for metaphysics in a more estimable manner" than founders of other religious traditions (WWRII p. 162). In summary, Schopenhauer looked upon the allegorical doctrines of the Indian religions as sacred vessels containing and communicating the insights of genius, or the *ṛṣis*' original perception of the Platonic Ideas.

Schopenhauer also credited the *ṛṣis* with having anticipated the twofold assumptions of his own philosophy, and therefore of all sound metaphysical enquiry. Having perceived that the objects of external experience are merely ideal or *māyā*, they "started from the *subject*, from *ātma*, from *jīvātman*" in their attempt to solve the riddle of existence and give content to the inner nature of the phenomenon (MRI p. 116). They thereby established the Indian tradition of metaphysical reflection on correct presuppositions, whose introduction into Europe had been attended by many false turns and fruitless meanderings, from Descartes through Kant and up to Schopenhauer himself, on account of the predominance of the realist view.[31] Realism engenders the belief that metaphysical need can be satisfied "through the relations of *objects*, especially through the *principle of sufficient reason or ground*", with the result that European philosophers have represented an external object, God, "as constructing the world, deciding the fate of men, and so forth." (MRI p. 116)

But apart from Schopenhauer's high estimation of the mental faculties of the *ṛṣis* and their early discovery of the methodical principles

---

[31] See the essay 'Sketch of a History of the Doctrine of the Ideal and the Real' for Schopenhauer's account of the difficulties that attended the introduction of the "fundamental view" of idealism into Europe (PPI pp. 3-28).

underpinning all valid metaphysical enquiry, he consistently referred to Hinduism and Buddhism as religions and never as philosophies, and for two reasons: initially, the form in which they have communicated the insights of the *ṛṣis* has been allegorical rather than conceptual, and even when this medium has approached the conceptual clarity of philosophy through refinement, as he thought it had in Buddhism, they have been defended on authority rather than supported through argument. As previously discussed, these two features were Schopenhauer's main criteria for distinguishing religious from philosophical interpretations of the world and existence.

Schopenhauer's contrast between the allegorical character of Indian thought and the conceptual form of European was hardly original for the time, and we have already encountered similar oppositions in the works of Herder, Friedrich Schlegel and Hegel. Even a scholar as seemingly sober as Sir William Jones ventured a version when he remarked that "reason and taste are the grand prerogatives of European minds, while the Asiaticks have soared to loftier heights in the sphere of imagination."[32] However, in opposition to Hegel, while in agreement with Romantics such as Herder and Schlegel, Schopenhauer persistently lamented European philosophy's tendency to dwell in the empyrean realm of abstractions, and its concomitant reluctance to descend to earth or perception, in order to check the credentials of concepts such as "substance, ground, cause, the good, perfection, necessity, possibility" (WWRII p. 40). Schopenhauer's conception of the origin, nature and value of concepts was almost the opposite to that of Hegel, for whom the Idea to which all philosophical thought aspires is only formally abstract, but as the union of different determinations of reality, it is in content the most concrete rather than the emptiest unit of knowledge.[33] This contrast between their respective notions of the nature and possibilities of conceptual thought is partly reflected in their opposing evaluations of the Indian tradition in relation to western metaphysics.

One consequence of Schopenhauer's occasional use of Indian thought as a benchmark for criticising the abstractions of European philosophy

---

[32] Jones (1789b) p. 407.

[33] Hegel (1974) p. 24. As we have seen, Schopenhauer also used the term Idea to refer to the Platonic archetypes of natural forces and kinds, or concrete universals embodied in and known through intuitive perception of particulars. Whereas, therefore, Schopenhauer's Ideas are eternal archetypes that pre-exist the particulars that instantiate them, and thus a unity prior to perception (WWRI p. 234-5), for Hegel the Idea is the consummation of the self-movement of the concept, or the dialectical development of speculative thought, and thus a unity consequent on thought.

was that he occasionally pressed his conception of the contrasting tendencies of the two traditions to unwarranted extremes. His belief that Indian metaphysics originated in the intuitive faculty of the *ṛṣis* encouraged him to think that it was exclusively concerned with problems of experience, while European philosophy expended its intellectual energies on pointless, logical or conceptual puzzles. This rigid contrast led to his outright dismissal of the story, reported by William Jones from Persian sources, that Aristotle's nephew Callisthenes had discovered a complete system of logic in India and sent it to his uncle, whereupon it had been incorporated into Aristotle's systemisation of the formal part of thinking (WWRI p. 48).[34] This was clearly motivated by Schopenhauer's concern to preserve the Romantic image of India in relation to Europe, since he was aware of the existence of a school of logic in ancient India, the Navya-Nyāya, having taken notes from Colebrooke's essay on it and cited other ideas from the essay in his published works (MRIII p. 701; WN p. 44). His public disregard for the logic of Navya-Nyāya enabled Schopenhauer to sustain his polemical and Romantic-inspired image of India as the intuitionist, mystical and ideal corrective to the overly abstract character of European thought, and its modern commitment to conceptual-technical concerns.

As a result, Schopenhauer never contributed to the debate initiated by Hegel concerning the superiority of Greek logic over the "Hindu syllogism" of Colebrooke's essay.[35] Instead, Schopenhauer constructed a speculative history to show "how the course of Greek culture had prepared for and led up to" the logic of Aristotle without outside influence from India or elsewhere (WWRI p. 48). He located the origin of European logic in the "pleasure of debate" found among the Eleatics, Megarics and Sophists, which led to the discovery of natural rules of reasoning, until someone "systematic to the point of pedantry" expressed these in a system of abstract propositions (WWRI p. 47). In "the dreary Middle Ages" Aristotelian logic was "elevated to the centre of all knowledge", thereby neutering philosophical wonder and its impulse to reflect on problems arising from life and experience, which represented a threat to the system of settled theological dogmas. Lacking "real knowledge" and the freedom to seek it, scholastic philosophy "feasted only on formulas and words" (WWRI p. 48), while the material part of scholastic metaphysics was derived from the allegories and fables of Holy Scripture, on

---

[34] Jones (1799) p. 163.
[35] For an account of which see Ganeri (1996): Hegel's discussion of Nyāya appears in Hegel (1974) pp. 141-4.

the basis of which it established its pseudo-rational conclusions (MRIII p. 501). Schopenhauer thought that scholastic hyper-rationalism and its tendency to conflate real and logical connections had remained a persistent feature of European philosophy up to the present, distorting the achievements and magnifying the errors of even the "great Kant" (WWRI p. 453). Since he hoped that the oriental renaissance would correct the endemic rationalism of European speculation, he felt obliged to characterise eastern thought as fundamentally different in kind, and lacking a systematic tradition of formal logic.

However, and contrary to the frequent implication that Schopenhauer's philosophy of religion employs antitheses that seem to be synonymous or related — between eastern religion and western philosophy, allegories and concepts, and exoteric and esoteric forms of metaphysics — he maintained that the distinction between a higher and lower metaphysics was found "even in India, the fatherland of metaphysics", on account of the fact that there "cannot be one philosophy for all as there is one mathematics or one physics for all." (MRIII p. 694) This confirms the tendency noted earlier when we suggested that Schopenhauer's revised estimation of the concept of *nirvāṇa* complicates his contrast between the allegories of Indian religion and the concepts of European philosophy. According to him the esoteric doctrine of Indian wisdom was the perennial philosophy of the ideality of the Many and the reality of the One, discovered by the *ṛṣis* and expressed in the Sanskrit maxim "*tat tvam asi*" or "that art thou". Schopenhauer further learnt from Sir William Jones that the Upaniṣadic doctrine of *māyā*, or the illusoriness of the Many, had been systematised by Vedānta in its teaching that the properties of matter, "solidity, impenetrability, and extended figure", have "no essence independent of mental perception; that existence and perceptibility are convertible terms",[36] which he heralded as an Indian equivalent to Kant's doctrine concerning "the compatibility of empirical reality with transcendental ideality." (WWRI p. 4)

But although Schopenhauer thought that some concepts and doctrines from the Indian religions were comparable to those of western philosophy, he still thought that the former fell short of the latter, on account of the fact that they lack argumentative bases. In his view the majority of people belonging to the twice-born castes accepted the metaphysical doctrine of the One in the Many second-hand, through scriptural records of the intuitions of the *ṛṣis*, whereas in contemporary Europe the same

---

[36] Jones (1799) p. 164.

doctrine was supported by strict proofs formulated by Kant (BM p. 209). Most Hindus and Buddhists therefore knew this philosophical truth in a non-philosophical way, on the authority of texts, teachers or mystical adepts, while post-Kantians in Europe were able to defend it through reasons, in agreement with Schopenhauer's claim that philosophy has "its verification and credentials *in itself*", while religious doctrines have external supports (WWRII p. 164).[37]

But if Schopenhauer thought that the twice-born castes accepted the metaphysics of One-in-All in the absence of strict proof, he thought that the mass of people were incapable of even understanding it. In lieu of its direct communication, therefore, the moods, evaluations and conduct warranted by it were impressed on the hearts and minds of the Indian populace through the exoteric doctrine of metempsychosis (PPI p. 111). Whereas the "great saying" of the *Upaniṣads* "*tat tvam asi*" expresses directly and without falsification the present metaphysical identity of all beings, metempsychosis represents this identity successively, and thus figuratively, insofar as it implies that the phenomenal forms of time and causality are real, in the sense of independent of the subject (WWRII p. 601). But this suggests that Schopenhauer regarded the popular or exoteric tradition of Indian metaphysics as realist rather than idealist, which accords with his observation that realism is "inborn" and the "original disposition of the intellect" (WWRI p. xxiii), but conflicts with other claims he makes. It especially contradicts his tendency to present the Indian religions as unabashedly and entirely idealist, and thus evidence of the merely local and contingent status of European realism, which has been sustained by the cultural dominance and educational privileges of the realist metaphysics of Judaeo-Christianity and the implications of creation out of nothing:

> [i]n India idealism is the doctrine even of popular religion, not merely of Brahmanism, but also of Buddhism; only in Europe is it paradoxical in consequence of the essentially and inevitably realistic fundamental view of Judaism. (FR pp. 50-1)

---

[37] As an aside, it might be noted that, irrespective of Schopenhauer's assertion that Kant's idealism is supported by proofs with "such a complete power of conviction that I number its propositions among the incontestable truths" (WWRI p. 437), a cursory reading of his 'Criticism of the Kantian Philosophy' leaves one confused as to which of Kant's proofs he considered completely compelling, since he seems to find fault with all of them. Ultimately, it seems that he thought that the strongest argument for idealism was the mutual implication of the terms subject and object (WWRI p. 434), which is, at the very least, a *petitio principii*.

It is difficult to know what to make of this contradiction, unless Schopenhauer is saying that believers in metempsychosis are virtual or implicit idealists. This is the likeliest explanation, but since he never commented on this issue, it can only be conjectural. Ultimately, the contradiction might be a consequence of Schopenhauer's overly casual and non-systematic presentation of the Indian religions, and of the difficulties he faced in satisfactorily assimilating them to the philosophical positions and contrasts he wanted them to serve.

In summary, Schopenhauer thought that, from the earliest period, the basic materials of the Indian religions consisted of the *ṛṣis'* intuitive and mystical apprehension of the ideality of the Many and the reality of the One, which was subsequently communicated through the esoteric doctrines of *māyā* and *"tat tvam asi"*, and exoterically to the masses through the doctrine of metempsychosis. The next major development in the intellectual history of India occurred when the Buddha demythologised the popular presentation of Indian wisdom and stripped away the allegorical veils and "merely mythological fictions" of Brahmanism (PPII p. 401). According to Schopenhauer, the Buddha managed to achieve this *without* at the same time forfeiting a mass following:

> If we go to the root of the matter, even the fantastic and sometimes strange Indian mythology, still constituting today as it did thousands of years ago the religion of the people, is only the teaching of the *Upaniṣads* which is symbolised, in other words, clad in images and thus personified and mythicised with due regard to the people's powers of comprehension. According to his powers of education, every Hindu traces, feels, surmises, or clearly sees through it and behind it…[t]he purpose of the Buddha Sakya Muni, on the other hand, was to separate the kernel from the shell, to free the exalted teaching itself from all admixture with images and gods, and to make its pure intrinsic worth accessible and intelligible even to the people. In this he was marvellously successful and his religion is, therefore, the most excellent on earth and is represented by the greatest number of followers. (PPII p. 225)

In Schopenhauer's estimation, the Buddha's contribution to Indian wisdom was therefore twofold. On the one hand he separated the popular doctrine of metempsychosis "from all admixture with images and gods" and represented it in a more adequate form, which, as we shall see later, Schopenhauer considered to have anticipated his own doctrine of the metaphysical permanence of the will (PPII pp. 276-7). On the other hand, the Buddha improved on the esoteric doctrine of *"tat tvam asi"* by defining the "that", or metaphysical principle of identity, in negative terms, as the cessation of the phenomenon or *nirvāṇa*. However, it is important to note that Schopenhauer did not regard Buddhism as an innovation: the Buddha did not discover or teach new, distinctly Buddhist, truths, nor did he do away with the experiential bases of Indian wisdom or formulate arguments in support of them. The Buddha merely clarified the form in which his predecessors, the *ṛṣis*, had deposited the content of their intuitions.

Schopenhauer's characterisation of Buddhism as "essentially a *Hinduism* that is clarified of the crazy stories of Indian mythology as well as of the caste system" (MRIV p. 48) would conflict with the view of most Buddhists,[38] and even T.R.V. Murti, a practising Hindu, attributed a greater degree of originality to the Buddha.[39] It might be noted, however, that Schopenhauer's theory that the Buddha merely communicated Upaniṣadic wisdom in a different form was common in the nineteenth century. Max Müller similarly argued that "the doctrines of the *Upaniṣads* are no doubt pure Buddhism, or rather Buddhism is on many counts the consistent carrying out of the principle laid down in the *Upaniṣads*."[40] This thesis was resurrected by the Neo-Vedāntins in the twentieth century, whose unified image of Indian wisdom served as the ideological accompaniment of the movement for India's independence. One of Neo-Vedānta's most prominent figures, Sir Sarvepalli Radhakrishnan, propagated the image of India's seamless wisdom when he depicted the Buddha as a closet Hindu, who cleansed rather than displaced the teachings of the *Upaniṣads*, but whose rationalist rejection of the authority of the *Vedas* obliged him to refer to the Absolute through negations rather than direct descriptions.[41]

---

[38] Rahula (1967) pp. 9-10.
[39] Murti (1974) p. 17.
[40] Quoted from Radhakrishnan (1996) vol. I, p. 470.
[41] Ibid.

CHAPTER 6

THE ORIENTAL RENAISSANCE

I. Cosmogony and Metaphysics

In his presentation of specific doctrines belonging to the Indian religions, Schopenhauer unabashedly assimilated them to his own philosophical positions. His interpretative practice implies a convergence on the material or perceptual level between the "fundamental wisdom" of Brahmanism and Buddhism and the "single thought" (*einziger Gedanke*) that unfolds throughout the four books of *The World as Will and Representation* (WWRI p. xii). In a manuscript note from 1831 he suggested that the intuitions that resulted in his pessimistic and godless philosophy had been prefigured in the experience of the Buddha centuries earlier, and that this was the basis of the conceptual agreement he detected between them:

> When I was seventeen, without any proper schooling, I was affected by the *misery and wretchedness of life*, as was the Buddha when in his youth he caught sight of sickness, old age, pain and death. The truth which the world clearly and loudly proclaimed soon threw off the jewish dogmas that had been stamped on my mind, and the result for me was that this world could not be the work of an all-bountiful, infinitely good being, but rather of a devil who had summoned into existence creatures in order to gloat over the sight of their anguish and agony. (MRIV p. 119)

In this chapter we focus on Schopenhauer's interpretation of the main doctrines of the Indian religions in detail, in order to construct a systematic picture of his understanding of Indian thought. Since the main thesis of this book is that Schopenhauer's philosophical sponsorship of the Indian religions was stimulated by his conviction of the intellectual and cultural decline of Judaeo-Christian monotheism, the following exposition of his interpretation will mirror, as closely as the material permits, the thematic structure and development of ideas in Chapters 3 and 4 on Christianity. In this section, therefore, we begin by looking at Schopenhauer's presentation of the mythical cosmogonies of Hinduism and what they imply about the Indian understanding of the inner nature of the world, before passing over to his account of how Buddhism improved on these myths by restating their basic conceptions without mythological admixture. In the following section we see how Schopenhauer situated these cosmogonical and metaphysical doctrines within his typology of pessimistic and optimistic *Weltanschauungen*, and how he related their teachings on the nature and value of the world and existence to the problem of evil and suffering. In the closing section of this chapter we look at Schopenhauer's assessment of the adequacy of Indian metaphysics in relation to two other criteria of metaphysical need; its ability to provide a satisfactory account of ethical virtue and asceticism, and its capacity to sustain a viable doctrine of immortality or continued existence.

In the last chapter we noted how Schopenhauer thought he had discovered the "fundamental view" of esoteric idealism in Sir William Jones' summary of the position of Vedānta as "existence and perceptibility are convertible terms",[1] as well as an esoteric form of metaphysical monism in the Upaniṣadic phrase "*tat tvam asi*" or "that art thou". According to him, this twofold view of the illusoriness of the Many and their unity in a metaphysical One had been communicated to the Indian masses in a number of ways — for a moral purpose through the doctrine of transmigration or metempsychosis, and for metaphysical edification in creation myths such as the *Puruṣa-Sūkta* from the *Ṛg-Veda*.[2] In this hymn the creation of the world is traced to a primal sacrifice and dismemberment of the Supreme Person (*puruṣa*), which leads to the view that the stuff of the universe or inner kernel of things is originally and essentially divine. Schopenhauer read the opening of this hymn in Colebrooke's translation:

> 1. 'The embodied spirit which hath a thousand heads, a thousand eyes, a thousand feet, stands in the human breast, while he totally pervades the earth.' 2. 'That being is this universe, and all that has been or will be; he is that which grows by nourishment, and he is the distributor of immortality.' 3. 'Such is his greatness; and therefore is he the most excellent embodied spirit: the elements of the universe are one portion of him; and three portions of him are immortality in heaven.' 4. 'That threefold being rose above (this world); and the single portion of him remained in this universe, which consists of what does, and what does not, taste (the reward of good and bad actions): again he pervaded the universe.' (MRAR p. 222)[3]

Schopenhauer distinguished the teaching of this myth from the monotheistic dogma of creation out of nothing, on the grounds that it communicates in the medium of allegory the exoteric doctrine that the world is an

[1] Jones (1799) p. 164.
[2] *Ṛg-Veda*, 10.90 i-iv (Doniger O'Flaherty (ed., 2005) pp. 29-32).
[3] Colebrooke (1803) p. 251.

appearance of a unitary principle, and therefore conveys in symbolic form the doctrine of the One in the Many that is explicitly transmitted through the doctrines of *māyā* and *tat tvam asi* (PPII p. 222).[4]

However, it is one thing for Schopenhauer to state that the ancient *ṛṣis* were the first to discover that the world is the appearance of a metaphysical One, conveyed to the masses through creation myths such as the *Puruṣa-Sūkta*, and another to claim that they conceptualised this unitary One in the same way that he did, as striving will-to-live. In the first edition of *The World as Will and Representation* Schopenhauer remarked that his metaphysics of the will was "the very first communication of an idea that has never previously existed" (WWRI p. 162): however, he seems to have meant by this that he was the first to communicate the doctrine *explicitly*, for he frequently discovered parallels to and implicit anticipations of it in an array of sources — including the findings of modern science, the theories of philosophical precursors, the insights of genius embodied in art and literature, and especially the doctrines of the Indian religions. The notes he took from the first nine volumes of *Asiatick Researches* between November 1815 and May 1816 show that he expected to find his own ideas confirmed by Indian sources from the period of his first encounter with them. He copied out verbatim Colebrooke's explanation of the Sanskrit term *asu* as "the unconscious volition, which occasions an act necessary to the support of life, as breathing, etc." (MRAR p. 243),[5] and quoted it twenty years later in *On the Will in Nature* as an external confirmation of his teaching that "organic life is unquestionably derived from the will." (WN p. 45) When, in the same article, Colebrooke translated a verse from the *Taittirīya Upaniṣad* as "[t]hat, whence all beings are produced: that, by which they live, when born: that, towards which they tend; & that, into which they pass; do thou

---

[4] Contrary to Schopenhauer's monist interpretation, the Vedānta theologian Rāmānuja used the *Puruṣa-Sūkta's* distinction between three portions of the Supreme Person in heaven and one portion that undergoes *karma* and rebirth (or "tastes" the rewards of "good and bad actions") as scriptural justification for his metaphysics of Viśiṣṭādvaita, or 'qualified non-dualism'. Rāmānuja's theology is monotheist, but his cosmogony has no exact parallel in western thought, being neither monism nor pantheism, nor even creation out of nothing. The clearest scriptural support for it appears in the *Bhagavad-Gītā*, where Kṛṣṇa as Supreme Lord teaches that he brought the world into being by activating his lower material nature, while his higher conscious Self transcends and governs the course of events (9.5-8). Schopenhauer often quoted from August Wilhelm Schlegel's 1823 Latin translation of the *Gītā*, but seems to have taken its references to a Supreme Lord (*summum dominum*) as literary personifications of an impersonal principle rather than evidence of Indian theism (BM p. 214).

[5] Colebrooke (1808) p. 426n.1.

seek, for that is <u>Brahme</u>",[6] Schopenhauer appended the marginal comment "[t]he will to live is the source and essence of things." (MRAR p. 247)

However, Schopenhauer might have been better advised to interpret these passages as anticipations of his doctrine of the universal subject of knowledge than as anticipations of his metaphysics, because Colebrooke's translations consistently lead up to the conclusion that the metaphysics of Hinduism is based on a conscious and intellectual rather than vital and blind principle.[7] For example, Colebrooke's explanation of the Sanskrit term *asu* appears in a footnote to a passage that first considers and then rejects *asu* or "unconscious volition" as a candidate for the inner essence of things, and which concludes with the statement that "all that is the eye of intelligence. On intellect [every thing] is founded; the world is the eye of intellect, and intellect is its foundation. Intelligence is [BRAHME] the great one."[8]

However, Schopenhauer did confine such speculative explorations of parallels between will and *asu* or <u>Brahme</u> to his manuscript notes, and did not broadcast them in the first edition of *The World as Will and Representation*. This suggests that, by 1818 at least, he was still fairly circumspect about the relation between the central concepts of his system and the metaphysical connotations of key Sanskrit terms.[9] The meaning of *māyā* was fairly unproblematic to him, and he used it as a synonym for the Kantian phenomenon at several points.[10] But nowhere in the first volume do we find the sort of positive assertions of equivalence between Sanskrit terms and the will that we find in his manuscript notes. However, he still gives some indication of his *a priori* expectation that a

[6] Ibid. pp. 455-6. The passage is from the Taittiriya Upaniṣad III.I.1.

[7] On only a few occasions did Schopenhauer use Indian texts as independent confirmations of his doctrine of the subject of knowledge, such as in the second, 1847 edition of *On the Fourfold Root of the Principle of Sufficient Reason* where — in opposition to the reflexivity of the subject presupposed by Fichte's and Schelling's intellectual intuition — he quotes from the *Bṛhadāraṇyaka Upaniṣad* in support of his view that the subject knows but is not known (FR p. 208; Bṛ.Up. III.7.23).

[8] Colebrooke 1808: p. 426. Schopenhauer copied out these closing sentences also, and underlined the idealist-sounding phrases, such as "<u>all that is the eye of intelligence</u>", "<u>On intellect every thing is founded: the world is the eye of intellect:</u>" (MRAR p. 244). The original is from the *Aitareya Upaniṣad* III.I.1-3.

[9] Which casts further doubt on Urs App's hypothesis (discussed in Chapter 1) that Friedrich Majer's German translation of Wilkins' *Bhagavad-Gītā* was "crucially important for the genesis of Schopenhauer's metaphysics of will" (App (2006b) p. 76).

[10] From Payne's index *māyā* is used as a synonym for the phenomenon or *principium individuationis* at WWRI p. 8, p. 17, p. 253, p. 284, p. 352, p. 365, p. 370, p. 373, pp. 378-9, p. 397, p. 399, p. 419, p. 420, p. 495.

dimly divined and mythologically expressed species of vitalism was the basis of Indian wisdom. At one point he argues that when Hesiod and Parmenides made Eros "the first, that which creates, the principle from which all things emerge", they thereby provided symbolic confirmation of his teaching that the "inner being of nature, the will-to-live, expresses itself most strongly in the sexual impulse"; for the same reason the "*māyā* of the Indians, the work and fabric of which are the whole world of illusion, is paraphrased by *amor*." (WWRI p. 330) The presuppositions of this connection are also operative in his exegesis of the significance and meaning of the creation myths featuring the Hindu god Brahmā. Colebrooke's translations informed Schopenhauer that Brahmā was a personification of the Hindu conception of the metaphysical One behind the Many, while the innumerable stories recounting Brahmā's lascivious acts further suggested that he was the Indian equivalent of Eros and a symbol of the sexual impulse.[11] The upshot was Schopenhauer's references to Brahmā as "the most sinful and lowest god" of the *Trimūrti*, symbolising "generation, origination" (WWRI p. 276) and "the sensual pleasure of procreation" (WWRI p. 399). This may explain why he described the soteriological goal of "reabsorption in *Brahman*" as an evasive myth or "meaningless" word (WWRI p. 411), for it conflicts with his own theory that salvation is attained through denial of the principle of generation as opposed to reunion with it.

Schopenhauer's later readings on Hindu mythology tended to confirm his early view of its implications for Hindu metaphysics. At some stage between 1818 and 1844 he read James Taylor's 1812 English translation of the Sanskrit drama the *Prabodha Chandrodaya*.[12] Written in the thirteenth century by Kṛṣṇa Miśra, this work not only became one of Schopenhauer's main sources for information on the significance of Brahmā, but also went some way towards verifying his maxim that religious texts communicate philosophical knowledge in the medium of allegory, since it belongs to a genre of Sanskrit works in which plot development and character stand for abstract or philosophical principles. Its influence is evident in Schopenhauer's comments that Brahmā created

---

[11] Schopenhauer referred to the story from the *Matsya Purāṇa* in which Brahmā's desire for his daughter leads to him sprouting four faces in order to see her better (WN p. 49n.1). Although this reference appears in a post-1854 redaction of *On the Will in Nature*, Schopenhauer's source for the story is an article by Captain Francis Wilford from volume VI of *Asiatick Researches*, which he first read between November 1815 and May 1816.

[12] Kṛṣṇa Miśra (2006).

the world "contrary to his will" (MRIV p. 149), that he "lives and suffers in you and me, in my horse and in your dog" (FR p. 184), that his sufferings persist until "the first beings he has begotten again pass out of existence through contemplation and chastity" (MRIV p. 149), and thereby bring about his redemption (PPII p. 300). Schopenhauer is clearly assimilating the cycle of Brahmā myths to his own philosophical drama of the blind will's objectification of itself in the medium of individuation, suffering and conflict, whereby it obtains knowledge of its inner nature in the reflective consciousness of human beings, and thereafter brings about its voluntary self-denial. In his notes he further speculated as to whether Brahmā might be "akin to the Italian *bramare* (ardent desire)" and thus

> also *Brahm* [or *Brahman*], the primary and original being from which the three gods [of the *Trimūrti*] originate: the origin and kernel of the world is then ardent desire, the vigorous and impetuous will. (MRIV p. 150)

In the late 1840s Schopenhauer found further confirmation of this interpretation in Max Müller's statement that "*'Brahman means originally force, will, wish, & the propulsive power of creation'*" (GB p. 405),[13] as well as in Müller's definition of Brahmā as "will, desire [*Willen, Begehr*]" (GB p. 414). In his last work of 1851, *Parerga and Paralipomena*, the figure of Brahmā is referred to as evidence of the radical discontinuity between the cosmogony of the Hindu *Purāṇas* and the creation myths of Judaism, Christianity and Islam, for the former teach

> no creator God, but a world-soul called *Brahman* (in the neuter). *Brahmā*... as part of the *Trimūrti*, is merely a popular personification of *Brahman* in the extremely transparent Indian mythology. He obviously represents the generation, the origin, of beings just as Viṣṇu does their acme, and Śiva their destruction and extinction. Moreover, his production of the world is a sinful act, just as is the world incarnation of *Brahman*. (PPI p. 127)

Moira Nicholls has argued that Schopenhauer knew that his depiction of Brahmā as an evil principle and his creation as a sinful act was

> an interpretation of Indian mythology rather than an actual statement of accepted Hindu doctrine. This is important since it is doubtful that the similarity between Brahmā and the will is nearly as strong as Schopenhauer thinks. While Hindu doctrine asserts that *Brahman* is the sustainer of the world, it also maintains that Brahman is the ground of all value, the core of the true, the good, and the beautiful.[14]

---

[13] Müller (1847) p. 9.
[14] Nicholls (1999) p. 184.

Nicholls is correct to state that Hindu doctrine teaches that *Brahman* is "the ground of all value", but it is not at all clear that Schopenhauer regarded his characterisation of Brahmā as an interpretation rather than "actual statement of accepted Hindu doctrine." Moreover, the sources available to him in combination with the interpretative interests he brought to them seem to justify his characterisation. This claim requires some elaboration.

Scholars of Hinduism have long recognised that the term is a nominal referent for the religious life of the sub-continent, and that 'Hindu' and 'Hinduism' are blanket categories with little stable or univocal reference.[15] Although, of course, other religions are not completely uniform, the very quantity of literature and the diversity of tendencies incorporated within Hinduism means that it is equally true to say that Hindus believe that the world is the product of a mistake or an act of evil as it is to maintain that they believe that creation is a gift of a Supreme Person worthy of worship and adoration.[16]

As previously mentioned, Schopenhauer's preferred source for the Brahmā myths was the *Prabodha Chandrodaya*, a thirteenth-century text written by Kṛṣṇa Miśra, an adherent of the non-dual or Advaitic school of Vedānta. Advaita is the only Hindu or even Vedānta school whose interpretation of *māyā* is identical with that of Schopenhauer, for Advaitins maintain that scriptural references to *māyā* signify a cosmic power of illusion or primal ignorance (*avidyā*) which conceals from beings the truth concerning the identity between their inner self (*ātman*) and the ultimate Self or reality (*Brahman*). This ultimate reality is described as 'without' ('*nir*') 'quality' ('*guṇa*'), form, external relations or internal differentiation, and is, as Nicholls says, the metaphysical "ground of all value, the core of the true, the good and the beautiful." Another Advaitin term for *nirguṇa Brahman* is *sat-cit-ānanda*, or "being-consciousness-bliss". They maintain that a combination of scriptural study, yogic meditation, chastity and abstention from meretricious pleasures will enable beings to discriminate the real from the unreal and the changing from the unchanging in the Self, overcome cosmic ignorance,

---

[15] Lipner (1998) Chapter 1.

[16] For details of the anti-cosmic view see Doniger O' Flaherty (1976) Chapter 3. Schopenhauer was familiar with texts which express the contrary, optimistic and theistic view of loving devotion (*bhaktimārga*) for the Supreme Person, such as the *Bhagavad-Gītā*. However, his reading of the *Gītā* was highly selective, and he usually referred to it in support of his monism and the ethics of compassion he founded upon it (WWRII p. 326; BM pp. 213-14).

attain release from the iron bonds of *karma*, repudiate the false attractions of *māyā*, and attain non-discursive, non-dual, super-mundane knowledge of their inner identity with *Brahman*. Advaita Vedānta's conception of *nirguṇa Brahman* as a fully-realised, quiescent cosmic consciousness, similar to the One of Plotinus or Aristotle's thought-thinking-itself, suggests that Schopenhauer's etymological speculation that *Brahman* originally signified "ardent desire, the vigorous and impetuous will" (MRIV p. 150) was simply false.

However if, as Advaitins say, *nirguṇa Brahman* — the ground or inner being of the world — is essentially still, quiescent consciousness, then whence cosmic ignorance, *karma* and *māyā*? Advaitins generally avoid explanations of the origin of this delusory world, arguing — as the Buddhists did before them — that it is more important to follow the path and attain liberation from *avidyā*, *karma* and *māyā* than enquire after their origin. However, in literary and non-technical texts written by Advaitins, such as Kṛṣṇa Miśra's *Prabodha Chandrodaya*, the origin of the world is frequently attributed to a personal creator, *saguṇa Brahman* (*Brahman* 'with qualities'), otherwise known as Brahmā. Advaitins claim, in opposition to other schools of Vedānta (such as Rāmānuja's Viśiṣṭādvaita), that Upaniṣadic texts in which *Brahman* is addressed as personal Lord and Creator are not, at the highest level, to be interpreted literally. In other words, they are steps on the ladder of metaphysical understanding, figurative concessions to the uncultivated religious consciousness that has not yet realised its inner identity with formless *nirguṇa Brahman*. And since the *Prabodha Chandrodaya* emerged from an Advaitin stable, it is no surprise to find it expressing the anti-cosmic tendency of Hinduism, explaining Brahmā's creation of the world as the product of his delusion, as an event contrary to his will, for which he must undergo atonement.[17] This suggests that Schopenhauer could often be an attentive reader of his Indian sources, and did not set out wilfully to misrepresent or over-interpret their content for his own purposes.

Schopenhauer's exegesis of the Brahmā myths suggests that he regarded Hindus as eastern Gnostics and therefore virtual atheists, since their principle of creation is an incompetent or malicious god unworthy of worship. But irrespective of his genuine admiration for Hindu mythology and his conviction of its ability to communicate his philosophical positions in the medium of allegory, he preferred what he took to be the outright and non-mythological atheism of Buddhism. We have already

---

[17] Doniger O'Flaherty (1976) p. 51.

mentioned his theory that the achievement of the Buddha consisted of discarding the allegorical casing of Indian wisdom, such as the "crazy stories" relating Brahmā's "sinful" creation of the world (MRIV p. 48; PPII p. 225). In one passage he indicates familiarity with the Buddhist story in which Brahmā appears as a vain and boastful deity, but whose proud assertions of his creative prowess fold under critical questioning from the Buddha, and who thereafter recognises the latter's superior wisdom and becomes a patron of the movement (WWRII p. 169).[18] Schopenhauer seems to have interpreted this story of the twilight of the Vedic gods as a symbolic declaration of Buddhist atheism, which he regarded as the religion's most interesting and distinctive attribute, and to which he referred on several occasions, citing the unanimous testimony of contemporary Buddhologists (FR p. 184; WN p. 134; WWRII p. 115; PPI pp. 116). He was equally pleased to find that Buddhism not only deconstructs the concept of divinity, but also rejects any doctrine of creation, and quoted from I. J. Schmidt to the effect that "'[t]he expression creation is foreign to Buddhism, since it knows only of world origins or formations'" (FR pp. 185). Buddhism's rejection of an absolute creator God made a very strong impression on Schopenhauer, and clearly influenced aspects of his philosophy of religion. It not only confirmed that the category of the divine is not a necessary condition for the satisfaction of metaphysical need, but Buddhism's successful amalgamation of atheism and morality also validated — and perhaps even served as the original inspiration for — Schopenhauer's religious typology, according to which it is irrelevant whether a religion is "monotheistic, polytheistic, pantheistic, or atheistic" (WWRII p. 170), since the "spirit and ethical tendency" are its essential elements, "not the myths in which it clothes them." (WWRII p. 623) These reflections led to his argument that "atheistic Buddhism is much more closely akin to Christianity than are optimistic Judaism and its variety, Islam" (WWRII p. 444), and thereby his theory of the Indian origin and essence of Christianity.

However, so far we have only seen Schopenhauer define Buddhism in accordance with what it is not — i.e., that it has no conception of the divine and no concomitant doctrine of creation. Do his works indicate the opposite — that he was acquainted with or in any way interested in

---

[18] Schopenhauer read this story in Alexander Csoma Körösi's synopsis of a Tibetan text, the *Kahgyur* (Körösi (1836)). Stories glorifying the Buddha's superior power and knowledge in relation to that of Brahmā date from the primitive origins of the religion, and were part of Buddhism's polemic against Vedic Hinduism and the caste order in India (for a Pali version of the tale, see the *Dīgha Nikāya* 1.215-23).

Buddhist accounts of the origin and inner nature of the world, or did he think that the negation of *nirvāṇa* and the silence of the sage was all that Buddhists had to say (or, rather, not say) on matters of metaphysics? The evidence contained in his published works is fairly sparse, since the passages in which Buddhism features prominently are almost always negative in intent, formulated to demonstrate monotheism's cultural specificity. However, it is to an extent possible to construct a positive image of Schopenhauer's conception of Buddhism from his tendency to contrast it with European metaphysics. Initially, in opposition to Friedrich Schlegel's assimilation of Buddhism to Jacobi's characterisation of Spinozistic pantheism (implied by Schlegel's comment that Buddhism teaches the morally debilitating doctrine of "the nothingness of all matter"[19]), Schopenhauer presents Buddhism as the contrary of pantheism, materialism or amoralism. For him pantheism is merely "a polite expression" for atheism (WN p. 132), for it presupposes theism as the norm and makes its appearance only after the breakdown of commonly approved procedures for validating the concept of God, but before the establishment of conditions that enable a confident rejection of the concept altogether. Pantheism is therefore a vacuous position, since to "call the world God is not to explain it, but only to enrich the language with a superfluous synonym for the word world." (PPII p. 99) By contrast, Schopenhauer's account of the intellectual history of classical India depicts Buddhism emerging from the virtual or practical atheism of Hinduism, in which Brahmā is depicted as an incompetent or "sinful" creator. This distinguishes the full-blooded and assured atheism espoused by Buddhism from the half-hearted unbelief of European pantheism, for "the Buddha did not regard as a theophany a world steeped in sin and suffering, whose beings, all doomed to die, exist for a short time in this way, that one devours the other." (WN p. 132)

Schopenhauer also — albeit indirectly — rebuffed Schlegel's argument that Buddhism supports moral fatalism by teaching "the nothingness of all matter". He shared Schlegel's moral objections to materialism, insofar as it denies the "essential thing of the whole of existence", namely "the morality of human conduct" (WN p. 139). However, Schopenhauer proclaimed Kant's idealism as a middle path which circumvents the disjunctive premise of the eighteenth century between materialism and fatalism or theism and moral freedom, thereby opening "the way to entirely different and deeper explanations of existence."

---

[19] Schlegel (1849) p. 489.

(WWRI p. 513) One such deeper explanation is contained in Buddhism, which spurns both theism and materialism and teaches the profounder doctrine of "the merely apparent existence of this world that is presented to our senses." (FR p. 187)[20] We saw previously that Schopenhauer thought that only idealism avoids the moral fatalism consequent on all systems of realism — whether theism or materialism — since only an idealist account of the phenomenon can ground our feelings of responsibility for what we have done on a transcendentally free act of self-constitution. And Schopenhauer found an implicit statement of his doctrine of transcendental freedom in Buddhism's ascription of "all changes in the world to the moral works of the animal beings" (WWRII pp. 169-170). Schopenhauer acknowledged that such an account of the origin of the world was likely to appear inscrutable to Europeans raised on a doctrine of creation out of nothing. As an instance he cited the story of the Dutch governor in Ceylon, whose faith prevented him from comprehending the "naïve, sincere and artless atheism" of the Sinhalese monks with whom he was discussing religious matters. When the governor asked them about the "supreme being who created the world", they replied that there is no higher being than the Buddha and that the world is not made but is

> self-created; and that nature spreads it out and draws it in again. They say that it is that, which existing, does not exist; that it is the necessary accompaniment of rebirths; but that these are the consequence of our sinful conduct. (FR p. 186)

In Schopenhauer's view therefore, the Buddhist theory of the nature and origin of the world is that it is the phenomenal unfolding of prior moral choice. Buddhism thus offers a solution to the central problem of western philosophy since Socrates, which is to

> connect the force which produces the phenomenon of the world and in consequence determines its nature, with the morality of the disposition or character, and thus to demonstrate a *moral* world-order as the basis of the *physical*. (WWRII p. 590)

And Buddhism traces the series of relations between antecedent moral choice and consequent world construction "to infinity", without termi-

---

[20] For this reason, one might say that Schopenhauer's assimilation of Buddhism to his version of transcendental idealism does have the corollary that it teaches the "nothingness of all matter" — or at least its nothingness apart from the subject, for Schopenhauer's idealism proclaims that "the intellect is that in the representation of which alone matter exists." (WWRII p. 16)

nating the series of conditions in a transcendent and objective First Cause, or all-powerful creator (WWRI p. 484). It is therefore one with esoteric Hinduism, insofar as both "assign to the world only a dreamlike existence and regard life as the consequence of our guilt." (PPII p. 378) However, Schopenhauer preferred Buddhism's exoteric presentation of this teaching to that of Hinduism, since the Buddha liberated "the exalted teaching...from all admixture with images and gods" (PPII p. 225) by explaining the form and content of the present as the ripening of prior choice or "consequence of our sinful conduct" (FR p. 186).

But if Schopenhauer thought that the Buddha had demythologised Hindu cosmogony by resolving the world on the sinful conduct of animal beings rather than the creative power of an incompetent god, in what way did he consider the Buddha to have improved on the ṛṣis' presentation of the metaphysical One animating nature's forms? In other words, did Schopenhauer discover an equivalent of his notion of will in Buddhist sources? His belief that the Buddha had demythologised the "crazy stories" of Hinduism featuring Brahmā, the personification of "ardent desire, the vigorous and impetuous will" (MRIV p. 150), combined with his understanding of Buddhist cosmogony as a system of moral becoming, would suggest that he had found a dim presentiment of his metaphysics in Buddhism. Furthermore, he had learnt that the Daoists — who he considered almost indistinguishable from the Buddhists on account of their mutual co-existence in China (WN p. 130) — deduced their concept of *T'ien*, or "the mind of Heaven", from "*the Will of mankind!*", which he hailed as a "striking and astonishing" confirmation of his metaphysics (WN p. 137).[21] However, Schopenhauer never explicitly claimed in his published works that Buddhism proclaims the will as the metaphysical essence of all phenomena, and the associations he made between his metaphysics and Buddhist doctrines were never as strong as those he made between the will and the mythical figure of the Hindu god Brahmā. Only in a private letter to his disciple Adam von Doss, written in 1856, did he draw explicit parallels between elements of his *Willensmetaphysik* and concepts from Buddhism. He maintained that Spence Hardy's gloss of the Buddhist term *upādāna* as "cleaving to existing objects"[22] indicated that it was identical to his will-to-live (*Wille zum Leben*), while "*Carma*" is the equivalent of his notion of the intelligible character, or

---

[21] Schopenhauer's main source on Daoism was an anonymous article of 1826, published in *Asiatic Journal and Monthly Register vol. XXII*. The author's discussion of the relation between *T'ien* and the human will appears on page 42.

[22] Hardy (1850) p. 409.

Idea of the individual without intellect. And in confirmation of his view that Buddhism avoids moral fatalism by promulgating a version of transcendental freedom, he cited Major C. Mackenzie's statement that "[t]he origine [sic!] of Karma is inconceivable",[23] and concluded by stating that "in general, the agreement with my teaching is amazing." (GB p. 384)

Although it is the stated aim of this study to remain as close as possible to the contextual issues, motivations and rationale of Schopenhauer's interpretation of the Indian religions, on closer analysis his discovery of an "amazing" convergence between aspects of Buddhist doctrine and his metaphysics does seem highly questionable. However, it was sufficiently plausible to induce an expert of the stature of Radhakrishnan to summarise Buddhist thought in palpably Schopenhauerian terms:

> As the world process is affiliated to conscious growth, so is the force of causality related to inner motivation...The difficulty of external causation is due to the fact that in the outside world our knowledge is confined to relations of phenomena. But in our inner consciousness we know that our will determines acts. The same force operates throughout. Schopenhauer calls it the 'will.' Buddha calls it 'karma.' It is the one reality, the thing in itself of which the whole world is the working out.[24]

However, Buddhists generally employ the term *upādāna* in a non-metaphysical context, to analyse the five personality-factors or mental and physical processes which, to the unenlightened consciousness, appear as a unified and stable Self, and are therefore grasped after as an 'I'.[25] In this context *upādāna* refers to a state of psychological grasping or attachment, which establishes a comparison with Schopenhauer's maxim that the "chief and fundamental incentive in man as in the animal...is craving for existence and well-being." (BM p. 131) However, Buddhists do not raise *upādāna* to the cosmic or metaphysical status of Schopenhauer's will in nature or will-to-live. That said, they do derive psychological attachment, or *upādāna*, from a more general 'craving' or 'thirst' pervading the natural universe, known as *trṣṇā* in Sanskrit and *taṇhā* in Pali. Schopenhauer would have been aware of this concept, since it appears in Spence Hardy's works, but he overlooked it and never referred to it in either his published works or notes. As the universal principle of which *upādāna* is the local and psychological manifestation, *trṣṇā* does have some features in common with Schopenhauer's will-to-live. In the *Dhammapada* thirst (*taṇhā*,

---

[23] Mackenzie (1809) p. 256.
[24] Radhakrishnan (1996) vol. I, p. 371.
[25] Harvey (1995) p. 4.

since the *Dhammapada* is a Pali text) is described as the "the builder of the house", or the force that constructs the world of experience:

> I have run through a course of many births looking for the maker of this dwelling and finding him not; painful is birth again and again. Now you are seen, O builder of the house, you will not build the house again. All your rafters are broken, your ridgepole is destroyed, the mind, set on the attainment of *nirvāṇa*, has attained the extinction of desires.[26]

But, irrespective of this similarity between Schopenhauer's will-to-live and Buddhist *tṛṣṇā*, there is a crucial difference between them that issues in a fundamental divergence between Schopenhauer's philosophy and Buddhism. This relates to the fact that the dominant outlook of Buddhism is phenomenalist, so that it does not characterise thirst as the inner nature of objects or the dynamic principle that sets the causal process in motion. Thirst is instead a very important but ultimately phenomenal cause in the twelve-fold chain that charts the *mutually dependent* arising and reinforcement of the wheel of ignorance, craving, attachment and suffering known as *pratītyasamutpāda* (usually translated as *dependent origination*). As Edward Conze comments:

> Schopenhauer teaches that the Will is the Thing-in-itself, whereas in Buddhism 'craving' operates within the conditioned and phenomenal world, and the unconditioned noumenon lies in *nirvāṇa*, which is quite calm as the result of the abolition of craving.[27]

Buddhists would therefore regard Schopenhauer's conceptions of the will as thing-in-itself, the will-to-live and intelligible character as suspiciously comparable to the cosmic Self (*ātman*) of Hindu doctrine, the rejection of which in the doctrine of no-Self (*anātman*) is the chief tenet of all Buddhist schools.[28] Schopenhauer was familiar with the Buddhist doctrine of

---

[26] *Dhammapada* 153-4 (see Radhakrishnan (ed., 1998) p. 110).

[27] Conze (1963) pp. 19-20.

[28] An exception to this is the idealist school of Yogācāra or Vijñānavāda, whose concept of the *ālaya-vijñāna* or storehouse-consciousness is in many ways analogous to (and the likely predecessor of) Vedānta theories of the Self. In the Introduction we quoted Murti's explanation of the *ālaya-vijñāna* as cosmic will; although questionable in some ways, Murti's gloss does illustrate the *ālaya-vijñāna's* function as world-ground and the storehouse for the ripening of *karmic* effects. However the *ālaya-vijñāna's* deepest aspect, the *param-ālaya*, seems to have more in common with the Advaita notion of *nirguṇa Brahman* as still and quiescent being-consciousness-bliss (see Harvey (1990) pp. 107-109). This may suggest a comparison between Schopenhauer's acknowledgement of a possible distinction between the thing-in-itself manifesting itself as will and the thing-in-itself apart from this manifestation, but, as discussed earlier, his philosophical standpoint prevented him from expanding on this distinction, so that he does not make positive statements about it. Its function is, as I argued above, ethically regulative.

no-Self, but interpreted it as simply a denial of individual personality.[29] Although the Abhidharma philosophy presented it in a similar way, explaining objects and persons as temporary assemblages of ultimate existents or *dharmas*, the Mādhyamikas universalised the cause-effect relation of *pratītyasamutpāda* to deny that even *dharmas* have the properties of a metaphysical Self, such as permanence or self-subsistence (*svabhāva*).[30] And this difference between the metaphysical status of will and *tṛṣṇā* is more than a hair-splitting point of purely theoretical relevance, for it opens up a further opposition between the ethical and soteriological doctrines of Schopenhauer and Buddhism. However, since discussion of Schopenhauer's account of Indian ethics appears in a later section of this chapter, I shall suspend further consideration of this issue until then.

II. Evil, *Karma* and Rebirth

For now we turn to Schopenhauer's account of the affective attitudes towards the world and life conveyed by the cosmogony and metaphysics of the Indian religions. We have already observed how, for Schopenhauer, a metaphysical *Weltanschauung* or world-view is at once and simultaneously a *Weltwertung* or world-assessment, and that this is *a fortiori* true of systems of religious metaphysics, "[t]he spirit and ethical tendency" of which "are the essentials...not the myths in which it clothes them." (WWRII p. 623) But Schopenhauer tended to assess *all* metaphysical views, religious *and* philosophical, according to whether they are optimistic and present "the existence of this world as justified by itself, and consequently praise and commend it", or pessimistic and

> consider it as something which can be conceived only as the consequence of our guilt, and thus really ought not to be, in that they recognise that pain and death cannot lie in the eternal, original, and immutable order of things, that which in every respect ought to be. (WWRII p. 170)

Given his exegesis of the inner meaning of Indian accounts of the origin and nature of the world, it is no surprise to find him placing Hinduism and Buddhism in the pessimistic category. Brahmā as "the most sinful

---

[29] Schopenhauer quoted the Buddha's saying "'[m]y disciples, reject the idea that I am this or this is mine.'" (WWRII p. 614; taken from Hardy (1853) p. 258) Elsewhere he suggested that *nirvāṇa* consists in a denial of individuality (WWRII p. 609).

[30] Nāgārjuna stated that dependent origination, or *pratītyasamutpāda*, established the emptiness of things as a middle way between eternalism and annihilationism (Nāgārjuna (1991) Dedicatory Verses, XXIV.18).

and lowest god" of the *Trimūrti* whose "production of the world is a sinful act" (WWRI p. 276; PPI p. 127), and the Buddha's demythologised version of this which explains the evolution of the world as "a consequence of our sinful desires" (FR p. 186), are unequivocal marks of a pessimistic world-view. Schopenhauer therefore regarded the inner spirit and ethical tendency of Hinduism and Buddhism as identical to that of true and original Christianity. According to him, all three religions have supported a high level of spiritual culture in their respective civilisations, teaching their followers to

> look beyond the narrow, paltry, and ephemeral life on earth, and no longer to regard that as an end in itself, but as a state or condition of suffering, guilt, trial, struggle and purification, from which we can soar upwards to a better existence, inconceivable to us, by means of moral effort, severe renunciation, and the denial of our own self. (WWRII pp. 627-28)

However, as we saw in Chapter 4, Schopenhauer thought that Christianity's historical entanglement with the optimistic monotheism of Judaism had led to "inconsistencies and contradictions" in its statement of pessimism, as a result of which its theologians have expended an inordinate amount of intellectual effort on the pointless task of reconciling the transcendent and revealed dogma of God's goodness with the immediately perceived suffering of the created order. For this reason he considered the metaphysical theories of Hinduism and Buddhism preferable to those of Christianity, insofar as they have a direct relation to concrete feeling conditioned by will and do not distort our awareness of want, suffering, and evil, and the certain knowledge that all this is crowned by death. Schopenhauer was aware that the Buddha had begun his discourses with "four fundamental truths", the first of which asserted the ubiquity of suffering in *saṃsāra* (WWRII p. 623). This suggested to him that the metaphysics of Indian wisdom is based on a 'bottom-up' inference from inner and outer experience, and is therefore favourable to the 'top-down,' privative theory of evil and suffering formulated by Christian theologians such as Augustine. This implied that the Indian religions concur with his view that "the want, the privation, the suffering is what is positive" and happiness a mere temporary respite from this (WWRI p. 320). He found this confirmed not only in the First Noble Truth of suffering or *duḥkha*, but also in the fact that Buddhism's ethical teachings "start not from the cardinal virtues, but from the cardinal vices, as the opposite or negation of which the cardinal virtues first make their appearance." (PPII p. 203) Indian wisdom therefore confirms his theory of the primacy of wrong-doing and egoism. Such open and direct pessimism sug-

gested to Schopenhauer that neither Hinduism nor Buddhism regards evil
and suffering as theoretical problems to be explained away by "lengthy and
diffuse sophisms that turn out to be mere words" (as he said of the theodicy
of Scotus Erigena — PPI p. 61). For them, evil and suffering are practical
problems, the solution to which is contained in their ethics and variously
presented theories of the "*redemption* of mankind and the world" (PPI
p. 62). Surveying various religious cosmogonies in relation to the problem
of evil, Schopenhauer made no secret of his preference for the honest and
direct pessimism of Hinduism and Buddhism over the optimism of monotheism:

> *Brahmā* produces the world through a kind of original sin, but himself remains
> in it to atone for this until he has redeemed himself from it. This is quite a
> good idea! In *Buddhism* the world comes into being in consequence of an
> inexplicable disturbance (after a long period of calm) in the crystal clearness
> of the blessed and penitentially obtained state of *nirvāṇa* and hence through a
> kind of fatality which, however, is to be understood ultimately in a moral
> sense; although the matter has its exact analogue and corresponding picture
> in physics, in the inexplicable arising of a primordial nebula, whence a sun is
> formed. Accordingly, in consequence of moral lapses, it also gradually
> becomes physically worse until it assumes its present sorry state. An excellent
> idea! To the *Greeks* the world and the gods were the work of an unfathomable
> necessity; this is fairly reasonable in so far as it satisfies us for the time being.
> *Ormuzd* lives in conflict with *Ahriman*; this seems not unreasonable. But that
> a God *Jehovah* creates this world of misery and affliction *animi causa* and *de
> gaieté de coeur*, and then applauds himself with a πάντα καλὰ λίαν, this is
> something intolerable. (PPII pp. 300-1)

Bryan Magee has disputed the propriety of Schopenhauer's procedure of
treating world-views as simultaneously world-assessments. Paraphrasing
Hume, Magee argues that since an 'is bad' cannot be derived from an
'is', Schopenhauer's pessimism "is logically independent of his philosophy" and therefore merely a matter of "vocabulary" or presentation.[31]
Without wishing to controvert the soundness of Magee's logic, Schopenhauer did not share his conception of the content and range of philosophical knowledge. Although he never acknowledged this explicitly, the
type and variety of insights that Schopenhauer attributes to the subject's
powers of apprehension and perception indicates the extent of his depar-
ture from Kant's epistemological model of perception as seeing or sens-
ing. This is, in part, a consequence of Schopenhauer's more inclusive
phenomenology and opposition to theories that present the subject of

[31] Magee (1983) p. 13.

knowledge as originally and simply a spectator of the world, or "winged cherub without a body". In his view the subject is primarily "rooted in the world", as

> an *individual*, in other words, his knowledge, which is the conditional supporter of the whole world as representation, is nevertheless given entirely through the medium of a body, and the affections of this body are, as we have shown, the starting-point for the understanding in its perception of this world. (WWRI p. 99)

When combined with his metaphysical theory that spatio-temporal objects are essentially visible will, Schopenhauer's emphasis on the embodiment of the subject leads to a naturalistic theory of perception which grounds judgements that go beyond the empirically indisputable properties of objects, on account of the fact that the intellect is shot through with feeling states and preconscious evaluations of the world and life (WWRI p. 271). These include the moods and attitudes encoded within the allegorical doctrines of the pessimistic religions, such as that the world and the human condition are fallen, that individual existence is a state of suffering that it were better never to have been, and that holiness consists in an ever-diminishing identification with the desires and promptings of the individual will experienced immediately within the depths of the body. Schopenhauer's concrete notion of the perceiving subject and the breadth of judgements available to it not only diverges from the epistemological models of Hume and Kant, but also prefigures Nietzsche's definition of the human as "the creature that measures values, evaluates and measures...the 'valuing animal as such'",[32] as well as Dilthey's notion of experience (*Erlebnis*) and, through this, Heidegger's conception of *Dasein's* "being-in-the-world" (*In-der-Welt-Sein*).

Of course, Schopenhauer's expanded and proto-hermeneutical model of the subject and philosophical knowledge does not lead to certain or incontestable conclusions, so that, as Magee says, it is logically possible to reformulate Schopenhauer's metaphysics "with equal accuracy in a vocabulary of optimism, or in a vocabulary agnostic as between the two."[33] However, as Christopher Janaway argues, "the basic materials for Schopenhauer's pessimism are indeed contained in his central metaphysical doctrine", following immediately from its depiction of existence as essentially conditioned by inalterable and insatiable, blind, striving will.[34] Janaway also draws attention to the fact that Schopenhauer's

---

[32] Nietzsche (1989) II.8.
[33] Magee (1983) p. 14.
[34] Janaway (1989) pp. 271-4.

emphatic vocabulary of pessimism, and his typological division between pessimistic and optimistic *Weltanschauungen*, were absent from the first statement of his system in 1818. They appeared only in the second, 1844 edition of *The World as Will and Representation*, in the context of distinguishing Judaism (and philosophy influenced by it) from the 'Indic' and world-denying religions, Hinduism, Buddhism and true and original Christianity.[35] This is not to say that Schopenhauer was unaware of the pessimistic consequences of his philosophy in 1818, but that he did not consider it necessary to press its pessimism or draw support from other pessimistic world-views at that time. It might be claimed that his intensive studies in comparative religion and formulation of an explicit philosophy of religion between 1818 and 1844 led to his mature view that the evaluative elements of a *Weltanschauung*, whether religious or philosophical, are intrinsic features of its obligation to provide a true interpretation of the world that simultaneously satisfies metaphysical need.

Schopenhauer regarded the doctrine of *karma* and rebirth (which he usually referred to as transmigration or metempsychosis) as the main vehicle for communicating Indian wisdom to the people,[36] insofar as it has an admirable capacity to satisfy almost all of the criteria of metaphysical need. In the context of Indic theodicy and the obligation to explain evil and suffering, metempsychosis avoids the suggestion implied by the Hindu creation myths that the individual sufferer is merely the innocent victim or pawn of wider, cosmic processes. Instead, metempsychosis locates the responsibility for present suffering within the sufferer himself, as the effect or ripening of evil acts performed by him in a previous existence. And with an economy that Schopenhauer considered the especial merit of metempsychosis, it simultaneously recommends moral observance by portraying freedom from future suffering as a consequence of good acts performed in the present (PPII p. 400).

However, in Schopenhauer's view metempsychosis is not strictly true, but truth wearing the garment of myth. It is the allegorical vehicle by which the moods, attitudes and motivations of the monist metaphysics of India have been conveyed to the people (WWRI pp. 355-6). Schopenhauer considered metempsychosis allegorically true because it makes use of perceptual pictures and the form of time to communicate the transcendental truth of metaphysical identity expressed directly in the *mahāvākya*, or "great word" from the *Upaniṣads*, "*tat tvam asi*":

---

[35] Janaway (1999) pp. 319f.
[36] A doctrine whose pessimistic implications are emphasised by the gruesome references to it as "re-death" (*punar-mṛtyu*) in Sanskrit literature — see the *Bṛhadāraṇyaka Upaniṣad* I.2.7, III.2.10.

> The doctrine of metempsychosis...deviates from the truth merely by trans-
> ferring to the future what is already now. Thus it represents my true inner
> being-in-itself as existing in others only after my death, whereas the truth
> is that it already lives in them now. (WWRII p. 601)

As a figural representation of metaphysical identity, Schopenhauer maintained that metempsychosis was taught to the Indian masses in the same
spirit in which Kant had offered his practical postulates and moral theology, in which a punishing and rewarding God is assumed as "a useful
and adequate *regulative scheme* for the purpose of explaining the serious,
deeply felt, and ethical significance of our conduct and also of directing
this conduct itself." But although Schopenhauer considered metempsychosis functionally analogous to Kant's practical postulates, he considered the Indian doctrine preferable for it contained "very much more
truth", was "of greater plausibility, and therefore of more immediate
value" (PPI p. 111). This is because Kant's moral theology is a patch-
work of doctrines whose weaknesses Kant himself had exposed in his
first *Critique* — namely, the Judaeo-Christian doctrines of God, freedom
and immortality. Metempsychosis attains the same end as Kant's scheme,
but without making use of "inconceivable" notions such as the will's
freedom of indifference to explain the disparity between the temperament
and conduct of one man in relation to another. Instead of claiming that
each created person is a *tabula rasa* who freely chooses to be "an angel
or a devil, or anything else that lies between the two", the *karmic* inheritance of metempsychosis communicates the transcendental truth that "all
genuine moral qualities, good as well as bad, are innate", in accordance
with the maxim "*operari sequitur esse*", or "action follows from being"
(PPII p. 238). It therefore makes use of fewer allegorical veils than the
Christian doctrines of the Fall and original sin to convey Schopenhauer's
doctrines of transcendental freedom, eternal justice, and the equivalence
of guilt and suffering.

In the 1850s Schopenhauer encountered a version of *karma* and rebirth
that he considered *sensu proprio* or strictly true — the esoteric version
of Buddhism of "a peculiar palingenesis resting on a moral basis"
(WWRII p. 502). He regarded this as an improvement on the exoteric,
Hindu theory of a transmigrating soul or ψυχή, because palingenesis
seemed to him to locate the human essence in the moral functions or will
rather than the intellect.[37] Although he acknowledged that the notion of

---

[37] Schopenhauer's characterisation of the Hindu version of *karma* and rebirth as transmigration of a soul or ψυχή is not exactly correct, although his understanding is no worse

a transmigrating will was "much more difficult to understand" than that of a transmigrating intellect, he preferred palingenesis to metempsychosis because it seemed to agree with his "doctrine of the metaphysical permanence of the will in spite of the intellect's physical constitution and fleeting nature" (PPII pp. 276-7).[38] And his discovery that the concept — or more accurately, the word — Παλιγγενεσία appeared in the New Testament, provided further confirmation of his theory of the Indian origin of the religion of Jesus (PPII p. 277).[39]

The preceding exposition of Schopenhauer's interpretation of Indian doctrines emphasises his procedure of drawing on their testimony for the negative purpose of attacking the sacred conceptions of European metaphysics. This might be considered unfortunate, but his impression of the extent to which monotheism had become embedded in the European psyche led him to welcome the contrary witness of Indian thought. Its grander and more ancient perspective offered fresh and novel solutions to familiar questions, while simultaneously revealing the merely local validity of Europe's catalogue of necessary truths. Indian metaphysics was an especially useful restriction on the universality that European philosophers had attributed to the transcendent abstractions of God, world and soul, inherited from Jewish revelation and systematised respectively in speculative theology, cosmology and rational psychology. Schopenhauer maintained that one of Kant's greatest merits was to have shown that reason cannot demonstrate the objectivity of these concepts or prove that they have transcendent referents (WWRI pp. 422f). However, he thought that Kant had vitiated this achievement when he made God, world and soul subjectively necessary Ideas, dialectically generated by reason's "concern" to ascend "from the conditioned synthesis...toward the unconditioned,"[40] and therefore useful tools for guiding our scientific

than that of his sources, since Colebrooke similarly affiliated the Hindu doctrine closely to Platonic metempsychosis (Colebrooke (2001) p. 229). But, as Klostermaier argues, the *ātman*, or transmigrating element in Hindu doctrine, has a complex meaning "that would not allow us to equate it with the term *soul* as normally used in the West." (Klostermaier (1994) p. 207)

[38] This is questionable since, as previously noted, Buddhists generally avoid concepts of metaphysical permanence. However, once again, Schopenhauer's understanding is only as good as his sources, since Spence Hardy's exposition of Buddhist *karma* and rebirth does suggest an analogy with Schopenhauer's doctrine of the permanence of the will (Hardy (1853) pp. 394-6).

[39] Παλιγγενεσία appears in Matthew 19:28 and Titus 3:5. However, in these verses it refers to eschatological and psychological regeneration respectively, rather than rebirth or Indian reincarnation — see Bauer (1979) p. 752.

[40] Kant (1998) A333/B390.

investigations of phenomena.[41] As Ideas natural to reason, Kant also put these concepts to regulative use as the practical postulates of God, freedom and immortality, belief in which arises from a need of reason in its practical aspect to entertain the possibility of the end of all moral action, the *summum bonum* of happiness proportioned to virtue.[42] The spectacle of Schelling and Hegel transforming Kant's regulative use of the Ideas into a constitutive theory of the Absolute frequently sent Schopenhauer into literary convulsions (FR pp. 168-9; PPI pp. 22-3). However, he consoled himself with the thought that, contrary to Kant's theory of reason's natural production of the Ideas, the testimony of Indian metaphysics proves that there is no concern of reason to ascend to the unconditioned ground of phenomena:

> the return to an unconditioned cause, to a first beginning, is by no means established in the nature of our faculty of reason...the original religions of our race, which even now have the greatest number of followers on earth, I mean Brahmanism and Buddhism, know nor admit such assumptions, but carry on to infinity the series of phenomena that condition one another. (WWRI p. 484)

And Schopenhauer seems to have arrived at this view of the dispensability of the Ideas as a consequence of his encounter with the Indian religions. In the first, 1813 edition of his doctoral dissertation he repeated Kant's theory, with some modifications, that the subject naturally generates unconditioned Ideas (FR1 p. 40). A few months later he read Anquetil's *Oupnek'hat*, wherein he encountered the Indian doctrines of *māyā* and *karma* and their assumption of the infinity of the apparent world. This contrary perspective led to his later view that Kant's characterisation of reason's concern as ascent from the conditioned to the unconditioned, or *ens realissimum*, was itself the effect of cultural conditioning.

III. Ethics and Immortality

If Schopenhauer expected the oriental renaissance through Sanskrit sources to correct the transcendent concerns and overly abstract character of European metaphysics, he also hoped that it would restrain the contemporary drift towards optimism and ethical *eudaemonism* he perceived

---

[41] Ibid. A616/B644.
[42] Kant (1997) 5:124-32.

in movements as diverse as contemporary materialism, rationalist Prot-
estantism and the subaltern of the latter, professorial philosophy (WWRII
p. 464; WN p. 143). For, in keeping with systems of metaphysics that
support a pessimistic assessment of the world, the ethical injunctions of
the Indian religions manifest an *"anti-cosmic tendency"* consummated in
their soteriological ideal of redemption from the human condition, a tendency that Schopenhauer also found in true and original Christianity.
However, Christianity's "open enemies...who have appeared in most
recent times", have tended to present its anti-natural ethics as its most
objectionable feature, leading Protestant theologians to disavow Christian
asceticism as extrinsic to Christianity proper (WWRII p. 615). But
whereas an ethical *eudaemonist* and open enemy of Christianity such as
Hume considered its "monkish virtues" and austerities to be simply consequences of believing in an aberrant system of theistic ideas,[43] in
Schopenhauer's view the fact that the godless religions of the east supported an identical ethical outlook indicated that such practices were
grounded in a universal and unconscious instinct rather than ideas subject
to chance and change. Such uniformity of conduct, embodied in the lives
of ascetics and saints of all religions, irrespective of the difference between
their dogmas, confirmed to him that his own solution to the riddle of
existence — the denial of the will-to-live — was not "an arbitrarily
invented freak", but expressive of an instinct grounded "in the very
nature of mankind", and requiring serious attention from any philosophy
that presumes to throw light on the inscrutable nature of existence (WWRI
p. 389).

Schopenhauer thought that the ability to account for and explain opposing ethical tendencies was an important criterion of any metaphysical
system. This is because it is "characteristic of man's nature" to evaluate
all theories in relation to their practical consequences, so that the ethical
portion of a system of metaphysics will often be considered its "most
serious" part, since it is here that we find its solution to the riddle of
existence, its theory of suffering and virtue, and its estimation of the
realism of our expectations of immortality and redemption. But irrespective of humanity's overriding interest in practical concerns, Schopenhauer thought that philosophy can only ever be theoretical, and that "to
become practical, to guide conduct, to transform character, are old claims
which with mature insight it ought finally to abandon." (WWRI p. 271)
This is because the medium of philosophy is the concept, and "the

---

[43] Hume (1993b) p. 181.

concept is unfruitful for the real inner nature of virtue, just as it is for art" (WWRI p. 368). Schopenhauer's maxim that concepts are ethically impotent follows from his reversal of the dominant (i.e., Cartesian) conception of the relation between intellect and will, which in turn leads to his doctrine that actions are not effects of free and lucid rational choices between different abstract motives, but visible appearances of the necessary operation of specific motives on the force of character or will from the outside. The greater force of the will in relation to the intellect means that maxims, concept-combinations and practical syllogisms (such as Kant's categorical imperative) are impotent to modify "the impulse of strong desires, the storm of passion, and the gigantic stature of egoism." (BM p. 62) Ethical philosophy must therefore avoid the temptation to prescribe, and must content itself with enquiry and description instead (WWRI p. 271).

But even though Schopenhauer counselled that *philosophy* should abandon its age-old obligation to become practical and guide conduct, he thought that *religious* modes of satisfying metaphysical need were inherently practical. The primacy of will over intellect may entail that "abstract dogmas are without influence on virtue," so that false ones do not disturb it and true ones do not cause it, but the allegorical dogmas of religion can and do "have a powerful influence on *conduct*, on outward actions" (WWRI p. 368). Although incapable of changing the nature or disposition of the will, abstract maxims deduced from religious dogmas are able to alter its direction or tendency. In this aspect they function as the "guiding star" of the "public standard of integrity and virtue," bringing the unenlightened to enlightened ends (WWRII p. 167). If, therefore, we want an incurable egoist to act on motives irresistible to the good person — motives of justice, compassion and loving-kindness — we need to persuade him that such actions contribute "indirectly in some way *to his own advantage*" (BM p. 193). Schopenhauer thought that this task of bringing an egoist to good ends through appeal to his egoism was a religious task, the allegorical schemes of which present action on good motives as the cause of reward and neglect of these motives as the cause of punishment. Although religious dogmas do not, thereby, bring about salvation, Schopenhauer considered this beyond the power of any species of mental content, whether a religious allegory or a philosophical concept:

> it would be a bad business if the principal thing in a man's life, his ethical worth that counts for eternity, depended on something whose attainment was so very much subject to chance as are dogmas, religious teachings, and philosophical arguments. (WWRI p. 368)

And in addition to duping the egoist to perform non-egotistical actions, religious allegories also provide an explanatory but erroneous scheme by which the non-reflective person of good character rationalises his or her innate disposition towards virtue (WWRI p. 369).

Therefore, in relation to ethics and outward conduct, Schopenhauer thought that it was crucial that an allegorical or religious scheme be shored up by a system of punishments and rewards, an obligation that monotheism had fulfilled through representations of the wrath of God and the love of God.[44] However, since modern culture and the death of God have deprived Christian ethics of its traditional, allegorical rationale, its "sacred contents must be saved in some way by another vessel, and preserved for mankind." (WWRII p. 629) Schopenhauer found in translations of Sanskrit works an alternative regulative scheme for guiding outward conduct in accordance with the immemorial ethical wisdom previously communicated by Christianity, one containing "very much more truth…of greater plausibility, and therefore of more immediate value… the dogma of Brahmanism, of a rewarding and punishing metempsychosis." In his view this restrains natural egoism and recommends virtue by teaching that "we must be reborn at some time in the form of every being that has been injured by us so that we may suffer the same injury." (PPI p. 111) And Schopenhauer expected metempsychosis to be a more effective cause of ethical action than God's will, since it uses perceptions to stand for transcendental doctrines, which have greater power over the imagination than the abstract, transcendent hypostases of theological ethics (WWRI p. 355; PPI p. 111).

On Schopenhauer's presentation therefore, the Indian doctrine of metempsychosis accounts for evil and suffering and explains and recommends moral conduct. But — and more importantly — it also fulfils the most important criterion of a system of metaphysics, which is to offer solace for the certain knowledge of death through a viable doctrine of continued existence. For, in agreement with the scholastic maxim "[n]othing comes out of nothing, and nothing can again become nothing!" (WWRII p. 487), metempsychosis assures every individual that his existence is of eternal duration, insofar as it connects present circumstances with those of other lives stretching into the infinite past *and* future.

---

[44] Schopenhauer's account of the practical instrumentality of religious dogmas often evokes the image of Dostoyevsky's Grand Inquisitor, cynically manipulating the hopes and fears of an unregenerate, child-like mass with the concepts *"miracle, mystery, authority"* (Dostoyevsky (1982) pp. 288-311).

It thereby confirms, in the medium of time and therefore allegorically, Schopenhauer's transcendental doctrine of the originality of our mode of existence.

However, as mentioned previously, Schopenhauer thought that the real and esoteric doctrine of Indian metaphysics was indistinguishable from his own, for the Upaniṣadic formula "*tat tvam asi*" (or "that art thou") indicates that individuality is *māyā* or illusion and that each person "is the original being himself, to whom all arising and passing away are essentially foreign". Schopenhauer claimed that this is why "we find in India a confidence and a contempt for death of which we in Europe have no conception." (WWRII pp. 463-4) Since both the exoteric and esoteric forms of Indian metaphysics sustain a theory of continued existence by making aseity an intrinsic property of the human essence, Schopenhauer thought they were better capable of offering consolation for death than the theistic doctrine of creation out of nothing, which renders immortality contingent by grounding it upon the will of a personal being who called our nature out of an original nothingness (WWRII p. 488).

It might, however, be objected that if Schopenhauer seriously offered the regulative scheme of metempsychosis as a replacement for personal immortality underwritten by God, then he was simply unrealistic and oblivious to the psychological weight of tradition and the 'ways of the forefathers'. To suggest that an entire culture overthrow its customary beliefs and appropriate new and very different forms is to expect it to enact a kind of violence upon itself. However, as mentioned previously, Schopenhauer thought that "Brahmanism and Buddhism" had been the original religions of Europe's ancestors (BM p. 44), as well as the perennial philosophy of the human race (WWRI p. 357). As a result, his prediction that Indian wisdom would supplant Jewish monotheism was offered in the spirit of a negation of a negation. Contemporary research into culture and religion was suggesting that metempsychosis was "worldwide", and "the belief of the great majority of mankind, in fact really... the doctrine of all religions" (WWRII p. 504). The central role it played in a variety of belief systems from ancient Egypt up to Papua New Guinea, combined with the enthusiastic response it had elicited from contemporary Europeans such as Lessing and Hume, encouraged Schopenhauer to make an inductive inference to the effect that metempsychosis is

> the natural conviction of man whenever he reflects at all in an unprejudiced way. Accordingly, it would actually be that which Kant falsely asserts of his three pretended Ideas of reason, namely a philosopheme natural to

human reason, and resulting from the forms of that faculty; and where this belief is not found, it would only be supplanted by positive religious doctrines coming from a different source. (WWRII p. 505)

As a result, Schopenhauer did not expect the introduction of metempsychosis into the scheme of European belief to constitute an imposition or meet with much resistance, insofar as the only element opposing it was "Judaism, together with the two religions that have sprung from it, inasmuch as they teach man's creation out of nothing." (WWRII p. 506) And, as we saw in Chapter 4, Schopenhauer thought that monotheism and its associated doctrines were currently in decline.

In Chapter 4 we also suggested that Schopenhauer had anticipated the present popularity of the belief that immortality consists of reunion with the forces of nature. We might further claim that his argument for the intuitive and natural status of metempsychosis similarly derives confirmation from the number of contemporary Europeans claiming to have been Queen Cleopatra or Emperor Nero in a previous life. However, as their choice of predecessor too readily indicates, current believers in metempsychosis seem more concerned with power and the exaltation of their ego than with the exclusively moral connotations that Schopenhauer associated with the doctrine.

For, in Schopenhauer's view, the meaning and end of metempsychosis is eminently moral: it presents in vivid, concrete images the conceptual and *sensu proprio* true transcendental ground of virtuous action. We mentioned earlier that he thought that the abstract motives of rational knowledge (*Wissen*) — such as the allegories of religion and the concepts of philosophy — were incidental to true virtue, insofar as they merely elicit character or will, or set it in motion without changing its fundamental disposition. In his view actions of genuine moral worth are effects of a different kind of knowledge, one that impacts upon the moral disposition of the will without passing through reason, and which consists of "immediate and *intuitive* knowledge [*Erkenntnis*] of the metaphysical identity of all beings" (WWRII pp. 600-1).

The metaphysical basis of morality is therefore the ancient doctrine of the One in the Many, "at all times the jest of fools and the endless meditation of sages." Schopenhauer hailed Kant's philosophy as the source for the "strict proof" of this doctrine, insofar as it demonstrated that plurality was an effect of the phenomenal forms of space and time — the principles of individuation or "veil of *māyā*" (BM p. 209). Under the influence of these forms ordinary consciousness interprets the separation between self and other as an absolute and real partition, thereby greatly serving and facilitating the presuppositions and requirements of egoism. However, since Schopenhauer grounded metaphysical unity on blind striving will rather than quiescent cosmic consciousness, his conception of the relation between metaphysics and morality is ultimately negative. Initially, moral virtue proceeds from a constraint of our inner nature as will, and even when it takes the form of compassionate action, it is awakened only by the sight of another's misfortunes or woes, and manifested in acts to remove the source of their suffering (BM p. 144). As a result, moral insight's ability to penetrate the veils of the phenomenon presupposes catastrophe, and primary egoism is displaced only by pre-cognitive apprehension of the identity between a sufferer and oneself. Although Schopenhauer maintained that the theoretical explanation of compassionate action was known only to post-Kantian philosophers, he attributed "immediate and intuitive knowledge" of it to the *ṛṣis*, which they expressed through the "*mahā-vākya* or Great Word" from the *Chāndogya Upaniṣad* "*tat tvam asi*", and communicated to the people through the doctrine of metempsychosis (PPII p. 219).[45] A corollary of this claim is that everyone who acts from disinterested motives of justice and compassion are implicit Schopenhauerians:

> to be just, noble, and benevolent is nothing but to translate my metaphysics into actions. To say that time and space are mere forms of our knowledge, not determinations of things-in-themselves, is the same as saying that the teaching of metempsychosis, namely that 'One day you will be born again as the man whom you now injure, and will suffer the same injury,' is identical with the frequently mentioned formula of the Brahmans, *Tat tvam asi*, 'This thou art.' (WWRII p. 600)

However, for Schopenhauer "the moral virtues are not really the ultimate end." The will's movement on motives of loving-kindness and compassion indicates only partial release from immersion in the *principium individuationis* and the realist and egotistical perspectives sustained by it. This is because compassionate action not only presupposes the reality of the other's ego, but serves its ends by alleviating its misfortunes. Moral virtue therefore merely "accompanies man as a light on his path from the

---

[45] Paul Hacker has argued that Schopenhauer misrepresents the moral outlook of premodern Hinduism when he identifies *tat tvam asi* as the basis for virtue (Hacker (1995) Chapter 13). However, since Hacker goes on to show that Neo-Vedāntins from Vivekananda onwards have, under the influence of Schopenhauer's reading, used the formula as a basis for morals, then Schopenhauer's misrepresentation seems to have been based on nothing more than ignorance of the history of Hindu doctrine, as opposed to the "logically impossible" connection Hacker accuses him of making (Ibid. p. 277).

affirmation to the denial of the will" (WWRII p. 608), for beyond virtue lies asceticism. However, the path is straight, since the transition from virtue to asceticism does not presuppose a severance from the standpoint of morality, but an intensification of its perception of "the identity of the will in all its phenomena" (WWRI p. 378). He who no longer recognises any distinction between his inner nature and others and compassionately identifies with their sorrows, soon realises that suffering is not a localised misfortune experienced by the few, but essential to life as such, being the necessary consequence of its inner nature. With the dawning of such awareness, the compassionate person apprehends the futility of all efforts to assuage misery in a groaning world. The realisation that the entirety of the phenomenon is "involved in a constant passing away, a vain striving, an inward conflict, and a continual struggle" impacts on his inner disposition and "becomes the *quieter* of all and every willing." His will "now turns away from life; it shudders at the pleasures in which it recognises the affirmation of life." (WWRI p. 379) The saint in whom the will has turned and denied itself spurns attachment to the pleasures of sex and wealth and the agitations that accompany their pursuit, embracing chastity and voluntary poverty instead.

However, Schopenhauer thought that salvation through knowledge could never be perfect, since the will, not the intellect, is the hegemon or controlling element in the human being: "suffering merely known" is the narrow gate to the denial of the will, while the more common way is through "suffering personally felt", or misfortune inflicted by the accidents of personal experience (WWRI p. 392). As a result, the path of the Schopenhauerian saint — whose body is visible will, or will translated into the forms of perception — must pass beyond mere resignation through knowledge and assume an activist quality of deliberate self-chastisement. He must constantly struggle against the possibility of the will's renewed arousal and reattachment to the objects in which it had previously invested value, and protect against the permanent possibility of backsliding by seeking out the repulsive, inviting insult and injury from others, and resorting to extreme acts of bodily mortification, such as

> fasting, and even to self-castigation and self-torture, in order that, by constant privation and suffering, he may more and more break down and kill the will that he recognises and abhors as the source of his own suffering existence and of the world's. (WWRI p. 382)

To substantiate his account of the methods of the saint who denies the will and life with it, as well as to fend off likely objections, Schopenhauer referred to the "enviable life of so many saints and great souls among the Christians, and even more among the Hindus and Buddhists" (WWRI p. 383). But irrespective of this almost universal testimony, he claimed that his soteriological ideal had attained "a more far-reaching development and a more decided expression" in Hinduism and Buddhism than in the Christian Church, because Indian asceticism was not "restricted by an element quite foreign to it, as the Jewish doctrine of faith is in Christianity." (WWRI p. 387) To give concrete form to his theory, Schopenhauer composed a catalogue of what he took to be specifically Indian acts of self-denial, ascending from "love in general, not limited to the human race, but embracing all that lives", through "abstinence from all animal food; perfect chastity and renunciation of all sensual pleasure for him who aspires to real holiness", up to

> voluntary penance and terrible slow self-torture for the complete mortification of the will, ultimately going as far as voluntary death by starvation, or facing crocodiles, or jumping over the consecrated precipice in the Himalaya, or being buried alive, or flinging oneself under the wheels of the huge car that drives around with the images of the gods amid the singing, shouting, and dancing of bayaderes. (WWRI p. 388)

This quote evokes a macabre spectacle of reckless self-destruction, which has a strange resonance with Nietzsche's description of Dionysian intoxication, which in the German Middle Ages manifested itself in "ever-growing throngs", roaming "from place to place, impelled by the same Dionysian power, singing and dancing as they went".[46] Schopenhauer's suggestion that such acts of self-destruction constitute the acknowledged ideals of Hinduism and Buddhism is overly cavalier; however, this is not to say that extreme practices similar to these have never occurred in India in the name of religion, just that they — like the sexual rituals of Tantra and the antinomian rituals of Śaivite sādhus[47] — are extremely rare and usually frowned upon by the mainstream. Despite the innumerable stories relating gruesome acts of mortification performed by Indian ascetics, only the Digambara sect of the Jains has theoretically sanctified and practised bodily self-mortification with consistent rigour, and for the explicit purpose of self-annihilation.[48]

Schopenhauer's theoretical discussion of the meaning and end of asceticism naturally presupposes his metaphysics of the will, which, as we have seen, he also detected in the religions of India, albeit in dim and

---

[46] Nietzsche (2007) 1.

[47] One of which is to use the skull of a Brahmin as a begging-bowl, in commemoration of Śiva's slaughter of Brahmā.

[48] See Dundas (2002) p. 165.

unsystematic form. However, his philosophical assumptions and interest in assimilating Indian ideas and practices to his own philosophy occasionally encouraged him to ignore certain theoretical and atmospheric differences between the intellectual traditions of east and west, and this is palpably evident in his account of the motives of Indian asceticism. As Edith Wyschogrod has argued, there is "for every psycho-social practice an episteme, a cluster of ideas often invisible, that is both the conceptual backdrop and the enabling mechanism for the emergence of ascetic life *in situ*."[49] Earlier we drew attention to an asymmetry between Schopenhauerian will and Buddhist thirst or *tṛṣṇā*, stemming from the fact that whereas the Buddhists position thirst *within* the twelve-fold phenomenal chain of *pratītyasamutpāda* or dependent arising, Schopenhauerian will is the metaphysical substratum of the series of causes or principle of sufficient reason of becoming. According to Buddhism, the weakest point in the chain of phenomenal causes, and therefore the focus for therapy, is ignorance rather than thirst or craving — a view that is shared by several prominent Hindu schools, including Advaita Vedānta. The Indian religions tend to stress the centrality of knowledge to salvation, depicting enlightenment as a power that completely burns desire or craving and releases the saint from its fetters and restraints *while still embodied*. Schopenhauer may have maintained that the denial of the will is possible through intuitive knowledge of the identity of beings, but this is only the narrow gate to salvation. In the majority of cases he thought that the will was too strong for knowledge, so that it "must be broken by the greatest personal suffering before its self-denial appears." (WWRI p. 392) And irrespective of whether salvation appears through knowledge or through experience of suffering, Schopenhauer's metaphysical theory of the body as visible will entails the permanent possibility of back-sliding, to protect against which the saint must resort to the safeguards of acts of self-torture and bodily mortification.

The presuppositions of Schopenhauer's metaphysics and ethics are derived from a tradition of anti-rationalist theological and philosophical reflection that has, since at least St Paul and Augustine, placed the will rather than the intellect at the centre of its speculative concerns.[50] For this

---

[49] Wyschogrod (1998) p. 16.

[50] St Paul and Augustine notoriously reversed Socrates' optimistic view of the primacy of intellect over will (implied in the principle that to know the good is to do it) when they lamented their weakness to act on higher motives: in the words of St Paul, "the good that I would I do not: but the evil which I would not, that I do." (Romans 7:15; see also Augustine (1961) 8.5). Western thought's twofold derivation from Greek philosophy on

tradition knowledge of the Holy Will of the metaphysical God has been the highest theoretical end, and negation of one's self-centred purposes and rebirth in God's life the consummate practical achievement. As a result, a greater number of ascetic practices aimed at breaking the will can be found in the annals of western monasticism than in the contemplative atmosphere of Indian soteriology. Whereas St Benedict resorted to the cure of throwing himself upon nettles and briars in order to break or kill the will manifested in his sexual longings, the Buddha expressly counselled against acts of self-mortification on the grounds that the bodily sufferings they induce are obstacles to the twofold task of conquering ignorance and attaining enlightenment.[51] Even the well-known and rather spectacular austerities of Hindu holy men — lying on a bed of nails, raising a limb until it is completely withered — are not considered to be deliberate acts of self-mortification, but are — perhaps paradoxically — pursued to accumulate psychophysical power and energy which, at the highest levels, confer supremacy even over the gods.[52]

And this difference between the intellectualist soteriology of Buddhism and Advaita and the voluntarism of parallel theories in the west indicates the point at which Schopenhauer and the Indian religions ultimately diverge. Although Hinduism and Buddhism acknowledge the soteriological importance of overcoming desire or thirst, they also maintain that they are simply causal processes of *māyā*, with the result that awareness of their phenomenal status contributes to permanent liberation from their grip. And whereas Schopenhauer's metaphysics depicts bodily life as a penitential state either frustrated by never-satisfied willing, or as a constant struggle to bring about its denial (a struggle that can, moreover, only cease at death), Hinduism and Buddhism console by offering knowledge of our inner essence as the being-consciousness-bliss of *Brahman*, or of the emptiness of existents and the possibility of attaining

---

the one hand and Jewish religion on the other has had the consequence that its history has frequently oscillated between a dominant tradition of rationalism and an equally potent undercurrent of voluntarism. As we have seen, the German Counter-Enlightenment's reaction against the intellectualism of the *Aufklärung* brought with it a resurgence of voluntarism, of which Schopenhauer was an important heir.

[51] Gregory the Great (1959) pp. 59-60; *Majjhima Nikāya* 1.240ff.

[52] For an account of the Hindu theory of asceticism as generation of power in the form of heat or energy (*tapas*), see Klostermaier (1994) p. 56. Nietzsche evidently knew something of this explanation, since he pointed to the legend of King Viśvamitra as confirmation of his theory that asceticism is an indirect expression of the will-to-power (Nietzsche (1989) III.10). Had Schopenhauer heard of this Hindu explanation of the purpose of asceticism, he might have remarked that the rational motives by which ascetics explain their actions rarely coincide with the real motives governing their conduct (WWRI p. 383).

nirvāṇa in this life.[53] It is, therefore, Schopenhauer's metaphysics of the will that places him firmly within the western intellectual tradition, and which is responsible for the variance between his soteriological theory and that of the religions of India. And it is therefore ironic, especially in the light of his Marcionite tendencies and opposition to Judaism, that the tradition of metaphysical voluntarism in which his philosophy stands has often been identified as the particular contribution of biblical or Hebrew monotheism to western thought.[54]

However, so far our exposition of Schopenhauer's theory of asceticism has relied entirely on the first edition of *The World as Will and Representation* published in late 1818. In the second edition of 1844, his statement of the ascetic denial of the will is far less extreme, and explicitly rejects acts of self-mortification and torture. He claims that since the "most complete exercise of moral virtues" brings "poverty, privations, and special sufferings of many kinds", then

> *asceticism* in the narrowest sense, the giving up of all property, the deliberate search for the unpleasant and repulsive, self-torture, fasting, the hairy garment, mortification of the flesh; all these are rejected by many as superfluous, and perhaps rightly so. Justice itself is the hairy garment that causes its owner constant hardship, and philanthropy that gives away what is necessary provides us with constant fasting. (WWRII p. 607)

Schopenhauer never made an explicit connection between this dilution of his early theory of asceticism and the limitations he placed on the status of the will as thing-in-itself in the same volume, but they seem to be related. If, as he concedes, the thing-in-itself may have "determinations, qualities, and modes of existence" apart from its appearance as will (WWRII p. 198), then the severer practices of bodily "self-castigation and self-torture" undertaken to "break down and kill the will" (WWRI

---

[53] Buddhists distinguish between two species of *nirvāṇa*: the first, called '*nirvāṇa* with substrate remaining' (*sopadhiśeṣanirvāṇa*), describes the Buddha's condition from enlightenment to death, during which period his previously accumulated *karma* sustains his perceptions of things, but realising that they are no-Self his interactions with them give rise to no further *karma*. With the exhaustion of his *karma* on the death of his body, the Buddha passes into '*nirvāṇa* without substrate remaining' (*nirupadhiśeṣanirvāṇa*). Nāgārjuna developed the implications of this distinction by arguing that recognition of the emptiness of phenomena leads to the realisation that *saṃsāra* and *nirvāṇa* are ultimately identical, for since both lack self-nature, there is nothing to distinguish them (Nāgārjuna (1991) XXV.19).

[54] Otto (1958) p. 6; Gillespie (1995) p. 24; Pattison (1996) pp. 11-25. Pattison specifically relates how Augustine expressed the biblical, voluntarist view in Platonic categories, and in a later chapter also locates Schopenhauer within this tradition (Pattison (1996) pp. 60-69).

p. 382) no longer seem necessary if it is possible that the thing-in-itself that we know as will in its affirmation might become something different in its denial. This point provides confirmation of the view defended earlier that the later limitations that Schopenhauer placed on his doctrine of the will partly proceeded from extended reflection on the theoretical implications of the possibility of moral conduct, rather than to formulate a transcendent and speculative theory of mystical union with an ineffable reality 'beyond' the will. And, with regard to Moira Nicholls' thesis that the later shifts in Schopenhauer's *Willensmetaphysik* were also partly effects of his growing knowledge and appreciation of the Indian religions, it seems significant that he follows his observation that many have rejected asceticism "in the narrowest sense" and "perhaps rightly so" with the explanation that this is why

> *Buddhism* is free from that strict and excessive asceticism that plays a large part in Brahmanism, and thus from deliberate self-mortification. It rests content with the celibacy, voluntary poverty, humility, and obedience of the monks, with abstinence from animal food, as well as from all worldliness. (WWRII p. 607)

He concludes by noting that Vedānta also "rightly says" that, with the arising of true knowledge, the ideal of perfect resignation is attained: no further works of self-mortification are necessary, for accumulated *karma* has been burned and rendered obsolete by saving knowledge.

If Nicholls' thesis that Schopenhauer revised his *Willensmetaphysik* under the partial and gradual influence of the Indian religions can also be used to explain his later repudiation of the extremer forms of asceticism, then it seems that Hindu and Buddhist doctrines encouraged Schopenhauer to move from a western, activist soteriology to an eastern, contemplative one. This implies a different model of his relation to his Indian sources than Pol-Droit's notion of an "abusive annexation", by which Schopenhauer is meant to have forcibly moulded Indian doctrines to an *a priori* and alien scheme.[55] The possibility that he displaced specific intellectual currents of his own tradition as a result of growing exposure to Indological works is a classic realisation of Gadamer's hermeneutical account of a fusion of intellectual horizons.[56] And if the intellectual traditions of east and west enjoyed their first, promising encounter in the works of Schopenhauer, then the historical effects of this event flowed into new streams and led to a new exchange of ideas after his death. However, we shall return to this point at the end of the Conclusion that follows.

---

[55] Pol-Droit (2003) p. 93.
[56] Gadamer (1989) pp. 302f.

CONCLUSION

Our contextual study of Schopenhauer's philosophy of religion has shown that it was a conservative response to the religious crisis of the age — one that recognised, assimilated, yet also passed beyond Enlightenment assaults on religion and Christianity. The conflict between the intellectual outlook of modernism and traditional monotheistic belief threatened the integrity and survival of Christianity's moral and spiritual values. It was therefore fortuitous that contemporary scholarship had begun to publicise the outlines of a more durable religio-allegorical scheme; one that not only supported the same values, but had also provided their original rationale. In other words, the oriental renaissance was Schopenhauer's solution to the death of God.

Schopenhauer's conservative philosophy of religion was only one of many to appear in Germany at that time. In 1784 Kant had expressed the spirit of the Enlightenment when he dared his contemporaries "to be wise",[1] to become rational, self-legislating monads in matters of law, politics and morality, and to subject all traditional authorities to criticism and reasoned judgement. However, the German *Aufklärer* were generally less hostile to religious ethics and spirituality than their British or French counterparts, and this moderate outlook is reflected in Kant's philosophy of religion. His idealist assault on natural theology may have been a foundational event leading up to the death of God, but his moral theology re-established Christian values on a novel base. In lieu of their traditional objectivist or external supports, such as revelation or speculative reason, Kant founded Christian morals on the universal and necessary conditions of subjectivity. As a result, Christian belief is validated insofar as it recommends observance of the transcendental moral law known immediately to every rational being: or, as Kant himself remarked, his philosophy of religion denied "knowledge in order to make room for faith".[2]

However, Kant's rational synthesis of belief and morals was soon challenged by the anthropology of the Counter-Enlightenment, according to which reason is not master in its own house, but the slave of vital feeling, desire, need, or — in Schopenhauer's idiom — *will*. This new perspective was the presupposition of Schopenhauer's theory of the permanence

[1] Kant (1991) p. 54.
[2] Kant (1998) Bxxx.

of metaphysical need, and his related presumption that the majority would be forever incapable of liberating themselves from childlike dependence on the judgement of others. In his view a religious system of myths and allegories is an essential component of all culture, necessary to fulfil the important tasks of explaining life, guiding the unenlightened to enlightened ends and offering consolation for the inevitability of suffering and death. Schopenhauer's attitude towards the rational religion of Kant and the proto-secularism of Enlightenment culture was therefore sceptical. He promoted the Indian religions as popular systems compatible with the advanced views of the age, and sufficient for the satisfaction of metaphysical need. But, irrespective of their divergent responses to the religious crisis of modernity, the motives governing Kant's and Schopenhauer's philosophies of religion were continuous. Just as Kant combined metaphysical agnosticism with a concern for the integrity of Christian ethics, so Schopenhauer supplemented atheism with an attempt to reconcile the spiritual kernel of Christianity with modern knowledge. An analogous synthesis of radicalism and conservatism appears in the religious thought of Schopenhauer's near-contemporaries Fichte, Schelling and Hegel, who similarly set out to preserve Christianity's inner core by confronting rather than retreating from the challenges of modernity.[3] Since the dawn of the twenty-first century, social scientists and journalists have been baffled by the failure of secularisation signified by the current resurgence and popularity of religious belief. It is significant that the central figures of German Idealism — otherwise so influential in conceptions of secular society and the proclamation of the death of God — should have recognised at the beginning of the nineteenth century the impossibility of secularism's ultimate triumph. In their view the spiritual and religious instincts are ineradicable: rather than surrender them, human beings will necessarily seek out new forms for their satisfaction and expression.

However, Schopenhauer's philosophy of religion differed from that of his German contemporaries by combining a pronounced opposition towards monotheism and concepts of God with a high evaluation of Christian ethics. Hinduism and Buddhism attracted him because they seemed to do the same. He considered them to be, like his own philosophy, *immanent* rather than *transcendent* systems of metaphysics, and the prototypes of a schema that relegates the world of individuals to the level of appearance, while simultaneously raising the inner essence of that which appears to the level of the original being itself. He thought that

---

[3] For a more detailed examination of this point see Hedley & Ryan (2009).

this contrast between the ideal and the real was a natural deduction from Kant's account of the forms and laws of the intellect, and therefore preferable to monotheism's merely revealed opposition between necessary and contingent being. This means that the Indian faiths are better able to withstand rational criticism, and therefore more suitable systems of belief in a culture of intellectual advancement.

His conviction of the superiority of India's metaphysical conceptions also led Schopenhauer to hail its religions as more efficient tools for the practical task of satisfying metaphysical need. The identity that Hinduism and Buddhism presents between the essence of appearances and the One justifies our feelings of moral responsibility by tracing conduct and character to a free act of transcendental self-constitution. It also enables them to explain genuine acts of virtue as effects of intuitive knowledge of metaphysical unity, and to offer consolation for suffering and death by teaching everyone "to regard himself as *Brahman*, as the original being himself, to whom all arising and passing away is essentially foreign" (WWRII p. 463). By contrast, the metaphysics of monotheism is incapable of explaining evil or moral responsibility without ultimately assigning them to the creator-God; of accounting for acts of compassion without reducing them to the egoistic intention of attracting the favour of God; or of offering a viable account of continued, post-mortem existence, since the "assumption that man is created out of nothing necessarily leads to the assumption that death is his absolute end." (WWRII p. 488)

Schopenhauer's contrast between an immanent and a transcendent system of metaphysics is paralleled by his epistemological opposition between truths obtained through intuitive perception and the conceptual dogmas of reason — an opposition that also provides the main presuppositions for his rejection of theism and concomitant endorsement of Indian metaphysics. He regarded the doctrines of Hinduism and Buddhism as allegorical vehicles for the intuitions of the *ṛṣis*, and the transcendent doctrines of Judaeo-Christianity as mere castles in the air. The monotheistic dogma of creation out of nothing opens up an absolute cleavage between God and the world, thereby denying any natural continuity between the metaphysical realm and the perceptual or experiential life of creatures. As a result, Judaism, Islam and historical Christianity have justified their teachings by elevating ancient manuscripts to the status of supernatural sources of knowledge, while philosophical theists have argued that natural knowledge of God is possible through speculation on an alleged *a priori* content. However, in agreement with the findings of recent biblical criticism, Schopenhauer considered religious scriptures as nothing more than records of the thoughts of sages, and therefore "subject to error, as is the lot of everything human." Although scriptures are an important adjunct to the popular communication of metaphysical truth, the literal belief that a being of a higher order had revealed the nature and purpose of existence to the priestly class of ancient nations could only be sustained by "a big child" (PPII p. 361). Schopenhauer thought that the Indian religions had no comparable doctrine of revelation, on account of his view that they entertained no literal notion of a Supreme Person. The format of scriptures such as the *Upaniṣads* seemed to confirm this, since they unequivocally present their teachings as the deliverances of sages — such as when Uddālaka Āruṇi instructs his son Śvetaketu on the nature of "the subtle essence" that this "whole world has for its self. That is the true. That is the self. That art thou (*tat tvam asi*)."[4]

Given his theory that the "advanced views of the age" necessitate a reassessment of the sources of philosophical and religious metaphysics, it is likely that Schopenhauer would have been dismayed by the contemporary theological tendency to celebrate monotheism's dependence on revelation as a mark of its superior distinction. A regrettable number of twentieth-century theologians have resurrected traditional doctrines of revelation in order to defend the uncritical position that scriptures (whether the Bible or *Qur'an*) contain more-than-human teachings, superior to the merely knowable and demonstrable doctrines of philosophy and science, and the idolatrous doctrines of other religions. It might, however, be argued that the militant emphasis on revelation which entered Christian theology through Karl Barth has simply fulfilled Schopenhauer's prediction of Christianity's cultural marginalisation through neglect of the modern imperative for doctrinal reform. The stir periodically created within theological circles by manifestoes outlining unquestioning commitment to principles of neo- or radical orthodoxy contrasts sharply with the complete indifference or mild bemusement they elicit outside theology. It compounds the impression that theologians simply do not want to understand the depth of their crisis, and are content to communicate only with one another. Such expressions of fundamentalist certainty in the integrity of the Bible and the tradition have frequently been accompanied by a polemical attitude that spurns disciplined enquiry and genuine reflection, and which sustains itself by overlooking the relevance of more than two centuries of historical and biblical criticism.

---

[4] *Chāndogya Upaniṣad* VI.8.7.

As for natural knowledge of the transcendent principle of theism, Schopenhauer thought that it resided upon manipulation of the indeterminate structure of concepts with little content — such as infinite, finite, being, cause, perfection, possibility, actuality and goodness. He welcomed Locke's nominalist account of concept-formation as a corrective to this, since Locke's theory showed that reason's innate content is merely formal, and that the material part of concepts is derived from primary perception (FR p. 174). Thought in the medium of concepts therefore involves thinking *less* than is given through perception, so that the abstractions of the ontological and cosmological arguments are little more than the empty husks of original perceptions, or, in Nietzsche's memorable phrase, "the last smoke of evaporating reality".[5] According to Schopenhauer, the favoured concepts of the western metaphysical tradition include so many possible determinations within them that "we can make of them whatever we like" (WWRII p. 83), presenting "what is inseparable...as separated, and what cannot be united as united" (WWRII p. 84). His criticisms of the unreliable medium and arbitrary procedures of western metaphysics imply that the concepts of the classical arguments for God's existence could just as easily be used to demonstrate his non-existence — a point substantiated by J.N. Findlay when he appropriated the concepts and premises of Anselm's proof to defend God's necessary non-existence.[6]

By contrast, Schopenhauer thought that the *ṛṣis* of ancient India had developed their doctrines by, on the one hand, starting from the subject, "from *ātma*, from *jīvātman*" (MRI p. 116), and on the other through "a universal perception of the world" (WWRI p. 419). They had thereby anticipated Schopenhauer's own revised conception of the sources and methods of post-Kantian metaphysics, which proceeds from the presupposition that

> the solution to the riddle of the world is possible only through the proper connexion of outer with inner experience, carried out at the right point, and by the combination, thus effected, of these two very heterogeneous sources of knowledge. (WWRI p. 428)

And despite the fact that Schopenhauer thought that the *ṛṣis* had produced their doctrines "as the direct utterance of their consciousness", presenting them "mythically and poetically" (WWRI p. 419), his assessment of their allegorical form turned out to be an important element in his conception of

---

[5] Nietzsche (1976) 3.4.
[6] Findlay (1968) pp. 119f.

an oriental renaissance. It meant that they were capable of standing as representatives of his conceptual system, and of communicating the moods of his philosophy in a form comprehensible to the unphilosophical majority.

Schopenhauer's posthumous influence on the intellectual life of Europe is difficult to assess, since he has often been a hidden source of specific themes, doctrines and tendencies in subsequent and, frequently, more popular thinkers. His philosophical star rose in 1851 on the publication of the two-volume *Parerga and Paralipomena*, from which time he was universally acknowledged as one of the most important philosophers on the continent. However, at the turn of the twentieth century his star rapidly descended again, especially in English-speaking nations, as a consequence of the advance of analytical philosophy. Although this school originated in a Schopenhauer-like repudiation of Hegel's metaphysics and an almost universal commitment to nominalism, the majority of analytical philosophers have not shared Schopenhauer's conception of philosophy as an experiential science that resolves the physical world on a moral quality. It is likely that he, in turn, would have regretted the fact that the nominalist bias of this school has encouraged most of its fellowship to resurrect what he considered to be Kant's "strange and unworthy definition of philosophy" as "a science *of* concepts" rather than "a science *in* concepts" (PPII p. 8; WWRI p. 453), surrendering investigation of the world to physics, chemistry and biology and confining philosophy to analysis of the methods and concepts of science. Even though the majority of analytical philosophers working on ethics have abided by Schopenhauer's tenet that ethics describes rather than prescribes, they have tended to confine their descriptions to the implications of moral language. However, the influence of Schopenhauer on Wittgenstein's theories of the subject, the limits of knowledge and the mystical in the *Tractatus* have often been noted,[7] and a further case might be made for arguing that Schopenhauer's naturalistic theory of concept-formation similarly influenced Wittgenstein's later anti-representationalism. In recent decades many scholars trained in analytical philosophy have produced studies of different aspects of Schopenhauer's system, amounting to a definite resurgence of interest in his thought. However, there has been little interest in his philosophy of religion, or the philosophical implications of his interest in the religions of India.

---

[7] By, for example, Bryan Magee (1983) pp. 286-315: see also Wittgenstein (2000) 5.631-5.633, 6.522.

And, despite the German medium and context of his work, the influence of Schopenhauer's pessimistic philosophy and interpretation of the Indian religions has not been much greater in Europe. His continental reputation tends to describe the same parabola as the fate of his philosophy in English-speaking circles, consisting of a rapid ascent succeeded by an equally rapid decline. After his death in 1860 several influential German theorists continued to pursue and develop his themes — including his estimation of the relevance of Indian thought to European philosophy — such as Eduard von Hartmann, Philip Mainländer, Otto Weininger and the Sanskrit scholar and philosopher Paul Deussen. However, this initial enthusiasm for Schopenhauerian pessimism and the Indian religions was soon exhausted as a result of the posthumous rise to fame of Nietzsche, Schopenhauer's most influential continental disciple. Although Nietzsche's philosophical prominence has ensured the abiding but hidden influence of Schopenhauerian themes on later philosophers (such as Heidegger), Nietzsche's discipleship has, in general, had a negative effect on perceptions of his educator. Nietzsche may have enlarged on Schopenhauer's opposition to metaphysical abstraction and emphasis on the immanence of philosophical enquiry, but he failed to be explicit about the extent to which his radical epistemology, *Kulturkritik* and philosophy of the will-to-power were elaborations of themes of his master. The majority of Nietzsche's references to Schopenhauer consist of assaults on his pessimism and ethics, which are characterised as symptoms of an ephemeral decadence consequent on the death of God.[8]

And Nietzsche's complex relation to Schopenhauer is reflected in his attitude towards the Indian religions. Although he praised Buddhism for its "strict phenomenalism" and remarked that it was "a hundred times more realistic than Christianity: posing problems objectively and coolly", he categorised it alongside Christianity as a decadent religion,[9] espousing a pessimism of weakness distinct from the pessimism of strength of sixth-century Greek culture.[10] Just as Hegel had attacked the Romantic extravagances of Friedrich Schlegel's enthusiasm for the orient, so Nietzsche's philhellenism prompted him to look upon Schopenhauer's oriental renaissance as a step too far eastwards. It is therefore odd to find that whereas recent scholarship on Schopenhauer and the Indian religions has emphasised their discontinuities, works on Nietzsche

---

[8] Nietzsche (1968) 17.
[9] Nietzsche (1976b) §20.
[10] Nietzsche (2007) An Attempt at Self-Criticism 1.

and the Indian or Asian traditions have usually sought (or created!) points of agreement.[11]

Schopenhauer's pessimism and endorsement of the Indian religions elicited a more sympathetic and enduring response from continental artists and thinkers working outside philosophy. Richard Wagner's devotion to Schopenhauer encouraged him to write a sketch of an opera on the life and mission of the Buddha named *The Victors* (*Die Sieger*), some of the themes from which were allegedly used in *Parsifal*.[12] And the novels of Hermann Hesse frequently incorporated aspects of the Indian religions championed by Schopenhauer. The third of the three tales composed by Joseph Knecht, Magister Ludi of Castilia in Hesse's *The Glass Bead Game*, is a skilfully illustrated presentation of the opposition between the realm of *māyā* and the yogi's liberation from its meretricious attractions through attainment of non-dual vision beyond subject and object. Lastly, Carl Gustav Jung's break with Freud was partially stimulated by his growing appreciation of the psycho-analytical potential of religious symbols, particularly those of the east. Jung made no secret of the depth of his debt to Schopenhauer, and his presentation of the contrast between Indian and European thought contains several Schopenhauerian motifs, not least when he claims that

> [i]t is quite possible that India is the real world, and that the white man lives in a madhouse of abstractions...Life in India has not yet withdrawn into the capsule of the head. It is still the whole body that lives.[13]

However, Jung's enthusiasm for eastern ideas never reached the level of Schopenhauer's oriental renaissance. Jung maintained that it was "sheer folly" for westerners to reject their scientific consciousness in favour of eastern mysticism and ethics, arguing that it would lead to "another uprooting of consciousness. Only by standing firmly on our own soil can we assimilate the spirit of the east."[14]

In the realm of theology and religious studies, Schopenhauer's philosophy of religion has had much less influence, almost none in fact. In Chapter 3 we noted that theological studies of his philosophy have tended

---

[11] Recent studies distinguishing Indian thought from Schopenhauer include those by Gestering (1986), Hacker (1995), Pol-Droit (2003), and Berger (2004a). Works attempting to forge links between Nietzsche and Buddhism include those by Mistry (1981) and Morrison (1997), while the volume edited by Parkes (1991) contains articles comparing themes between Nietzsche's philosophy and Asian thought generally.

[12] Welbon (1968) pp. 176-8.

[13] Jung (1978) p. 90.

[14] Ibid. p. 51.

to conceal the extent of his hostility towards monotheism, setting out instead to find tacit or deep commitment to theism in his works. They have commonly focussed on Schopenhauer's concession that ethical conduct and mysticism may indicate a distinction between the thing-in-itself manifesting itself as will and the thing-in-itself apart from this manifestation. The latter is frequently compared with theological conceptions of God beyond God, with Mannion in particular asserting an analogy between the thing-in-itself apart from will and Rahner's doctrine of God's incomprehensibility.[15] Even theological reflection influenced by Heidegger's critique of onto-theology and turn towards an immanent mode of philosophising (or, in Heidegger's idiom, "thinking") has tended to overlook the fact that Schopenhauer initiated this line of critique and conception of metaphysics, which Heidegger inherited from Nietzsche.[16]

As for European culture and religious practice, it need hardly be said that Schopenhauer's prediction that the decline of monotheism would be succeeded by an oriental renaissance did not occur. There are currently no ministers of a Europe-wide religion giving sermons on the auspicious rebirths to be reaped through acts of compassion or self-sacrifice, and no temples carrying symbols of the metaphysical identity of all beings or the denial of the will to live (apart from, perhaps, crucifixion altarpieces in Christian churches). And it is likely that Schopenhauer would have been very surprised to find that the Anglican Church is considered wet and overly liberal in some quarters, for this contrasts with his presentation of its clergy as aggressively self-serving and narrow-minded (PPII pp. 222-5).

Of course, the religions of India *have* enjoyed a sort of vogue in the west since Schopenhauer's death in 1860, and — as he predicted — frequently as the result of a break with theistic doctrines. However, western enthusiasm for India has never attained the status of an established church, and the turn to Indian motifs, symbols and practices has occasionally expressed little more than a vague mystical posturing or toying with esoteric exotica, rather than a genuine yearning for a spiritual outlet or disciplined religious commitment. However, this has not always the case, for many westerners have sought and found sincere spiritual nourishment in Hinduism and Buddhism, including the followers of Swami Bhaktivedānta's International Society for Kṛṣṇa Consciousness and the

---

[15] Mannion (2003) pp. 274-7.

[16] For example, in a recent collection of essays devoted to Heidegger's critique of onto-theology, Schopenhauer's name is mentioned only once, by Robert Pippin, in the context of noting that Nietzsche rejected his "romantic pessimism"—see Pippin (2003) p. 20.

members of the Friends of the Western Buddhist Order established by Sangharakshita (a.k.a. Dennis Lingwood). The success and expansion of such orders in the west might be seen as a vindication of Schopenhauer's theory of the permanence of metaphysical need, but whether they count as a fulfilment of his prediction of an oriental renaissance is another matter. From an alternative perspective it could be argued that they are simply symptoms of the religious fragmentation consequent upon the decline of Christian monotheism, a decline that Schopenhauer not only discussed at length, but also helped to bring about.

However, Schopenhauer's endorsement of the Indian religions did ignite a renaissance of Indian wisdom in one part of the world — and, oddly enough, in India itself. European eulogies on the superiority of Hinduism and Buddhism in relation to Christianity influenced young Indian intellectuals to reclaim their heritage and reformulate its essential teachings. They not only aimed to show that the metaphysics of the Indian tradition is equal to European philosophy in speculative rigour and sophistication, but that it produces experiences of profounder spiritual depth than Christianity. These objectives are especially evident in the writings of figures attached to the Hindu reform movement known as Neo-Vedānta. We have already referred to Murti's study of the Mādhyamika, in which he argued that Nāgārjuna had anticipated the methods and doctrines of the German idealists.

But a more striking and practical instance of Schopenhauer's influence on the revitalisation of the Indian heritage is reflected in the career of the theoretical founder of Neo-Vedānta, Swami Vivekaṇanda. A disciple of the mystic Rāmakṛṣṇa, Vivekananda was one of the foremost spokesmen of Neo-Hinduism in the late nineteenth century. He set out to represent the monist metaphysics of Vedānta so that it recommended an activist approach to the problems of contemporary life. As a monism of consciousness, Vedānta had traditionally conferred no more than relative or interim value on ritual or moral action, presenting it as a mere preliminary to spiritual self-perfection and the renunciation of all obligation.[17] In the interests of modernising the Indian inheritance, Vivekananda sought resources in the tradition that would justify a positive basis for moral and social engagement as an end in itself. Such a reinterpretation would not only rebuff European claims that Indian metaphysics warrants an attitude of soporific passivity, but simultaneously provide an ideological

---

[17] This theory has some points in common with Schopenhauer's account of the path from morality to asceticism outlined in the previous chapter.

standpoint for opposition to British rule. Paul Hacker has charted the relation between Vivekananda's meeting and acquaintance with Schopenhauer's disciple Paul Deussen in September 1896, and the appearance of Schopenhauer's interpretation of *tat tvam asi* as the metaphysical basis of ethics in Vivekananda's subsequent works.[18] Hacker has also shown how subsequent Neo-Vedāntins influenced by Vivekananda's appropriation tended to consider the ethical interpretation of *tat tvam asi* as the traditional outlook of ancient Hinduism, oblivious to its original formulation in the works of a nineteenth-century German idealist.[19] The Neo-Vedāntins' success in constructing a coherent and sophisticated *Weltanschauung* that was simultaneously Hindu, universal, and geared towards moral and social action, became an important ideological feature of Indian Nationalism. Sir Sarvepalli Radhakrishnan, the most prolific and probably most influential of the twentieth-century Neo-Vedāntins, not only promulgated this interpretation of the Indian tradition in the scholarly works he wrote while Spalding Professor of Eastern Religions and Ethics at the University of Oxford, but also embodied its ideals during his presidency of independent India from 1962 to 1967.

In this way, Schopenhauer's conception of an oriental renaissance through the study of Sanskrit sources had an unexpected and unusual consequence. Although it helped to stimulate a limited amount of interest in the Indian religions in western nations, his prediction that it would produce a fundamental change in life, knowledge and thought was ultimately fulfilled not in Europe, but in the original homeland itself.

[18] Hacker (1995) pp. 294-7.
[19] Ibid. pp.298ff.

BIBLIOGRAPHY

Works by Schopenhauer

References in the text cite the page numbers of the editions of Schopenhauer's works listed below.

Werke in zehn Bänden: Schopenhauers Zürcher Ausgabe (Zürich: Diogenes, 1977).
Schopenhauer's Early Fourfold Root (1813 edition), translated by F.C. White (Aldershot: Avebury, 1997).
On the Fourfold Root of the Principle of Sufficient Reason (1847 edition), translated by E.F.J. Payne (La Salle Illinois: Open Court, 1997).
The World as Will and Representation 2 vols., translated by E.F.J. Payne (New York: Dover, 1969).
On the Will in Nature, translated by E.F.J. Payne (Oxford: Berg, 1995).
On the Basis of Morality, translated by E.F.J. Payne (Oxford: Berghahn Books, 1995).
Prize Essay on the Freedom of the Will, translated by E.F.J. Payne (Cambridge: Cambridge University Press, 1999).
Parerga and Paralipomena 2 vols., translated by E.F.J. Payne (Oxford: Clarendon Press, 2000).
Der Handschriftliche Nachlass vol. V (Frankfurt-am-Main: Waldemar Kramer, 1968).
Manuscript Remains 4 vols., translated by E.F.J. Payne (Oxford: Berg, 1988-1989).
Manuscript Remains: notes from vols. 1-9 of Asiatick Researches (unpublished manuscript notes: box XXIX, pp. 205-250, Schopenhauer-Archiv, Frankfurt-am-Main).
Philosophische Vorlesungen: vier Bänden (München; Zürich: Serie Piper, 1986).
Gesammelte Briefe (Bonn: Bouvier Herbert Grundmann, 1978).

Secondary Bibliography

Editions of Sacred Texts cited.
Ṛg-Veda, translated and edited by W. Doniger O'Flaherty (London: Penguin, 2005).
The Principal Upaniṣads, translated and edited by S. Radhakrishnan (New Delhi: Indus, 1994).
Bhagavad-Gītā, translated by S. Mitchell (London: Rider, 2000).
Dīgha Nikāya, in *Dialogues of the Buddha* 3 vols., translated by T.W. & C.A.F. Rhys Davids (London: Pali Text Society, 1899-1921).

Majjhima Nikāya, in *Middle Length Sayings* 3 vols., translated by I.B. Horner (London: Pali Text Society, 1954-9).
The Dhammapada, translated and edited by S. Radhakrishnan (New Delhi: Oxford Indian Paperbacks, 1998).

Journals
Asiatic Journal & Monthly Register vol. XXII (London: Kingsbury, Parbury & Allen, 1826).
Asiatick Researches vols. I-X (London: P. Elmsly, 1789-1809).
Transactions of the Royal Asiatic Society of Great Britain and Ireland vols. I-III, (London: Parbury, Allen & Co., 1827-1835).

Abelson, P. (1993) 'Schopenhauer and Buddhism', *Philosophy East and West* 43, pp. 255-278.
Anselm (1990) *Proslogion*, translated by W.E. Mann, in S.M. Cahn (ed.), *Classics of Western Philosophy*, 3rd edition (Indianapolis/Cambridge: Hackett), pp. 365-381.
App, U. (1998a) 'Notes and Excerpts by Schopenhauer Related to Volumes 1-9 of the *Asiatick Researches*', *Schopenhauer-Jahrbuch* 79, pp. 11-33.
—, (1998b) 'Schopenhauers Begegnung mit dem Buddhismus', *Schopenhauer-Jahrbuch* 79, pp. 35-56.
—, (2003) 'Notizen Schopenhauers zu Ost-, Nord-, und Südostasien vom Sommersemester 1811', *Schopenhauer-Jahrbuch* 84, pp. 13-39.
—, (2006a) 'Schopenhauer's India Notes of 1811', *Schopenhauer-Jahrbuch* 87, pp. 15-31.
—, (2006b) 'Schopenhauer's Initial Encounter with Indian Thought', *Schopenhauer-Jahrbuch* 87, pp. 35-76.
Aquinas, T. (1911) *Summa Theologica vol. I*, translated by Fathers of the English Dominican Province (London: R. & T. Washbourne Ltd.).
Aristotle (1991) *The Art of Rhetoric*, translated by H. Lawson-Tancred (Harmondsworth: Penguin).
Armstrong, K. (2007) *The Bible: The Biography* (London: Atlantic Books).
Atwell, J.E. (1990) *Schopenhauer: The Human Character* (Philadelphia: Temple University Press).
—, (1995) *Schopenhauer on the Character of the World: The Metaphysics of Will* (Berkeley, California; London: University of California Press).
Atzert, S. (2007) 'Schopenhauer und seine Quellen. Zum Buddhismusbild in den frühen *Asiatick Researches*', *Schopenhauer-Jahrbuch* 88, pp. 15-27.
Augustine (1953) *On Free Will*, translated by J.H.S. Burleigh, in J. Baillie, J. T. McNeill & H. P. van Dusen (eds.), *The Library of Christian Classics vol.VI* (London: SCM Press), pp. 102-217.
—, (1961) *Confessions*, translated by R.S. Pine-Coffin (Harmondsworth: Penguin).
—, (1972) *City of God*, translated by H. Bettenson (Harmondsworth: Penguin).
Barth, K. (1960) *Anselm: Fides Quaerens Intellectum: Anselm's Proof of the Existence of God in the Context of his Theological Scheme*, translated by I.W. Robertson (London: SCM Press).
Batchelor, S. (1994) *The Awakening of the West: The Encounter of Buddhism and Western Culture: 543 B.C.E. – 1992* (London: Aquarian).

Bauer, W. (1979) *A Greek-English Lexicon of the New Testament and other Christian Literature*, 2nd edition revised and augmented by F. W. Gingrich & F.N. Danker (Chicago: University of Chicago Press).

Berger, D.L. (2004a) *"The Veil of Māyā" : Schopenhauer's System and Early Indian Thought* (Binghamton, N.Y.: Global Academic Publishing).

—, (2004b) '"The Poorest Form of Theism": Schopenhauer, Islam and the Perils of Comparative Hermeneutics', *Islam and Christian-Muslim Relations* 15/1, pp. 135-146.

—, (2007) 'Does Monism Do Ethical Work? Assessing Hacker's Critique of Vedāntic and Schopenhauerian Ethics', *Schopenhauer-Jahrbuch* 88, pp. 29-37.

Berman, D. (1998) 'Schopenhauer and Nietzsche: Honest Atheism, Dishonest Pessimism', in C. Janaway (ed.), *Willing and Nothingness: Schopenhauer as Nietzsche's Educator* (Oxford: Clarendon Press), pp. 178-195.

Boswell, J. (1992) *The Life of Samuel Johnson* (London: Everyman).

Braithwaite, R.B. (1964) 'An Empiricist's View of the Nature of Religious Belief', in J. Hick (ed.), *The Existence of God* (London: Macmillan), pp. 228-252.

Buchanan, F. (1801) 'On the Religion and Literature of the Burmas', *Asiatick Researches vol.VI* (London: P. Elmsly), pp. 163-308.

Bullock A. (1993) *Hitler and Stalin: Parallel Lives* (London: Fontana Press).

Bultmann, R.K. (1985) *New Testament and Mythology: and other Basic Writings*, translated by S. M. Ogden (London: SCM Press).

Bykhovsky, B. (1984) *Schopenhauer and the Ground of Existence*, translated by P.Moran (Amsterdam: B.R. Grüner).

Caputo, J.D. (1993) 'Heidegger and Theology', in C. Guignon (ed.), *The Cambridge Companion to Heidegger* (Cambridge: Cambridge University Press), pp. 270-288.

Cartwright, D.E. (2003) 'Locke as Schopenhauer's (Kantian) Philosophical Ancestor', *Schopenhauer-Jahrbuch* 84, pp. 147-156.

Colebrooke, H.T. (2001) *Essays on the Religion and Philosophy of the Hindus* (London: Ganesha).

—, (1803) 'On the Religious Ceremonies of the Hindus, and of the Brahmens especially', *Asiatick Researches vol.VII* (London: P. Elmsly), pp. 232-285.

—, (1808) 'On the Vedas, or Sacred Writings of the Hindus', *Asiatick Researches vol. VIII* (London: P. Elmsly), pp. 369-476.

—, (1809) 'Observations on the Sect of Jains', *Asiatick Researches vol. IX* (London: P. Elmsly), pp. 287-322.

—, (1827) 'On the philosophy of the Hindus. Part III. MĪMĀNSĀ', *Transactions of the Royal Asiatic Society of Great Britain and Ireland vol. I* (London: Parbury, Allen & Co.), pp. 439-466.

Conze, E. (1963) 'Buddhist Philosophy and its European Parallels', *Philosophy East and West* 13:1, pp. 9-23.

Copleston, F.C. (1975) *Arthur Schopenhauer: Philosopher of Pessimism*, 2nd edition (London: Search Press).

—, (1991) *Aquinas* (Harmondsworth: Penguin).

Cupitt, D. (1980) *Taking Leave of God* (London: SCM).

—, (1982) *The World to Come* (London: SCM).

—, (1994) *The Sea of Faith*, 2nd edition (London: SCM).

Dauer, D. (1969) *Schopenhauer as Transmitter of Buddhist Ideas* (Berne: Herbert Lang).

Deussen, P. (1894) *The Elements of Metaphysics*, translated by C.M. Duff (London: Macmillan).

—, (1906) *Philosophy of the Upanishads*, translated by A.S. Geden (Edinburgh: T. & T. Clark).

—, (1911) *Die Geheimlehre des Veda: ausgewählte texte der Upanishad's* (Leipzig: F.A. Brockhaus).

Deussen P. (ed.) (1897) *Sechzig Upanishad's des Veda*, aus dem Sanskrit Übersetzt und mit einleitungen und anmerkungen versehen von Dr. P. Deussen (Leipzig: F. A. Brockhaus).

Doniger O'Flaherty, W. (1976) *The Origins of Evil in Hindu Mythology* (Berkeley; London: University of California Press).

Dostoyevsky, F. (1982) *The Brothers Karamazov*, translated by D. Magarshack (Harmondsworth: Penguin).

Dumoulin, H. (1981) 'Buddhism and Nineteenth-Century German Philosophy', *Journal of the History of Ideas* 42, pp. 457-70.

Dundas, P. (2002) *The Jains*, 2nd edition (London: Routledge).

Duperron, A.H.A. (1801-02) *Oupnek'hat: Secretum Tegendum* 2 vols. (Agentorati: Levrault).

Feuerbach, L. (1957) *The Essence of Christianity*, translated by G. Eliot (New York: Harper Torchbooks).

Fichte, J.G. (1956) *The Vocation of Man*, translated by W. Smith (New York: Bobbs-Merrill).

Findlay, J.N. (1968) 'Can God's Existence be Disproved?', in A. Plantinga (ed.), *The Ontological Argument: From St. Anselm to Contemporary Philosophers* (London: Macmillan), pp. 111-122.

Fox, M. (ed.) (1980) *Schopenhauer: His Philosophical Achievement* (Brighton: Harvester Press).

Flew, A. (1955) 'Death', in A. MacIntyre & A. Flew (eds.), *New Essays in Philosophical Theology* (London: SCM Press), pp. 267-272.

—, (1964) 'Theology and Falsification', in J. Hick (ed.), *The Existence of God* (London: Macmillan), pp. 224-228.

—, (1976) *The Presumption of Atheism* (London: Elek/Pemberton).

Flew, A. & MacIntyre, A. (eds.) (1955) *New Essays in Philosophical Theology* (London: SCM Press).

Freud, S. (1991) *Beyond the Pleasure Principle*, translated by J. Strachey, in A. Freud (ed.), *The Essentials of Psycho-Analysis* (Harmondsworth: Penguin), pp. 218-268.

—, (1985) *The Future of an Illusion*, translated by J. Strachey, in A. Dickson (ed.), *Civilization, Society and Religion: Group Psychology, Civilization and its Discontents and Other Works* (Harmondsworth: Penguin), pp. 183-241.

Gadamer, H. (1989) *Truth and Method*, 2nd edition, translation revised by J. Weinsheimer & D.G. Marshall (London: Sheed & Ward).

Ganeri, J. (1996) 'The Hindu Syllogism: Nineteenth Century Perceptions of Indian Logical Thought', *Philosophy East and West* 46/1, pp. 1-16.

Gardiner, P. (1963) *Schopenhauer* (Harmondsworth: Penguin).

Geertz, C. (2002) 'Religion as a Cultural System' in M. Lambek (ed.), *A Reader in the Anthropology of Religion* (London: Macmillan), pp. 61-82.

Gestering, J.J. (1986) *German Pessimism and Indian Philosophy: A Hermeneutic Reading* (Delhi: Ajanta Publications).

Glasenapp, H. Von (1960) *Das Indienbild Deutscher Denker* (Stuttgart: K.F. Koehler).

Gonzales, R.A. (1992) *An Approach to the Sacred in the Thought of Schopenhauer*, (San Francisco: Mellen Research University Press).

Gregory the Great (1959) *Dialogues*, translated by O.J. Zimmerman (New York: The Fathers of the Church, Inc.).

Gruber, E.R. & Kersten, H. (1995) *The Original Jesus: The Buddhist Sources of Christianity* (Shaftesbury: Element Books Ltd.).

Hacker, P. (1995) *Philology and Confrontation: Paul Hacker on Traditional and Modern Vedānta*, translated by W. Halbfass (Albany, NY: State University of New York Press).

Haffmans, G. (ed.) (1977) *Über Arthur Schopenhauer* (Zürich: Diogenes).

Halbfass, W. (1988) *India and Europe: An Essay in Understanding* (New York: State University of New York Press).

Hamlyn, D.W. (1980) *Schopenhauer* (London: Routledge & Kegan Paul).

Hardy, S. (1850) *Eastern Monachism* (London: Partridge & Oakey).

—, (1853) *A Manual of Buddhism* (London: Partridge & Oakey).

Harrison, P. (1999) *The Elements of Pantheism: Understanding the Divinity in Nature and the Universe* (Shaftesbury: Element).

Hartshorne, C. (1962) *The Logic of Perfection, and Other Essays in Neoclassical Metaphysics* (La Salle, Illinois: Open Court).

Harvey, P. (1990) *An Introduction to Buddhism: Teachings, History and Practices* (Cambridge: Cambridge University Press).

—, (1995) *The Selfless Mind: Personality, Consciousness and Nirvāṇa in Early Buddhism* (Surrey: Curzon Press).

Hayman, R. (1995) *Nietzsche: A Critical Life* (London: Pheonix Giants).

Hecker, M.F. (1897) *Schopenhauer und die Indische Philosophie* (Cologne: Hübscher und Teufel).

Hedley, D. (2008) *Living Forms of the Imagination* (London; New York: T & T Clark International).

Hedley, D. & Ryan, C. (2009) 'Nineteenth-Century Philosophy of Religion', in G. Oppy and N. Trakakis (eds.), *A History of Western Philosophy of Religion vol. IV*, (Stocksfield: Acumen Publishing Ltd.), pp. 1-19.

Hegel, G.W.F. (1977) *Phenomenology of Spirit*, translated by A V. Miller (Oxford: Clarendon Press).

—, (1956) *The Philosophy of History*, translated by J. Sibree (New York: Dover Publications).

—, (1975) *Logic: Part I of the Encyclopaedia of the Philosophical Sciences (1830)*, translated by W. Wallace (Oxford: Clarendon Press).

—, (1985) *Philosophy of Mind: Part III of the Encyclopaedia of the Philosophical Sciences (1830)*, translated by W. Wallace (Oxford: Clarendon Press).

—, (1987) *Lectures on the Philosophy of Religion: vol. II, Determinate Religion*, translated by R.F. Brown, P.C. Hodgson & J.M. Stewart with the assistance of H.S. Harris (Berkeley; Los Angeles; London: University of California Press).

—, (1988) *Lectures on the Philosophy of Religion: one-volume edition (the Lectures of 1827)*, translated by R.F. Brown, P.C. Hodgson & J.M. Stewart with the assistance of H.S. Harris (Berkeley; Los Angeles; London: University of California Press).

—, (1974) *Lectures on the History of Philosophy: vol. I, Greek Philosophy to Plato*, translated by E.S. Haldane & F.H. Simson (New York: Humanities Press).

—, (1995) *On the Episode of the Mahābhārata known by the name Bhagavad-Gītā by Wilhelm von Humboldt*, translated by H. Herring (New Delhi: Indian Council of Philosophical Research).

Heidegger, M. (1955) *What is Philosophy?* translated by W. Kluback & J.T. Wilde (London: Vision Press).

—, (1968) *What is called Thinking?* translated by J.G. Gray & F.D. Wieck (New York: Harper & Row).

—, (1971) 'A Dialogue on Language between a Japanese and an Inquirer', translated by P.D. Hertz, in *On the Way to Language*, (New York: Harper & Row), pp. 1-54.

—, (2000) *Introduction to Metaphysics*, translated by G. Fried & R. Polt (New Haven, Conn.; London: Yale University Press).

Herder, J.G. (1800) *Outlines of a Philosophy of the History of Man*, translated by T. Churchill (London: J. Johnson).

—, (1993) *Against Pure Reason: Writings on Religion, Language, and History*, translated by M. Bunge (Minneapolis: Fortress Press).

Hesse, H. (1972) *The Journey to the East*, translated by H. Rosner (London: Panther Books).

—, (1998) *Siddhartha*, translated by H. Rosner (London: Macmillan).

—, (1979) *The Glass Bead Game*, translated by R. & C. Winston (Harmondsworth: Penguin).

Hick, J. (1991) *An Interpretation of Religion: Human Responses to the Transcendent* (London: Macmillan).

Hick, J. (ed.) (1964) *The Existence of God* (London: Macmillan).

Hübscher, A. (1989) *The Philosophy of Schopenhauer in its Intellectual Context: Thinker against the Tide*, translated by J.T. Baer & D.E. Cartwright (Lewiston, N.Y.; Lampeter: Edwin Mellen Press).

Hueffer, F. (1876) 'Arthur Schopenhauer', *Fortnightly Review* 20, pp. 773-792.

Hume, D. (1978) *A Treatise of Human Nature* (Oxford: Clarendon Press).

—, (2000) *An Enquiry Concerning Human Understanding* (Oxford: Clarendon Press).

—, (1966) *An Enquiry Concerning the Principles of Morals* (La Salle, Illinois: Open Court).

—, (1993a) *Dialogues Concerning Natural Religion*, in J.C.A. Gaskin (ed.), *Dialogues and Natural History of Religion* (Oxford: Oxford University Press), pp. 29-130.

—, (1993b) *The Natural History of Religion*, in J.C.A. Gaskin (ed.), *Dialogues and Natural History of Religion* (Oxford: Oxford University Press), pp. 134-193.

—, (1993c) *My Own Life*, in J.C.A. Gaskin (ed.), *Dialogues and Natural History of Religion* (Oxford: Oxford University Press), pp. 3-10.

Husserl, E. (1970) *The Crisis of European Sciences and Transcendental Phenomenology: An Introduction to Phenomenological Philosophy*, translated by D. Carr (Evanston: Northwestern University Press).

James, W. (1979) *The Will to Believe and Other Essays in Popular Philosophy* (Cambridge, Mass.; London: Harvard University Press).

Janaway, C. (1989) *Self and World in Schopenhauer's Philosophy* (Oxford: Clarendon Press).

—, (1998) 'Schopenhauer as Nietzsche's Educator', in C. Janaway (ed.), *Willing and Nothingness: Schopenhauer as Nietzsche's Educator* (Oxford: Clarendon Press), pp. 13-36.

—, (1999) 'Schopenhauer's Pessimism', in C. Janaway (ed.), *The Cambridge Companion to Schopenhauer* (Cambridge: Cambridge University Press), pp. 318-343.

—, (2007) *Beyond Selflessness: Reading Nietzsche's Genealogy* (Oxford: Clarendon Press).

Janaway, C. (ed.) (1998) *Willing and Nothingness: Schopenhauer as Nietzsche's Educator* (Oxford: Clarendon Press).

—, (1999) *The Cambridge Companion to Schopenhauer* (Cambridge: Cambridge University Press).

Joinville, J.E. de (1803) 'On the Religion and Manners of the People of Ceylon', *Asiatick Researches vol.VII* (London: P. Elmsly), pp. 397-444.

Jones, W. (1789a) 'On the Gods of Greece, Italy and India', *Asiatick Researches vol. I* (London: P. Elmsly), pp. 221-275.

—, (1789b) 'Second Discourse on the Philosophy of the Asiaticks', *Asiatick Researches vol. I* (London: P. Elmsly), pp. 405-414.

—, (1789c) 'On the Hindus', *Asiatick Researches vol. I* (London: P. Elmsly), pp. 415-431.

—, (1790) 'On the Antiquity of the Indian Zodiac', *Asiatick Researches vol. II* (London: P. Elmsly), pp. 289-306.

—, (1799) 'On the Philosophy of the Asiatics', *Asiatick Researches vol. IV* (London, P. Elmsly), pp. 160-176.

Jung, C.G. (1978) *Psychology and the East*, translated by R.F.C. Hull (Princeton, N.J.: Princeton University Press).

Kahn, C. H. (1988) 'Discovering the Will from Aristotle to Augustine' in J.M. Dillon & A.A. Long, *The Question of "Eclecticism": Studies in Later Greek Philosophy* (Berkeley; Los Angeles; London: The University of California Press), pp. 234-259.

Kant, I. (1998) *Critique of Pure Reason*, translated and edited by P. Guyer & A.W. Wood (Cambridge: Cambridge University Press).

—, (1990) *Prolegomena to any Future Metaphysics*, translated by P. Carus, in S.M. Cahn (ed.), *Classics of Western Philosophy*, 3rd edition (Indianapolis/Cambridge: Hackett), pp. 933-1008.

—, (1997) *Critique of Practical Reason*, translated by M. Gregor (Cambridge: Cambridge University Press).

—, (1987) *Critique of Judgement*, translated by W.S. Pluhar (Indianapolis/Cambridge: Hackett).

—, (1960) *Religion within the Limits of Reason Alone*, translated by T.M. Greene & H.H Hudson, 2nd edition (La Salle, Illinois: Open Court).

—, (1991) *An Answer to the Question: 'What is Enlightenment?'*, translated by H.B. Nisbet, in H. Reiss (ed.), *Political Writings* (Cambridge: Cambridge University Press), pp. 54-60.

Kaufmann, W. (1974) *Nietzsche: Philosopher, Psychologist, Antichrist*, 4th edition (Princeton, N.J.: Princeton University Press).

Kierkegaard, S. (1962) *Philosophical Fragments*, translated by D.F. Swenson & H.V. Hong (Princeton, N.J.: Princeton University Press).

King, A (2005) 'Philosophy and Salvation: The Apophatic in the Thought of Arthur Schopenhauer', *Modern Theology* 21:2, pp. 253-274.

Kiowsky, H. (1996) 'Parallelen und Divergenzen in Schopenhauers Ethik zur buddhistischen Erlösungslehre', *Schopenhauer-Jahrbuch* 77, pp. 255-60.

Klostermaier, K.K. (1994) *A Survey of Hinduism*, 2nd edition (Albany, N.Y.: State University of New York Press).

Körösi, A.C. (1836) 'Analysis of the *Dulva*, a Portion of the Tibetan Work Entitled the *Kah-Gyur*', *Asiatick Researches vol. XX* (Calcutta: H.T. Huttmann), pp. 41-93.

Lambek, M. (2002) *A Reader in the Anthropology of Religion* (Oxford: Blackwell Publishers).

Kṛṣṇa Miśra (2006) *Prabodha Chandrodaya or Rise of the Moon of Intellect: A Spiritual Drama*, translated by J. Taylor (Montana: Kessinger Publishing).

Lange, N. de (1986) *Judaism* (Oxford: Oxford University Press).

Larson, G.J. (1988) 'The Age-Old Distinction between the Same and the Other', in G.J. Larson & E. Deutsch (eds.), *Interpreting Across Boundaries: New Essays in Comparative Philosophy* (Princeton, N.J.: Princeton University Press), pp. 3-19.

Lipner, J.J. (1998) *Hindus: Their Religious Beliefs and Practices* (London: Routledge).

MacIntyre, A. (1966) 'Is Understanding Religion Compatible With Believing?', in J. Hick (ed.), *Faith and the Philosophers* (London: Macmillan), pp. 115-133.

—, (1969) 'The Debate about God: Victorian Relevance and Contemporary Irrelevance', in A. MacIntyre & P. Ricoeur, *The Religious Significance of Atheism* (New York; London: Columbia University Press), pp. 1-55.

Mack, M. (2003) *German Idealism and the Jew: The Inner Anti-Semitism of Philosophy and German Jewish Responses* (Chicago; London: University of Chicago Press).

Mackenzie, C. (1809) 'An Account of the Jains', *Asiatick Researches vol.IX* (London, P. Elmsly), pp. 244-286.

McCutcheon, R.T. (ed.) (1999) *The Insider / Outsider Problem in the Study of Religion: A Reader* (London: Cassell).

Magee, B. (1983) *The Philosophy of Schopenhauer* (Oxford: Clarendon Press).

Mainländer, P. (1876) *Die Philosophie der Erlösung* (Berlin: T. Grieben).

Malter, R. (1987) *Faksimilenachdruck der 1. Auflage der Welt als Wille und Vorstellung mit einen Beiheft zur Einführung in das Werk* (Frankfurt: Insel).

Mann, T. (1939) *The Living Thoughts of Schopenhauer* (London: Cassell).

—, (1996) *Buddenbrooks*, translated by H.T. Lowe-Porter (London: Minerva).

Mannion, G. (2003) *Schopenhauer, Religion and Morality: The Humble Path to Ethics* (Aldershot: Ashgate).

Meisig, K. (2007) 'Der Irrtum von der Passivität der Inder', *Schopenhauer-Jahrbuch* 88, pp. 39-48.

Merkel, R.F. (1948) 'Schopenhauers Indien-Lehrer', *Schopenhauer-Jahrbuch* 32, pp. 158-181.

Meyer, U.W. (1994) *Europäische Rezeption indischer Philosophie und Religion: Dargestellt am Beispiel von Arthur Schopenhauer* (Berne: Peter Lang).

Mill, J. (1858) *The History of British India vol.I* (London: James Madden).

Mistry, F. (1981) *Nietzsche and Buddhism: Prolegomenon to a Comparative Study* (Berlin; New York: Walter de Gruyter).

Mockrauer, F. (1928) 'Schopenhauer und Indien', *Schopenhauer-Jahrbuch* 15, pp. 3-26.

Morrison, R. (1997) *Nietzsche and Buddhism: Ironic and Elective Affinities* (Oxford: Clarendon Press).

Müller, F.M. (1847) *On The Veda and Zend-Avesta* (London: Spottiswoodes & Shaw).

Murti, T.R.V. (1974) *The Central Philosophy of Buddhism: A Study of the Mādhyamika System* (London: George Allen & Unwin Ltd.).

Nāgārjuna (1991) *Mūlamadhyamakakārikā*, translated by D.J. Kalupahana (Delhi: Motilal Banarsidass).

Ñāṇajīvako (1970) *Schopenhauer and Buddhism* (Kandy: Buddhist Publication Society).

Navia, L. (1980) 'Reflections on Schopenhauer's Pessimism', in M. Fox (ed.), *Schopenhauer: His Philosophical Achievement* (Brighton: Harvester Press), pp. 171-182.

Nicholls, M. (1994) 'The Kantian Inheritance and Schopenhauer's Doctrine of Will', *Kant-Studien* 85:3, pp. 257-279.

—, (1999) 'The Influence of Eastern Thought on Schopenhauer's Doctrine of the Thing-in-Itself', in C. Janaway (ed.), *The Cambridge Companion to Schopenhauer* (Cambridge: Cambridge University Press), pp. 171-212.

Nietzsche, F. (2007) *The Birth of Tragedy*, translated by R. Speirs (Cambridge: Cambridge University Press).

—, (1974) *The Gay Science*, translated by W. Kaufmann (New York: Vintage Books).

—, (1989) *On the Genealogy of Morals*, translated by W. Kaufmann & R.J. Hollingdale (New York: Vintage Books).

—, (1976a) *Twilight of the Idols*, translated by W. Kaufmann, in W. Kaufmann (ed.), *The Portable Nietzsche* (Harmondsworth: Penguin), pp. 464-563.

—, (1976b) *The Antichrist*, translated by W. Kaufmann, in W. Kaufmann (ed.), *The Portable Nietzsche* (Harmondsworth, Penguin), pp. 568-656.

—, (1968) *The Will to Power*, translated by W. Kaufmann & R.J. Hollingdale (New York: Vintage Books).

Otto, R. (1958) *The Idea of the Holy: An Inquiry into the non-rational factor in the idea of the divine and its relation to the rational*, translated by J.W. Harvey (Oxford: Oxford University Press).

Oxenford, J. (1853) 'Iconoclasm in German Philosophy', *The Westminster Review* New Series 3, pp. 388-407.

Parkes, G. (ed.) (1991) *Nietzsche and Asian Thought* (Chicago and London: The University of Chicago Press).

Pascal, B. (1995) *Pensées*, translated by A.J. Krailsheimer (Harmondsworth: Penguin).

Pattison, G. (1996) *Agnosis: Theology in the Void* (London: Macmillan).

—, (2005a) *A Short Course in Christian Doctrine* (London: SCM Press).

—, (2005b) *Thinking About God in an Age of Technology* (Oxford: Oxford University Press).

Phillips, D.Z. (1976) *Religion without Explanation* (London: Basil Blackwell).

Pippin, R. (2003) 'Love and Death in Nietzsche', in M.A. Wrathall (ed.), *Religion after Metaphysics* (Cambridge: Cambridge University Press), pp. 7-28.

Plantinga, A. (1977) *God, Freedom, and Evil* (Michigan: William B. Eerdmans Publishing Co.).

Plantinga, A. (ed.) (1968) *The Ontological Argument: From St. Anselm to Contemporary Philosophers* (London: Macmillan).

Plato (1987) *The Republic*, translated by D. Lee (Harmondsworth: Penguin).

Pol-Droit, R. (2003) *The Cult of Nothingness: The Philosophers and the Buddha*, translated by D. Streight & P. Vohnson (Chapel Hill; London: University of North Carolina Press).

Popper, K.R. (1968) *Conjectures and Refutations: The Growth of Scientific Knowledge*, 3rd edition (London: Routledge and Kegan Paul).

Radhakrishnan, S. (1996) *Indian Philosophy* 2 vols. (New Delhi: Oxford Indian Paperbacks).

Rahula, W. (1967) *What the Buddha Taught*, 2nd edition (Bedford: Gordon Fraser Gallery Ltd.).

Ray, M.A. (2003) *Subjectivity and Irreligion: Atheism and Agnosticism in Kant, Schopenhauer and Nietzsche* (Aldershot: Ashgate).

Rollmann, H. (1978) 'Deussen, Nietzsche and Vedanta', *Journal of the History of Ideas* 39, pp. 125-132.

Royce, J. (1892) *The Spirit of Modern Philosophy* (Boston: Houghton, Mifflin).

Safranski, R. (1991) *Schopenhauer and the Wild Years of Philosophy*, translated by E.Osers (Cambridge, Mass.: Harvard University Press).

Said, E. (1985) *Orientalism* (Harmondsworth: Penguin).

Schelling, F.W.J. (1966) *On University Studies*, translated by E.S. Morgan (Athens: Ohio University Press).

—, (1936) *Of Human Freedom*, translated with a critical introduction and notes by J. Gutman (Chicago: Open Court).

—, (1977) *Schellings Philosophie der Offenbarung 1841/2*, edited by M. Frank (Frankfurt-am-Main: Suhrkamp).

—, (1857) *Philosophie der Mythologie*, *Sämmtliche Werke* 2/2 (Stuttgart und Augsburg: G. Cotta'scher).

Schlegel F. von (1968) *Gespräch über die Poesie* (Stuttgart: Metzler).

—, (1849) *On the Language and Wisdom of the Indians*, translated by E.J. Millington, in E.J. Millington (ed.) *The Aesthetic and Miscellaneous Works of Friedrich Schlegel* (London: Henry G. Bohn), pp 425-526.

—, (1846) *The Philosophy of History*, translated by J.B. Robertson (London: Henry G. Bohn).

Schleiermacher, F.D.E. (1998) *Hermeneutics and Criticism and other Writings*, translated by A. Bowie (Cambridge: Cambridge University Press).

Scheiffele, E. (1991) 'Questioning One's "Own" from the Perspective of the Foreign', in G. Parkes (ed.), *Nietzsche and Asian Thought* (London and Chicago: The University of Chicago Press), pp. 31-47.

Schimmel, A. (1975) *Mystical Dimensions of Islam* (Chapel Hill, North Carolina: University of North Carolina Press).

Schmidt, A. (1986) *Die Wahrheit im Gewande der Lüge: Schopenhauers Religionsphilosophie* (München; Zürich: Serie Piper).

Scholz, W. (1996) *Arthur Schopenhauer – ein Philosoph zwischen westlicher und östlicher Tradition* (Frankfurt-am-Main: Peter Lang).

Schwab, R. (1984) *The Oriental Renaissance: Europe's Rediscovery of India and the East, 1680-1880*, translated by G. Patterson-Black and V. Reinking (New York: Columbia University Press).

Sedlar, J.W. (1982) *India in the Mind of Germany: Schelling, Schopenhauer and their Times* (Washington: University Press of America).

Simmel, G. (1991) *Schopenhauer and Nietzsche*, translated by H. Loiskandl, D. Weinstein & M. Weinstein (Illinois: University of Illinois Press).

Singh, R. Raj (2007) *Death, Contemplation and Schopenhauer* (Aldershot: Ashgate).

Smart, N. (1979) *The Philosophy of Religion* (London: Sheldon Press).

Son, G. (2001) *Schopenhauers Ethik des Mitleids und die indische Philosophie: Parallelität und Differenz* (Freiburg; München: Karl Alber).

Sontag, F. (1967) 'The Meaning of Argument in Anselm', *Journal of Philosophy* 64:15, pp. 459-486.

Soskice J. M. (2006) 'Athens and Jerusalem, Alexandria and Edessa: Is there a Metaphysics of Scripture', *International Journal of Systematic Theology* 8:2, pp. 149-162.

Sprigge, T.L.S. (1991) *Theories of Existence* (Harmondsworth: Penguin).

Strauss, D.F. (1906) *The Life of Jesus Critically Examined*, translated by G. Eliot (London: Swan Sonnenschein & Co.).

Swinburne, R. (1993) *The Coherence of Theism*, revised edition (Oxford: Clarendon Press).

Taylor, R. (1985) 'Arthur Schopenhauer', in N. Smart, J. Clayton, S. Katz & P. Sherry (eds.), *Nineteenth Century Religious Thought in the West vol.I* (Cambridge: Cambridge University Press), pp. 157-180.

Thomas, M.M. (1969) *The Acknowledged Christ of the Indian Renaissance* (London: SCM Press).

Thundy, Z.P. (1993) *Buddha and Christ: Nativity Stories and Indian Traditions* (Leiden; New York: E. J. Brill).

Tillich, P. (1957) *Systematic Theology vol.II* (London: James Nisbet & Co. Ltd.).

Tuck, A.P. (1990) *Comparative Philosophy and the Philosophy of Scholarship: On the Western Interpretation of Nāgārjuna* (Oxford: Oxford University Press).

Turner, D. (1995) *The Darkness of God: Negativity in Christian Mysticism* (Cambridge: Cambridge University Press).

Überweg, F. (1909) *Grundriss der Geschichte der Philosophie des Altertums*, 10th edition (Berlin: Ernst Siegfried Mittler und Sohn).

Vallée, G. (1988) *The Spinoza Conversations Between Lessing and Jacobi: Text with Excerpts from the Ensuing Controversy* (Lanham; New York; London: University Press of America).

Ward, K. (1987) *Images of Eternity: Concepts of God in Five Religious Traditions* (London: Darton, Longman & Todd).

—, (1996) *Religion and Creation* (Oxford: Clarendon Press).

Welbon, G.R. (1968) *The Buddhist Nirvāṇa and its Western Interpreters* (Chicago: University of Chicago Press).

Wilford, F. (1801) 'On Mount Caucasus', *Asiatick Researches vol.VI* (London: P. Elmsly) pp. 455-536.

Wimbush, V.L. & Valantasis, R. (eds.) (1998) *Asceticism* (Oxford: Oxford University Press).

Windelband, W. (1903) *Lehrbuch der Geschichte der Philosophie*, 3rd edition (Tübingen und Leipzig: J.C.B. Mohr).

Wittgenstein, L. (2000) *Tractatus Logico-Philosophicus*, translated by D.F. Pears & B.F. McGuinness (London: Routledge).

Wrathall, M.A. (ed.) (2003) *Religion after Metaphysics* (Cambridge: Cambridge University Press).

Wynne-Tyson, E. (1970) *The Philosophy of Compassion: The Return of the Goddess* (London: Centaur P).

Wyschogrod, E. (1998) 'The Howl of Oedipus, the Cry of Héloïse: From Asceticism to Postmodern Ethics', in V.L. Wimbush & R. Valantasis (eds.), *Asceticism* (Oxford: Oxford University Press), pp. 16-30.

Young, J. (1987) *Willing and Unwilling: a Study in the Philosophy of Arthur Schopenhauer* (Dordrecht: Martinus Nijhoff).

—, (1992) *Nietzsche's Philosophy of Art* (Cambridge: Cambridge University Press).

—, (2005) *Schopenhauer* (London: Routledge).

—, (2006) *Nietzsche's Philosophy of Religion* (Cambridge: Cambridge University Press).

Zeller, E. (1914) *Die Philosophie der Griechen in ihrer geschichtlichen Entwicklung*, 11th edition (Leipzig: O.R. Reisland).

INDEX

Abelson, P. 15

Abhidharma 15, 201

Absolute (concept of) 42-43, 100, 115, 170, 208

Anselm of Canterbury 108-111, 225

apophaticism (*see* negative way)

App, U. 27n.

appearance/reality distinction (*see* phenomenon thing-in-itself distinction)

Aquinas, T. 113-115, 117-118

Aristotelian philosophy 85, 158

Aristotle 59, 70, 113-114, 181, 194

asceticism (*see also* will, denial of) 5, 142, 209, 215-220, 230n.

Asiatick Researches 24, 28, 159, 176, 189

atheism (*see also* God, death of) 93-94, 112-113, 123, 126, 138, 194-197

Aufklärung (*see* Enlightenment)

Augustine of Hippo 92, 124-130, 202, 217, 219n.

Barth, K. 13n., 68, 108-109, 224

Berger, D. 93, 161-162, 174n., 176

Berman, D. 93-94

Bhagavad-Gītā 24, 27n., 38n., 99, 189n., 193n.

Bible 6, 12-13, 224; Genesis 80, 89, 111, 146, 153; New Testament 12, 80, 151, 153; Old Testament 12, 48, 98, 103-104, 152

Bopp, F. 152

Brahmā 190-195, 203

Brahman 40, 192-194, 218

Brahmanism (*see* Hinduism)

Bruno, G. 76, 175

Buddha 113, 153, 172, 184-185, 195, 218

Buddhism 15-17, 52, 174, 194-203, 206-207, 217-218, 227

Buddhology 6, 44, 165, 169, 195

Bultmann, R. 151

Burnouf, E. 165, 169

Bykhovsky, B. 161

causation (law of causality) 113-117, 131-132, 144, 183, 200

character 131, 209-211, 213; empirical 132-134; intelligible 134-137, 197-198, 200

Christianity 11-12, 77-78, 87-88, 145-146, 224; 'historical' 74-75, 81-82, 90, 143, 151, 216; 'true and original' 80, 88, 90-91, 132-133, 140-142, 151-155, 209

Colebrooke, H. T. 25, 80n., 181, 188, 191, 207n.

contingency (metaphysical) 117-118, 130, 223

Conze, E. 200

Copleston, F. 95n., 114-115, 167

creatio ex nihilo, doctrine of 48, 97-99, 126-128, 133-135, 143, 154, 203

Cupitt, D. 53, 81

Daoism 165, 198

Descartes, R. 65, 77, 106

Deussen, P. 26, 231

Dhammapada 199-200

Dionysius the Areopagite 111, 175

Dostoyevsky, F. 138n., 211n.

Duperron, A. H. A. 25-26

Eckhart, Meister 112-113, 171

egoism 5, 72, 139, 210-211

Empedocles 174

STUDIES IN PHILOSOPHICAL THEOLOGY

1   H. de Vries, *Theologie im Pianissimo & zwischen Rationalität und Dekonstruktion*, Kampen, 1989
2   S. Breton, *La pensée du rien*, Kampen, 1992
3   Ch. Schwöbel, *God: Action and Revelation*, Kampen, 1992
4   V. Brümmer (ed.), *Interpreting the Universe as Creation*, Kampen, 1991
5   L.J. van den Brom, *Divine Presence in the World*, Kampen, 1993
6   M. Sarot, *God, Passibility and Corporeality*, Kampen, 1992
7   G. van den Brink, *Almighty God*, Kampen 1993
8   P.-C. Lai, *Towards a Trinitarian Theology of Religions: A Study of Paul Tillich's Thought*, Kampen, 1994
9   L. Velecky, *Aquinas' Five Arguments in the* Summa Theologiae *Ia 2, 3*, Kampen, 1994
10 W. Dupré, *Patterns in Meaning. Reflections on Meaning and Truth in Cultural Reality, Religious Traditions, and Dialogical Encounters*, Kampen, 1994
11 P.T. Erne, *Lebenskunst. Aneignung ästhetischer Erfahrung*, Kampen, 1994
12 U. Perone, *Trotz/dem Subjekt*, Leuven, 1998
13 H.J. Adriaanse, *Vom Christentum aus: Aufsätze und Vorträge zur Religionsphilosophie*, Kampen, 1995
14 D.A. Pailin, *Probing the Foundations: A Study in Theistic Reconstruction*, Kampen, 1994
15 M. Potepa, *Schleiermachers hermeneutische Dialektik*, Kampen, 1996
16 E. Herrmann, *Scientific Theory and Religious Belief. An Essay on the Rationality of Views of Life*, Kampen, 1995
17 V. Brümmer & M. Sarot (eds.), *Happiness, Well-Being and the Meaning of Life. A Dialogue of Social Science and Religion*, Kampen, 1996
18 T.L. Hettema, *Reading for Good. Narrative Theology and Ethics in the Joseph Story from the Perspective of Ricoeur's Hermeneutics*, Kampen, 1996
19 H. Düringer, *Universale Vernunft und partikularer Glaube. Eine theologische Auswertung des Werkes von Jürgen Habermas*, Leuven, 1999
20 E. Dekker, *Middle Knowledge*, Leuven, 2000
21 T. Ekstrand, *Max Weber in a Theological Perspective*, Leuven, 2000
22 C. Helmer & K. De Troyer (eds.), *Truth: Interdisciplinary Dialogues in a Pluralist Age*, Leuven, 2003
23 L. Boeve & L.P. Hemming (eds.), *Divinising Experience. Essays in the History of Religious Experience from Origen to Ricœur*, Leuven, 2004
24 P.D. Murray, *Reason, Truth and Theology in Pragmatist Perspective*, Leuven, 2004
25 S. van Erp, *The Art of Theology. Hans Urs von Balthasar's Theological Aesthetics and the Foundations of Faith*, Leuven, 2004
26 T.A. Smedes, *Chaos, Complexity, and God. Divine Action and Scientism*, Leuven, 2004
27 R. Re Manning, *Theology at the End of Culture. Paul Tillich's Theology of Culture and Art*, Leuven, 2004
28 P. Jonkers & R. Welten (eds.), *God in France. Eight Contemporary French Thinkers on God*, Leuven, 2005
29 D. Grumett, *Teilhard de Chardin: Theology, Humanity and Cosmos*, Leuven, 2005
30 I.U. Dalferth, *Becoming Present. An Inquiry into the Christian Sense of the Presence of God*, Leuven, 2006

PRINTED ON PERMANENT PAPER • IMPRIME SUR PAPIER PERMANENT • GEDRUKT OP DUURZAAM PAPIER - ISO 9706

N.V. PEETERS S.A., WAROTSTRAAT 50, B-3020 HERENT